The One Possible Basis
for a Demonstration
of the Existence of God

THE JANUS LIBRARY

Lorenzo Valla, DE VOLUPTATE (ON PLEASURE).
Maristella Lorch and A. Kent Hieatt

* * *

Rene Descartes, LE MONDE (THE WORLD).
Michael Sean Mahoney,

* * *

Immanuel Kant, DER STREIT DER FAKULTÄTEN
(THE CONFLICT OF THE FACULTIES). Mary J.
Gregor and Robert E. Anchor

* * *

Thomas Hobbes, DE CORPORE (PART FIRST).
Aloysius Patrick Martinich; with an inquiry into
Hobbes' Theory of Language, Speech and Reason-
ing by Isabel C. Hungerland and George R. Vick

* * *

Immanuel Kant, DER EINZIG MÖGLICHE BEWEIS-
GRUND (THE ONE POSSIBLE BASIS FOR A
DEMONSTRATION OF THE EXISTENCE OF
GOD). Gordon Treash

* * *

Etienne Bonnot de Condillac, LA LOGIQUE (LOGIC).
W. R. Albury

* * *

Nicholas de Cusa, IDIOTA DE MENTE. Clyde Lee
Miller

* * *

Johannes Reuchin, DE ARTE CABBALISTICA. Martin
Goodman

* * *

Johannes Kepler, MYSTERIUM COSMOGRAPHICUM,
E. J. Aiton and A. M. Duncan

* * *

Marsilio Ficino, DE VITA. Carol Kaske

* * *

Immanuel Kant, FORTSCHRITTE DER METAPHYSICK
(PROGRESS IN METAPHYSICS). Ted B. Humphrey

IMMANUEL KANT

Der einzig mögliche Beweisgrund

TRANSLATION AND INTRODUCTION BY GORDON TREASH

The One Possible Basis for a Demonstration of the Existence of God

luv
9-1-81

Contents

PART THREE

ACKNOWLEDGEMENTS

A great many of the notes appended to the text of the translation are taken with only slight alteration from Paul Menzer's edition of the essay for the Prussian Academy edition. In common with most twentieth-century students of Kant, I much appreciate the considerable advantages that edition offers.

Much of the initial work of translating Kant's essay was done in 1972-1973, during a sabbatical year spent in Bonn. I am grateful to Mount Allison University and to the Canada Council for support which made possible a substantial start on the work, and to Professor Hans Wagner, Director of the *Philosophisches Seminar* at Bonn, for his kindness in making available the facilities of the University. The encouragement afforded by his examination of an early draft of the translation was a considerable contribution to the ultimate completion of the project.

Finally, it is a special pleasure to record here my debt and my gratitude to Professor Lewis White Beck, Burbank Professor of Intellectual and Moral Philosophy at the University of Rochester. The value of the assistance rendered through his patient and incisive criticism of both the translation and the introduction is far beyond measure.

Gordon Treash
Mount Allison University
Sackville, New Brunswick

Introduction

Kant's Ontological Argument

Kant published this essay in the latter part of December 1762, and in accordance with established practice it was dated the following year. By then he was a man of some thirty-eight years and a scholar of considerable achievement, having already published well over a dozen treatises and monographs in both German and Latin. The essay was, however, the first one of his works to attract much attention in influential circles of central Europe. Moses Mendelssohn reviewed the book favorably and described its author as an "independent thinker," recommending that he undertake constructing an enduring philosophical system of his own. In Vienna the essay was noticed in a quite different way—by being placed on the index of forbidden books because of the sentiment with which it concludes.[1]

So far as the age of its author is concerned the work certainly is not a bit of juvenilia, and Kant's remark in the preface that it represents the results of "long reflection" suggests that when it was published he regarded it as being an accurate—even if not a complete—summary of his thought. If so, the essay has obvious significance for understanding the development of Kant's philosophy. It may also be of importance to the critical thought of Kant's maturity. For although toward the end of his life Kant seems not to have

placed much value on the work he had accomplished prior to the dissertation of 1770,[2] some conclusions important to this essay do recur in the *Critique of Pure Reason,* and the earlier manifestations of such conclusions illuminate the later.

I

Translation of Kant's title for this essay is not an easy task. The key expression *Beweisgrund* may be rendered in English as "evidence," "ground of proof," "argument," or "premise," and to choose one term consistently as the appropriate translation inevitably obscures the ambiguity of the original. What is primarily important so far as the title of the book is concerned is the tentative and incomplete nature of what is being offered. As Kant insists in his preface, the book is not a complete demonstration. That would require a systematic analysis, which is not intended. All that he is undertaking is "to sketch the first strokes of a master plan," and all he expects to offer is the "painstakingly assembled material for building" a demonstration. It is as the foundation or the basis for a systematic demonstration that the *Beweisgrund* is a premise. The entire essay is to be seen as preparation for the systematic demonstration which can be derived from it.

To be thoroughly effective the basis or premise for any demonstration of God's existence must permit no doubt of the conclusion based upon it. This means it will have to be an a priori argument, for only such a one is able to ground a proof rigorous in the fullest sense.

It is impossible to deny what cannot not be, that is, what is necessary. If it can be established that God is the one entity whose non-existence is impossible, it will be absolutely

10

necessary to recognize his existence as an element of reality, and this will provide the basis required for a systematic demonstration. The purpose of Kant's essay is to prepare the foundation for a systematic demonstration, and accordingly it will have to employ the conception of a necessary being.

The conception of God as that being which necessarily exists is at least as old as Augustine and had figured prominently in several seventeenth-century systems. Kant was not ignorant of the modern systems and their use of the notion. A cursory reading of the text of this one essay alone makes that abundantly clear. And so the first question the book raises is what the grounds are for Kant's categorical statement that the desired demonstration has not hitherto been discovered.[3] We must ask what Kant regarded in 1762 as being the fatal defect of the ontological argument as it had been proposed and why that classical formulation was not able to be the foundation or groundwork being sought. The answer to that question takes us a very considerable way towards understanding Kant's thought at the time this essay was published.

The major systems of the seventeenth century demonstrated the necessity of God's existence as an immediate consequence of conceiving him as the perfect being. Such a definition is on precisely the same ground as the other foundations of rational thought, for example the axioms of geometry. The truth of such a definition is obvious to all rational beings. And just as geometry is not possible unless the axioms and postulates are granted, metaphysics requires that God be understood as the being in which all perfections are united. Once this definition is admitted, existence follows immediately, for it is but one of the implications logically entailed by perfection; and, since necessary being is a greater perfection than contingent existence, the absolutely perfect being is one which cannot not be.

11

That characterization of the argument is an accurate summary of Descartes's thought, for the proofs of God's existence provided by both the third and the fifth *Meditations* turn upon analysis of perfection. The third *Meditation* invokes the agency of God as the cause of our finite conceptions of perfection. Precisely because of what is entailed by the finite idea of perfection Descartes is confident that at least this one idea must be the ectype of an actual divine archetype. And the fifth *Meditation* is an uncomplicated statement of the ontological argument in its traditional form. The non-existence of the perfect being, it maintains, is as inconceivable as a four-sided triangle: God's existence is as necessary as that any triangle have three sides.

Leibniz accepted the ontological argument with the qualification that God necessarily exists provided that it is possible that he exist. Since the possibility of that being which knows no limitation, no negation and no contradiction cannot be challenged, it is clear that God is the necessary existent.[4] In one respect, Leibniz went further than Descartes, the *Monadology* adding to the conclusion of the ontological argument that God's understanding is the source and the foundation not only of all that exists but of all possibility as well, "insofar as there is something real in possibility."[5] Nonetheless Leibniz's position is founded upon analysis of the notion of perfection precisely as Descartes's had been. Indeed only analysis of that conception makes it apparent that the essence of God involves his existence.[6]

It is the attempt to deduce the existence of God from a conception, even from a conception which all rational beings must entertain, which is the focus of Kant's criticism. In this essay, he is contending that such an argument can never be more than the account of what is entailed by the conception, and so it will not be able to proceed beyond such conceptions or

notions to actuality. The traditional forms of the ontological argument had, of course, claimed to do just that, but as early as 1755 Kant was aware of the problem the argument creates. In his *Habilitationschrift* [7] of that year he remarked: "I know, of course, that the concept of God is invoked through which one allows his existence to be determined. But it may easily be seen that this happens in the notion, not in reality." [8]

He is not, by any means, the first thinker to have criticized the ontological argument for this. Gaunilon, Thomas, and several of Descartes's critics had covered the same ground. Unlike these critics, however, Kant employs the criticism as the first step in revision of the ontological argument, not as evidence that the conclusion is impossible to achieve; and throughout the present work he erects signposts to guide the reader to that re-interpretation which alone can provide the basis for demonstrating God's existence.

One of the clearest of these occurs in the concluding observation of the first part of the book. There Kant notes that he has provided a properly "genetic" foundation for demonstrating the existence of God, genetic because it has been derived only from the characteristics of absolute necessity. The existence of the absolutely necessary being is known through what constitutes the being's necessity. [9] The one foundation for demonstrating this existence is to be uncovered by analysis of how that being functions in the world. That God is the necessary being will be shown by proving that there is a function which is absolutely essential and can be assumed only by a being which cannot not be.

The procedure involves analysis of actuality, but it will be sharply distinguished from those arguments which move from contingent matters of fact in the world to God as their efficient cause. That would be no argument a priori, but one dependent upon contingent existents. Rather than begin with the

contingent things, Kant's strategy is to show that God is necessary because some things are possible.

That there are possibilities or potentialities for things is not a difficult premise to defend. Even in a thoroughly determined world things may become what they are not now. If so, the character they come to have but do not now possess is not at present actual. It is only a possibility or a potentiality for some future determination. This possible character cannot be actual, of course, for then it would not be a possibility for the things' determination, but rather one of their actual characteristics. The character must somehow be possible, and yet not actual. It can be, if some entity be recognized which serves as the foundation for this unrealized possibility. Without that entity, unrealized possibility would not be anything. Just as clearly, that being which is the basis or ground of possibility cannot fail to exist, for were its being denied not only all existence but also all possibility would disappear.

The groundwork here laid out is categorical. It is not possible for there to be nothing, for the very possibility of total non-being would itself have to be at least a possibility.[10] If sheer non-being is impossible, whatever is requisite as ground for even the possibility of anything actual is necessary. The argument is entirely a priori, by which it supplies the first desideratum of a foundation for the systematic demonstration. But more than that, the necessity of God follows not from how God is conceived but rather from the nature of possibility itself. In terms Kant developed only much later, inference to the existence of God is not analytic but synthetic.

The answer to the question of how Kant's argument diverges from the familiar forms of the ontological argument is that although they are a priori they are also merely analytic and based upon a conception of perfection. His, by contrast, is intended to be synthetic and the result of discovery of the true

14

natures of possibility and actuality.

The first part of the essay is complicated since thought is something possible. So if all possibility be negated then the possibility of thought is also thereby canceled. But it is because thought requires something to be thought that the complete absence of possibility would negative thought as it would render everything else quite literally impossible. A primordial and necessary being is requisite if there is to be any thinking or conception. That necessity is prior to thought just as it precedes everything else.

II

In the final section of the essay Kant contrasts the argument he has defended with the traditional version, which he terms the "Cartesian" argument.

The Cartesian method proceeds from the possibilities of things as a ground to the existence of the primordial actuality as a consequence derived from this ground. The Kantian argument completely inverts the process. It moves from the possibilities, as consequences, to the necessary being as their ground. If it can be shown that the former method is not possible, the basis provided by the first section of the treatise is demonstrated to be the only tenable one.

There are two distinct but associated reasons why the Cartesian procedure is impossible, and these reasons take Kant considerably beyond the intuitive complaint against deriving existence from conceptions, or actuality from thought. The first of the reasons may be loosely described as being a logical one, and the second has to do with the connection between thought and existence. In that degree it is ontological.

(1) The logical reason for the impossibility of the Cartesian argument is the result of its form. It begins with a conception of the perfect being. In contradistinction to the actuality with

15

which the argument concludes, this premise is only a "bare possibility." Actuality or existence of the primordial being can be deduced from the mere possibility only through analysis of what is entailed by that concept. The analysis will yield the desired conclusion only when existence is regarded as a real predicate of the concept. It is decisively shown in the first portion of the essay, however, that existence can never be a real predicate.

The argument used to prove that existence is no predicate is identical with the one which was to appear nearly twenty years later in the *Critique of Pure Reason*.   There is no conception or predicate attaching to an existent thing that does not constitute its determination as a mere possibility. The complete conception of the hero Julius Caesar must include all his determining predicates. These determine him both as an actual, historical character and as a merely possible one. Nothing at all is added to that determination which delineates Caesar from Brutus when the former is recognized to be a real and actual being. Hence although "existence" may sometimes be employed as a predicate in grammar, it is not a real predicate. And so it will never be possible to derive the existence of any entity from the concept of that entity, be that concept what it may.

The Cartesian argument does precisely this, for it begins with the conception of the perfect being as the foundation of the argument and deduces the actuality of the being as a consequence. Descartes's argument is mentioned as exemplifying a type of argument, but arguments of this kind have in common that the actuality of God is already present in the possibility. This requires existence to be considered a real predicate. Since it is not, any argument which is Cartesian in form is doomed. Although Kant does not call special attention to Leibniz's revision of the argument, that too must be included

under the general censure, for it only appends to the classical form of the argument the priviso that God must be recognized as possible, and the necessity of his existence is entailed in the possibility of a perfect entity.

(2) The realization that existence is no real predicate is a special case of the general problem of determining what connection, if any, there is between thought and existence. The Cartesian form of the ontological argument contended that in the case of the perfect being existence may be deduced from an idea or a conception. The *One Possible Basis* shows it is impossible to argue coherently in this way, but the book is also much concerned with the general problem. The seventh proposition of the second book of Spinoza's *Ethics* is an explicit statement of that position. There Spinoza undertakes to demonstrate that "the order and connection of ideas is the same as the order and connection of things." To know and to understand the logical order is one with knowing and understanding the order of the things thought and conceived. Thought which is adequate is an apt reflection of how things are, and conversely the way things are is exactly mirrored in true and adequate ideas.

Despite sharp attacks on Spinoza, Leibniz adapted that axiom to his own thought. If what is and what is thought are correlative, as Spinoza had held, the characteristics of things must be fully expressed in the predicates attributed to these things. This is true whether the things concerned are actual or possible entities. The complete notions of both the actual and the possible will include all the characteristics of that actuality or possibility. Leibniz frequently calls upon this doctrine to develop his theory of substance. In the *Discourse on Metaphysics* and in correspondence with Arnauld, he repeats time and again the proposition that any true and adequate conception of a subject must include a clear notion of that

subject's predicates, for a true proposition merely makes explicit what is always implicit in the subject.

> Every true predication has some basis in the nature of things, and when a proposition is not an identity, that is to say when the predicate is not expressly contained in the subject, it must be included in it virtually. . . . So the subject term must always include the predicate term in such a way that anyone who understands perfectly the concept of the subject will also know that the predicate pertains to it.

> In every true affirmative proposition, whether necessary or contingent, universal or particular, the notion of the predicate is in some way included in that of the subject. *Praedicatum inest subjecto;* otherwise I do not know what truth is.

In this view the law of non-contradiction assumes great importance and Leibniz recognizes that it does. If every true proposition is one in which the predicates that pertain to the subject are already found in the notion of the subject, whatever is internally consistent with the subject and amongst its predicates is a possible determination of the subject. Nothing contradictory is possible, and, so long as the stress upon the analytic aspect of judgment which is implicit in the rule *praedicatum inest subjecto* is sustained, any subject will be possible whose predicates are internally consistent with one another. Those predicates free from contradiction are compossible.

The law of non-contradiction must of course be augmented by the other fundamental axiom of Leibniz's metaphysics, the law of sufficient reason. The latter principle demands that there be a sufficient reason for the enactment or the realization of possibilities. This law is a principle of actualization or actuality invoked to explain why this, rather than any other possible

world, has been chosen for enactment. Its importance is evident. But still, all the other worlds which are not chosen are possible ones because their conceptions are free of contradictions.

The axiom that possibility is constituted by freedom from contradiction is of considerable significance to the development of Leibniz's own metaphysical system, but for present purposes the significance of it lies in its appearance and modification in Baumgarten. Kant had employed Baumgarten's *Metaphysica* as the basis for his own lectures on metaphysics and in 1756 recommended it as being the "most useful and thorough of all handbooks of its kind despite the difficulties of obscurity which surround it."[16] Two volumes of the Academy Edition are devoted to Kant's handwritten notes, made over the period of several years, on the content of the handbook, and the strength of its influence upon Kant is indisputable.

Baumgarten begins, as Leibniz did, by insisting upon the primacy of the principle of non-contradiction in the explication of possibility: nothing contradictory is possible, and no possibility can be contradictory. But there is the suggestion of something more than the identification of possibility with logical consistency in Baumgarten's account. For he insists very early in the book that the possible not only is free from contraction but also can be represented, or is representable. To be possible is to be *repraesentabile,* representable.[17]

Baumgarten subjected this concept to no special analysis since he regarded it as being synonymous with other descriptions of possibility, i.e., whatever is not absurd, repugnant, or contradictory. As another expression of the principle of non-contradiction it is "absolutely primitive."[18] But although it is not further analyzed, the notion is highly suggestive when understanding Kant's conception of possibility in 1762.

Baumgarten is concerned with describing what constitutes the possibility of entities, and not only propositions and concepts. As he sees it, the possible determinatives of things are the characters that may serve as determinations or definitions of that thing.[19] If it is to be possible for an entity to be determined in some one way, the proposed determinations must be possibilities for it. Since possibilities must be representable, it follows that these possible determinatives must be representable as defining or determining that thing.

If an entity is possible, it is possible as this thing and not as something else, and so a character will be the possible determinative of an entity only if it harmonizes with the complete determination of the being. If it does not, it cannot be represented as determinative of that thing even though it may not stand in formal logical contradiction with its other possible determinatives.

Ordinary experience provides examples in which some characteristics are not possible for a thing because they cannot be harmoniously integrated with the other determinations of that being. The motion of a body in one direction with a given velocity and the motion in the opposite direction with the same velocity are opposed to one another. Yet such opposition is not logical contradiction, for both motions may simultaneously be present in a body. If they are, they will physically cancel each other and the body will remain at rest. Rest is the consequence of real opposition between two possible determinations of the body, and not the logical opposition of two contradictory propositions.

Baumgarten did not proceed this far with his analysis but Kant did, explicitly invoking twice the example just cited of real opposition in a body in static equilibrium. The case is cited in this essay [20] and again in a shorter paper on negative quantities written within a few months of publication of *The One Possible*

Basis.[21] He was thus fully aware of the implications of what Baumgarten had done.

The evidence that Kant had adopted Baumgarten's terminology is unmistakable. Baumgarten provides German glosses for significant Latin terms and he suggests that what is possible in itself (per se possibility) is to be described as "an und vor sich, innerlich, unbedingt möglich,"[22] possible in and for itself, internally or unconditionally possible. Precisely that language appears in the present essay. The second observation of the first part of the book is entitled "On internal possibility insofar as it presupposes an existence," and in this section of the first part Kant develops the basis from which the demonstration of God's existence may proceed by pushing the account of internal possibility much farther than Baumgarten had done.

Absence of contradiction is essential for the possibility of an entity, of course, but that alone does not establish the real possibility of any thing. Such logical consistency provides only the form of possibility. Form always requires its correlate, matter; and so, Kant maintains, in addition to the formal element in possibility there must also be the material or the data of it. This material, necessary to determine an entity as possible, is what provides the real element of possibility,[23] and it is in the employment of that conception that Kant most fully calls upon the connection between possibility and representability that Baumgarten had suggested. This step is essential for the revision of the ontological argument.[24]

The matter or data of every possibility must be given if anything is to be possible. But all such matter must be given through something else since in itself it is not actual but only the matter for the possible determination of actuality. There must be some actuality, then, through which such matter for possibility is given and which will be absolutely prior to all

possibility. Such a ground of all possibility cannot be a contingent being, for the possibility of its existence would demand a further ground. It must necessarily exist.

This suggests another reason why the Cartesian form of the ontological argument must be rejected. Freedom from contradiction is not a sufficient mark of possibility. The material or the data of any possible entity must be given, and if so it will not be possible to deduce God's possibility from a conception of him, as Leibniz had thought to be able to do. The conception may be free from contradiction, but such freedom fulfills only the formal condition of any possibility, even the possibility of God's existence. And, as is true for any other entity, the material for God's possibility must be given in addition to the form. Yet God is the ground in which all possibility is given, and it would be absurd were his possibility to be given by something else.[25]

In this regard Kant's treatise, defending as it does what he terms at times the ontotheological[26] argument, has important affinities to books *Theta* and *Lamba* of Aristotle's *Metaphysics*. In *Theta* Aristotle insists that actuality is prior to potentiality or the possible in substance, in definition, and even in time. Part of what is intended by such priority is that potentiality depends upon the actual in that it must be given through actuality. Only in this way can the potentials avoid being separate Platonic forms, a problem Aristotle was fully aware required careful attention.[27] Book *Lambda* confirms the dependence of potentiality upon the actual by insisting that for living beings what is prior is not the seed from which living beings are produced but the necessarily actual "perfect creature."[28]

Although the expression "ground of all possibility" or "ground of potentiality" does not explicitly occur in the Aristotelian text, that conception is implicit in Aristotle's

position, and Aristotle has clearly seen that such a ground of potentiality cannot itself be a potential being. It must exist and is a necessary being.[29]

Kant's argument proceeds, as Aristotle's had, from analysis of the condition which must obtain in order for there to be any possibility, and not from analysis of a notion which it is claimed all rational creatures must entertain. For this reason Kant is able to insist that the argument he is proposing avoids any reference to perfection[30] and is a genetic account of what constitutes the necessity of that being which cannot not be. Such an account cannot be provided by the classical forms of the argument precisely because they begin where the present argument ends, by assuming rather than demonstrating what constitutes the perfection of the necessary being.

III

Unless one is prepared to accept major philosophical accomplishments springing completely formed and without precedent from the heads of their creators, the recurrence of earlier work in later statements is not unexpected. Insofar as the understanding of possibility is concerned, the *Critique of Pure Reason* retains the achievement of the 1762 essay by insisting that possibility involves both a formal and a material aspect but it significantly amends the results of the earlier essay.

When the *Critique* is concerned explicitly with possibility, it is so first with the possibility of concepts and derivatively with the possibility of things. In these terms the logical aspect is apparent: conformity to the law of non-contradiction, as such non-contradiction had been the formal element of the possibility of things envisioned by *The One Possible Basis*. Of course conformity to this condition establishes no more than

freedom from self-contradiction. "For the objective reality of the concept, this logical condition is far from sufficient."[31] As Kant had argued in 1762, possibility requires a material aspect to provide the "objective reality" of the possibility.

For the earlier essay the field of possibility is wide. All that is given by or through the necessary being is material for possibility. The book does not proceed further to discuss how such possibility is grounded in the primordial being, but it requires no great interpretative leap to conclude that it is grounded in God's conceptualization.[32] If so, whatever God conceives is a possibility when possibility is understood as the previous sections argue it must be. The first *Critique*, by contrast, imposes much more specific conditions upon the possible. Only those elements which correspond to the possibility of an experience in general, that is, only those elements capable of being found in space and time, are possible objects of experience. "The possibility of things demands that the concept of the things agree with the formal conditions of an experience in general."[33] In short, only potential objects of sensible experience are the material of possibility.

This is an important difference between the position occupied by the transcendental philosophy and Kant's pre-critical conception. But that difference ought not to obscure the outline of the earlier essay in the critical account. The portion of the *Dialectic* in which Kant refutes the classical form of the ontological argument fills the outline to a considerable degree. The section opens with the assertion that: "You have already perpetrated a contradiction when you try to include the concept of existence in the concept of a thing which you want to think simply by its possibility, no matter under what surreptitious name."[34] As becomes clear immediately, the contradiction involved is the conflation of possibility and existence. Since Descartes's argument has undertaken to deduce

the actual from the concept of perfection alone, it is guilty of the contradiction.

This is to repeat that it is contradictory to treat existence as a predicate deducible from the concept of the subject by the use of the law of non-contradiction. The possibility of anything requires the material element, and such an element for the first *Critique* is intimately associated with sensation. It is impossible then to discover what is by means of the law of non-contradiction alone. No real possibility, as defined in the "Postulates of Empirical Thought" in the first *Critique*, is constituted by lack of contradiction. Insistence upon both material and formal aspects of possibility stands behind the conclusion that existence is not a real predicate in the *Critique*, just as it had supported the identical assertion in the 1762 essay.

The section of the *Critique* entitled "The Ideal of Pure Reason" returns to the question of the conception of the possibility of things. Here Kant repeats that the principle of contradiction is merely the logical condition of any possible determination of things. To this logical requirement must be added "the fundamental principle of thoroughgoing determination," der *Grundsatz der dürchgangigen Bestimmung*, a principle which concerns the content and not only the form of the possibility: "This is the fundamental principle of all predicates that constitute the complete concept of things . . . . "[35] Such a principle contains the presupposition of "the material for *all possibility* which must contain *a priori* the data for the particular possibility of every thing." The possibility of determination of finite things requires that there be presupposed a completeness of possibility, *ein Inbegriff der Möglichkeit*. This is so essential if anything is to be fully or completely known that Kant concludes it "prescribes to the understanding the rule of its complete use."[36]

Thus for the critical philosophy, as for the essay of 1762,

possibility of each particular determination demands inference beyond that individual determination to something else. For *The One Possible Basis* this is an actuality which cannot fail to be. By contrast the *Critique* has limited what can properly lie beyond such potentiality to an Ideal located only in the reason. As such it can never be represented as an element of categorial experience, but it is nonetheless a condition essential to the operation of the understanding. From *The One Possible Basis* to the *Critique of Pure Reason*, a time span of nearly twenty years, the notion persists that all determination of individual things presupposes a totality of possibility: if not an actuality which necessarily exists in order to ground possibility, then an idea of a presupposed completeness of possibility is a necessary condition of the knowledge of individual things. The revision of critical thought according to which the totality at the base of experience and knowledge is "founded upon an idea which has its seat purely in the reason,"[37] does not so much deny the doctrine of 1762 as it rests it upon the foundation of a critical transcendental philosophy and not a classical ontology.

For Kant's moral theology, God is a postulate necessary to complete the account of the ethical life. This is, of course, a major accomplishment of the critical program. The Ideal of Pure Reason proposes a speculative analogue of that morally demanded postulate. Thought of any objects of sense, no less than morality, requires the assumption of God although such an assumption is only an ideal, not an object of knowledge.[38] This speculative analogue of the practical postulate is a revision of the doctrine Kant's treatise of 1762 had defended.

Such a relationship between this earlier work and the *Critique of Pure Reason* provides a basis for answering the question why Kant undertook to attack in the *Critique* only the form of the ontological argument which he had seen to be impossible nearly twenty years earlier, leaving the stronger form

of the argument unmentioned by the second book of the Transcendental Dialectic. [39]

The *Critique's* demonstration that God is the Ideal of Reason and a subjective condition of understanding manifestly contradicts the conclusion of *The One Possible Basis*; but to defend the later position is the work of the entire *Critique of Pure Reason*. Consequently there can be no single convincing argument which will demolish the conclusion of *The One Possible Basis* as the formula "existence is no predicate" had demolished the Cartesian one.

Existence, possibility, and necessity are postulates of empirical thought for the *Critique*; and like the other elements of the Transcendental Analytic, they are to be employed only in their connection to sensibility. No matter how essential the *ens realissimum* is to the function of the understanding, it is no principle pertaining to objects, and so none of the modal quantifiers apply to it. To assume that they do is to fall prey to the temptation of taking subjective conditions of our thought for objective conditions, which of course is the essence of dialectical illusion. [40]

Viewed from the standpoint of the *Critique of Pure Reason* the defect of *The One Possible Basis* is the error of all dogmatic ontology, and although its positive conception of God as the ground of all possibility is preserved, the dogmatic foundation upon which that conclusion rests is rejected. If that be so, Kant's answer to his earlier position will remain implicit in the *Critique* although the direction it must take is clear. [41]

IV

Because of the direction in which his thought had developed by 1762, Kant was in a particularly strong position to exploit the implications of the doctrine according to which God

is the primordial principle of actuality. Much of his work had been devoted to elucidation of the principles by which nature and natural phenomena are to be understood. This included efforts which would be recognized by contemporary academic categorizing as falling within the domain of empirical science as well as the explorations of the philosophic implications of such science. The first book he had published (in 1747) was concerned to provide a way of truly estimating living forces, *vis viva*, and further interest in substantive scientific problems is reflected in the *Universal Natural History and Theory of the Heavens* (1755), an essay on the nature of fire (the same year), *An Attempt to Introduce Negative Quantities into Philosophy* (1763), and several essays explaining the nature of space and time.

Since the necessary being is an essential principle of all actuality, it will perforce be a fundamental principle of nature. No account of nature can be complete if it ignores this essential element, and elsewhere Kant strongly insists that metaphysics is indispensable to a complete physics.[42] Thus natural phenomena provide evidence for the existence of God since such phenomena are derived from the order and coherence of the necessary being. This means that the empirical or a posterori argument from things in the world to their source has great merit if only it be properly interpreted, although it must be admitted that it can never provide a demonstration with the rigor of a mathematical proof.[43] The second section of the *One Possible Basis*, and by far the longest of the three, is devoted to exploration of the utility of the ground staked out in the first portion of the essay for an understanding of nature. It will show that natural phenomena are most fully understood when they are regarded as constituting a system which, owing to its derivation from the primordial actuality, is orderly, harmonious, and coherent.

Customarily, the a posteriori argument observes a certain order and coherence in the world and regards that as justification for inferring a wise creator of such order. But there are, Kant insists, two defects of such a method which prevent it from achieving what might be accomplished by the a posteriori argument when it is properly constituted.

1) The order and coherence which customarily provide the basis for the argument are always judged from the human perspective. Thus the procedure inevitably leaves its defender open to the charge of having confused human advantage with divine purpose.

2) In addition, the a posteriori argument usually involves a depreciation of natural science. For if all natural order be the result of immediate divine intent, or even if it may be the result of such divine intention, research into causes and principles in nature is vain. The causes of natural phenomena are as ineffable as the will of the divine from which the a posteriori argument usually sees them as following.

By contrast, the great utility of the argument offered in the first section of the essay is its view of natural order as dependent upon the derivation of things from one common source. Since the internal nature of things is derived from the principle of actuality, what these things become and how they behave are ingredients in the nature of actuality. The characteristics and behavior of natural entities are the results of the realization or actualization of possibility, which is located only in the primordial necessary being. Since such actuality cannot not be, the order derived from it is necessary for the phenomena so ordered. Thus mechanical laws, general in their application, will characterize and explain the behavior of natural phenomena.

In the second section of the essay Kant argues that scientific laws, the laws of nature, have exactly the necessity.

which is to be expected in what follows from the very essence of things. As consequences of the necessary being the laws can be the subject of rational inquiry, and inquiring minds need not stand off from the most extensive investigation into the connections of things for fear of intruding into the realm of divine intent. There must be choice in determination of one order rather than any other. But once that is granted, phenomena will follow from the order chosen with systematic necessity. There will be extensive connection of things which appear diverse.

This is the metaphysical basis for regarding diverse effects as the results of a single general provision, and Kant is prepared to concede that general laws have a wider range of application than had previously been thought.

Mathematics, of course, is the paradigm instance in which simple foundations result in extensive consequences, consequences constituting an elegant unity once their order and mutual dependence upon a single source is adequately seen. In such a whole the results or consequences may resemble their foundations slightly or not at all.

Precisely this sort of unity and cohesion is characteristic of the other sciences too.

In biology, for example, there is good reason to think that not only development of living individuals, but their propagation as well—that is, not only their continuation but their origination—may be understood through general natural laws.[44] In physical science the case is even stronger for a single general law, or for a very few highly general laws, as explanatory of many physical phenomena. The seventh observation of the second part of this book is a brief summary of the work Kant had published in 1755 on the evolution of the solar system. In both the original essay and in the summary appended here he argues that the very origination of solar

systems, in which the various planetary motions constitute a harmonious whole, are consequences of general dynamic laws, not phenomena specially ordained by God. Newton, he insists, had thought it necessary to invoke the intention of God as the ultimate reason for the harmony manifested in the solar system as a systematic unit.[45] But that is an oversight owing to Newton's failure to recognize that space, which now appears empty, may have been full in an earlier epoch. If it was, then the mutual contact necessary to allow mechanical origination of the solar system would have been possible; and Kant demonstrates how the order of the phenomena would be a consequence of general scientific law. The evidence for such a hypothesis is strong, he argues, and that hypothesis permits him to concede considerably more to the governance of natural law than Newton had done. It is the first section of the book, Kant insists, which has provided the foundation of such an advance.

V

The essay went through three different editions as a separate book during Kant's lifetime. The editions were published by Kanter in Königsberg, in 1763, 1770, and 1794. In addition to these publications as a separate book, there were two collections of his shorter essays published while Kant was still alive, both editions including this treatise. A chronological edition of his essays appeared in 1797-1798. The *One Possible Basis* is in the second volume of the edition (pages 115-288), and it is also found in the second volume (pages 55-229) of Heinrich Tieftrunk's edition published in Halle in 1779.

The standard contemporary edition of Kant's works is published by the Prussian Academy. The essay, edited by Paul

Menzer, is in the second volume of that edition (pages 62-163). The German text of this edition is that of the Academy Edition. Wilhelm Weischedel edition of Kant's works in six volumes, published by the Wissenschaftliche Buchgesellschaft includes the essay in volume one (pages 621-738), and a paperback edition published by Felix Meiner in 1963 edited by Klaus Reich offers a text and introduction. In 1914 Fredrich Michael Schiele included this essay with several other of Kant's shorter works on religion for an edition published by Felix Meiner in Leipzig. Three other editions of the book have been included in editions of Kant's work published in this century. Cassirer's edition of 1912 includes the essay in volume two (pages 67-172) and Felix Gross included it in volume four (pages 113-232) of his 1921 edition of Kant's shorter works for the Insel Verlag. The Vòrlander edition published in Leipzig by Meiner also includes the text of this essay. There has been one previous translation into English by A.F.M. Willich in 1798 but that has not been reissued and is virtually inaccessible. A translation into French, *l'Unique Fondement Possible d'Une Demonstration de l'Existence de Dieu* by Paul Festugiere, was first published in 1931 and reissued by J.Vrin in 1963.

NOTES FOR THE INTRODUCTION

1. Karl Vörlander, *Immanuel Kants Leben* (Hamburg, 1974), p. 53.

2. In October 1797 Kant insisted to Heinrich Tieftrunk that a collection of his shorter works, which Tieftrunk was planning, should exclude everything written before 1770 and thus begin with the inaugural dissertation. Tieftrunk ignored this request. The second volume of his edition published in Halle in 1799 includes this essay.

3. See below, p. 2.

4. *Monadology,* Sec. 45.

5. Ibid., sec. 43.

6. Ibid., sec. 44.

7. *Principiorum primorum cognitionis metaphysicae nova dilucidatio,* K.G.S. I, 385-416. The essay has been translated into English by F.E. England in his book *Kant's Conception of God* (London, 1929).

8. *"Verum hoc idealiter fieri, non realiter.,"* *Nova dilucidatio,* note to Proposition 6, Scholium, K.G.S. I:394.

9. See below, p. 41.

10. See below, p. 23.

11. A592/B620-A603/B631.

12. The source of the formula "existence is no predicate" has been a matter of considerable debate. At the end of the last century and the beginning of this one Karl Groos suggested and Bruno Erdmann denied that Kant may have derived it from reading Hume's *Treatise*

(Karl Groos, "Hat Kant Hume's *Treatise* gelesen?" *Kant Studien,* vol. 5, 1901, pp. 177-181; and Bruno Erdmann, "Kant und Hume um 1762," *Archiv für Geschichte der Philosophie,* vol. 1, 1888, pp. 62-77 and 216-230). There are significant similarities between Kant's formula and the text of Hume's first work. However, were Hume the original source of this insight for Kant it would mean that Kant had read the *Treatise* in English, for it was translated into German only in 1790. There is little reason to suppose that Kant was able to read any English and certainly not a work in which the nuances of the language are as important as they are in Hume's writing.

Robert Wolff has shown ("Kant's Debt to Hume via Beattie," *Journal of the History of Ideas,* [January 1960], pp. 117-123) that the examples Groos cites as evidence of Kant's familiarity with the *Treatise* may well be based on a source available to both Hume and Kant. Certainly this is true of the use made of Julius Caesar (Hume, *Treatise,* I, 3, 7; Kant below, p. 11.) But although the example of Caesar does occur in sec. 13 of Leibniz's *Discourse on Metaphysics,* Kant is the only one of the three thinkers—Leibniz, Hume, and Kant— to employ it in connection with the question of whether existence can be a predicate. Hume's argument proceeds by maintaining that existence adds nothing to the idea already entertained of an object. On the other hand, existence is explicitly termed a predicate by Christian August Crusius. In his *Entwurf der notwendigen Vernunft-Wahrheiten* (1745) he defines existence as "that predicate of a thing by virtue of which the thing is to be encountered somewhere and at some time outside thought" (sec. 46). While declining to examine further in this essay the "proposition that whatever exists must be somewhere and somewhen," Kant remarks that such a definition is insufficient to distinguish possibilities from actualities (below, p. 19). If existence is that element which allows an entity to be encountered outside thought in space and time, then it is not analytically deduced from concepts. And if so Crusius may not only provide the terminology for Kant's formula denying that existence may be a genuine predicate, but at the same time he would be anticipating considerations important to the first *Critique* (see Lewis White Beck, *Early German Philosophy* [Cambridge, Massachusetts, 1969], p. 398).

13. *Discourse on Metaphysics* sec. 8. in Loemker, *Leibniz: Philosophical Papers and Letters* (Dordrecht, 1969), p. 307.

14. Letter of 14 July 1686 to Arnauld, in Loemker, *Letters, p. 337*. Leibniz may well have borrowed this principle from Arnauld's *Port Royal Logic*. See L.E. Loemker, "A Note on the Origin and Problem of Leibniz's *Discourse,*" *Journal of the History of Ideas* (October 1947), reprinted in *The Philosophy of Leibniz and the Modern World,* I. Leclerc, ed., (Nashville, 1973).

15. There are clear deviations from strict observation of this rule. The *New Essays* introduces the notion of disparates, those "propositions which state that the object of one idea is not the object of another idea as *that heat is not the same thing as color.*" Disparate propositions are relevant to the present issue since it is impossible for the objects of such disparate propositions to be identical: the identity of heat and color is not a possibility. Yet such an impossibility is "asserted independently of all proof or of reduction to opposition or to the principle of contradiction" (*New Essays Concerning Human Understanding,* tr. A.G. Langley [LaSalle, Illinois, 1949], p. 405). The ambiguity of Leibniz's position and the manifestations of such ambiguity in Wolff and Crusius as well as the influence of these two thinkers upon Kant's mature theory is fully explored by Lewis White Beck in his paper, "Analytic and Synthetic Judgments before Kant" in *Reflections on Kant's Philosophy,* W.H. Werkmeister, ed., (Gainsville, 1975), pp. 2-27.

16. K.G.S. I, 503.

17. "Nonnihil est aliquid repraesentabile, quicquid non involvit contradictionem, quicquid non est A et non-A, est possibile" (*Metaphysica* sec. 8, K.G.S. XVII, 24).

18. *Metaphysica,* sec. 8, K.G.S. XVII, 24.

19. *Metaphysica,* sec. 35-37, K.G.S. XVII, 34-35.

20. Below, p. 34.

21. *Versuch den Begriff der negativen Grössen in die Weltweissheit einzuführen,* K.G.S. II, 165-204. Baumgarten's influence is highly apparent in the essay on negative magnitudes. There Kant argues that where formal contradictions are posited, "die Folge dieser logischen Verknüpfung ist gar nichts (nihil negativum irrepraesentabile". On the other hand, the second sort of opposition, that is, real opposition, is that in which one predicate cancels what is proposed by the other: "Allein die Folge ist Etwas (cognitabile)" And such a something is *repraesentabile* (K.G.S. II, 172). This repeats exactly Baumgarten's terminology of *Metaphysica* sec. 7 and sec. 8.

22. K.G.S. XVII, 29.
23. Below, p. 69.
24. On the relation of Kant to Baumgarten, see Joseph Schmucker, "Die Frühgestalt des kantischen ontotheologischen Arguments in der *Nova dilucidatio* und ihr Verhältnis zum *Einzig Möglichen Beweisgrund von 1762,*" in *Studien zu Kants Philosophischer Entwicklung,* Heimsoeth, Henrich, and Tonelli, eds. (Hildesheim, 1967).

Schmucker argues against Klaus Reich that the conception of possibility with which Kant is operating in the essay is presaged by his *Habilitationschrift* of 1755 and is a development of Baumgarten's doctrine. This position seems to be fully supported by the texts concerned.

25. Another of the *Reflexionen,* dated by Adickes as falling into the period 1764-1766, emphasizes the two-fold nature of possibility and the implication of such a dual nature:

"The possibility of a thing is two-fold: Either, 1. when what exists will be found in a certain way according to laws which already obtain in it thanks to its own properties. For example, if wood exists then a house made of wood is possible—or also that an effect flows from powers. 2. The possibility where nothing exists because then there is no material for anything, and thus the concept of nothing can develop. Thus the concept of possibility is certainly *logically* prior to the actuality, but in *reality* it does not precede all actuality. Thus there is a being which contains the material for all possibility and with which to distinguish possibility from actuality is just as absurd as

when one takes space away from an object. It cannot be said that this being is possible" *Reflexion* 3809, K.G.S. XVII, 300).

26. *Reflexion* 4647, K.G.S. XVII, 624.

27. *Metaphysics* 1050 B35-1051 A.

28. *Metaphysics* 1072 B30.

29. *Metaphysics* 1050 B6-1050 B20.

30. Below, pp. 39-40.

31. A220/B268.

32. "Finite substances stand in no relation to each other through their existence alone, and have no communion except insofar as they are retained in reciprocal relations by the common ground of their existence, namely the divine understanding" (*Nova dilucidatio*, Proposition XIII, K.G.S. I, 412-413). "The will of God contains the real basis for the existence of the world" (*Negative Grössen, Negative Quantities*, K.G.S. II, 202).

33. A220/B267.

34. A597/B625.

35. A573/B601.

36. A573/B601.

37. A573/B601.

38. "An object of the senses can be thoroughly determined only if it is compared with all predicates of appearance and through them represented affirmatively or negatively. But because that which constitutes the thing itself (in appearance) namely the real, must be given, and without it cannot even be thought, and because that in

which the reality of all experience is given is the single all-encompassing experience, the matter for possibility of all objects of sense must be presupposed as given in an essence [*ein Inbegriff*]" (A581-582/ B609-610).

"All possibilities presuppose the notion of a most real being (*ens realissimum*). And this notion presupposes a concept of existence, since without being given realities can not be thought in sensation, but what is given in sensation exists. Absolute necessity rests upon the presupposition of the condition of all possibility, not upon the identity of a concept with itself from which no existence follows" (*Reflexion* 5518, 1776-1778, K.G.S. XVIII, 205).

"God is not something that exists outside of me, but rather [is] my own *thought*. It is absurd to ask whether God exists. A personal expression is appropriate only to grammar." (*Nachlasswerk,* 1796 or later, K.G.S. XXI, 153).

39. There is one allusion to the book. At A625/B653 the ontological argument is called the "one possible ground of proof which no human reason can forebear." The words *der einzig mögliche Beweisgrund* are printed in *Sperrdruck.*

40. A292/B353.

41. Klaus Reich proposes much the same solution to the problem both in the introduction to the Felix Meiner edition of the essay (Hamburg 1963, pp. ix-xiii) and in his earlier monograph, *Kants einziger möglicher Beweisgrund zu einer Demonstration des Daseins Gottes: Ein Beitrag zum Verständnis des Verhältnisses vom Dogmatismus und Kritizismus in der Metaphysik* (Leipzig, 1937).

42. "It is metaphysics—which a great many think can be dispensed with in the field of physics — which alone is of assistance and provides illumination" (*The Physical Monadology,* "Preliminary Remarks," K.G.S. I, 475).

43. The cosmological argument offers "comprehension of a common, true concept, [and] the vivacity of its impression and excellence and attraction for the moral drives of human nature . . . "

And since "it is without a doubt of more importance to vitalize mankind with elevated sentiments which are productive of noble activity . . . than to instruct it with carefully measured syllogisms . . . the famous cosmological proof cannot be denied the preference of general utility" (below, p. 237).).

44. Despite serious reservations about the details of their systems, Kant was impressed by the work of Buffon and Maupertuis which suggested that mechanical explanation has a wider scope in biology than was ordinarily imagined. (see below, pp. 193-197.) On the other hand, "it is not possible to discover the natural causes through which the most lowly cabbage is generated according to completely mechanical laws. . . . No Philosopher has ever been in a position to render any of the laws of growth or inner movement of . . . a plant as distinct and mathematically certain as those to which heavenly bodies conform" (below, p. 191).

45. Now by the help of these Principles [of motion], all material Things seem to have been composed of the hard and solid Particles above-mentioned, variously associated in the first Creation by the Counsel of an intelligent Agent. For it became him who created them to set them in order. And if he did so, it's unphilosophical to seek for any other Origin of the World, or to pretend that it might arise out of a Chaos by the mere Laws of Nature; though being once form'd, it may continue by those Laws for many Ages. For while Comets move in very excentrick Orbs in all manner of positions, blind fate could never make all the Planets move one and the same way in Orbs concentrick, some inconsiderable Irregularities excepted . . . such a wonderful Uniformity in the Planetary System must be allowed the Effect of Choice" (Isaac Newton, *Optiks,* [New York, 1952] Query 31, p. 402).

Der

einzig mögliche Beweisgrund

zu einer

Demonstration

des

Daseins Gottes

von

M. Immanuel Kant.

Vorrede.

Ne mea dona tibi studio disposta fideli,
Intellecta prius quam sint, contempta relinquas.
LUCRETIUS.

Ich habe keine so hohe Meinung von dem Nutzen einer Bemühung, wie die gegenwärtige ist, als wenn die wichtigste aller unserer Erkenntnisse: **Es ist ein Gott,** ohne Beihülfe tiefer metaphysischer Untersuchungen wanke und in Gefahr sei. Die Vorsehung hat nicht gewollt, daß unsre zur Glückseligkeit höchstnöthige Einsichten auf der Spitzfindigkeit feiner Schlüsse beruhen sollten, sondern sie dem natürlichen gemeinen Verstande unmittelbar überliefert, der, wenn man ihn nicht durch falsche Kunst verwirrt, nicht ermangelt uns gerade zum Wahren und Nützlichen zu führen, in so fern wir desselben äußerst bedürftig sind. Daher derjenige Gebrauch der gesunden Vernunft, der selbst noch innerhalb den Schranken gemeiner Einsichten ist, genugsam überführende Beweistümer von dem Dasein und den Eigenschaften dieses Wesens an die Hand giebt, obgleich der subtile Forscher allerwärts die Demonstration und die Abgemessenheit genau bestimmter Begriffe oder regelmäßig verknüpfter Vernunftschlüsse vermißt. Gleichwohl kann man sich nicht entbrechen diese Demonstration zu suchen, ob sie sich nicht irgendwo darböte. Denn ohne der billigen Begierde zu erwähnen, deren ein der Nachforschung gewohnter Verstand sich nicht entschlagen kann, in einer so wichtigen Erkenntniß etwas Vollständiges und deutlich Begriffenes zu erreichen, so ist noch zu hoffen, daß eine dergleichen Einsicht, wenn man ihrer mächtig geworden, viel mehreres in diesem Gegenstande aufklären könnte. Zu diesem Zwecke aber zu gelangen muß

Preface

Ne mea dona tibi studio disposta fideli,
Intellecta prius quam sint, contempta reliquas.
LUCRETIUS. [1]

I have no exaggerated opinion of the utility of an endeavor such as the present one is—as though the most important of all our knowledge, *that there is a God*, would totter and be in serious danger without the aid of profound metaphysical inquiries. Providence has not intended that the insights most necessary for human blessedness should rest upon the subtlety of refined inferences, but rather has immediately provided such insights to natural common sense which, if it is not confused by false artifice, does not fail to lead directly to the true and the useful insofar as we most urgently require them. Thus that employment of common sense which is still well within the limits of ordinary insights readily yields sufficiently convincing proofs for the existence and the properties of this being, although the subtle investigator will everywhere miss the demonstration and the exactitude of precisely defined concepts or regularly connected syllogisms. Nevertheless one is not able to avoid seeking whether this demonstration does not somewhere emerge. For without even mentioning the reasonable desire, which a mind accustomed to thorough investigation cannot forego, of achieving something complete and distinctly conceived in such important knowledge, still if that same insight be mastered it may be hoped that much more in the object could be explained. Achievement of this goal, however, requires that one venture into the fathomless abyss of

man sich auf den bodenlosen Abgrund der Metaphysik wagen. Ein finsterer Ocean ohne Ufer und ohne Leuchtthürme, wo man es wie der Seefahrer auf einem unbeschifften Meere anfangen muß, welcher, so bald er irgend= wo Land betritt, seine Fahrt prüft und untersucht, ob nicht etwa unbe= merkte Seeströme seinen Lauf verwirrt haben, aller Behutsamkeit unge= achtet, die die Kunst zu schiffen nur immer gebieten mag.

Diese Demonstration ist indessen noch niemals erfunden worden, welches schon von andern angemerkt ist. Was ich hier liefere, ist auch nur der Beweisgrund zu einer Demonstration, ein mühsam gesammeltes Bau= geräth, welches der Prüfung des Kenners vor Augen gelegt ist, um aus dessen brauchbaren Stücken nach den Regeln der Dauerhaftigkeit und der Wohlgereimtheit das Gebäude zu vollführen. Eben so wenig wie ich das= jenige, was ich liefere, für die Demonstration selber will gehalten wissen, so wenig sind die Auflösungen der Begriffe, deren ich mich bediene, schon Definitionen. Sie sind, wie mich dünkt, richtige Merkmale der Sachen, wovon ich handele, tüchtig, um daraus zu abgemessenen Erklärungen zu gelangen, an sich selbst um der Wahrheit und Deutlichkeit willen brauch= bar, aber sie erwarten noch die letzte Hand des Künstlers, um den Defi= nitionen beigezählt zu werden. Es giebt eine Zeit, wo man in einer solchen Wissenschaft, wie die Metaphysik ist, sich getraut alles zu erklären und alles zu demonstriren, und wiederum eine andere, wo man sich nur mit Furcht und Mißtrauen an dergleichen Unternehmungen wagt.

Die Betrachtungen, die ich darlege, sind die Folge eines langen Nach= denkens, aber die Art des Vortrages hat das Merkmal einer unvollendeten Ausarbeitung an sich, in so fern verschiedene Beschäftigungen die dazu er= forderliche Zeit nicht übrig gelassen haben. Es ist indessen eine sehr ver= gebliche Einschmeichlung, den Leser um Verzeihung zu bitten, daß man ihm, um welcher Ursache willen es auch sei, nur mit etwas Schlechtem habe aufwarten können. Er wird es niemals vergeben, man mag sich ent= schuldigen, wie man will. In meinem Falle ist die nicht völlig ausgebildete Gestalt des Werks nicht sowohl einer Vernachlässigung als einer Unter= lassung aus Absichten beizumessen. Ich wollte nur die erste Züge eines Hauptrisses entwerfen, nach welchen, wie ich glaube, ein Gebäude von nicht geringer Vortrefflichkeit könnte aufgeführt werden, wenn unter geübtern Händen die Zeichnung in den Theilen mehr Richtigkeit und im Ganzen eine vollendete Regelmäßigkeit erhielte. In dieser Absicht wäre es un= nöthig gewesen, gar zu viel ängstliche Sorgfalt zu verwenden, um in ein=

metaphysics. This is a dark ocean without coasts and without lighthouses where one must begin like a mariner on a deserted ocean who, as soon as he steps on land somewhere, must test his passage and investigate whether perhaps unnoticed currents have confused his course despite all the care which the art of navigation can command.

This demonstration has, however, not yet been discovered —which has already been noted by others. What I provide here is only the basis for such a demonstration [*Beweisgrund*] [2] the painstakingly assembled material for building which is presented for the appraisal of experts in order that through it they may execute the building according to the rules of durability and harmonious adaptation. And as I do not wish what I am here providing to be taken for the demonstration itself, so should the analyses of concepts that serve me not be taken as definitions. They are, as I believe, correct characteristics of the things with which I am dealing, and as such are apt to lead to exact definitions. In themselves they are useful for truth and distinctness, but they await the final artistic touch to be counted definitions. There is a time in a science like metaphysics when one trusts oneself to explain and demonstrate everything; but again there is another time when one ventures upon that same undertaking only with fear and diffidence.

The considerations which I present are the results of long reflection. But the manner of presentation itself has the characteristic of an uncompleted endeavor insofar as diverse concerns have not left the time required for perfecting it. It is, however, most futile ingratiation to beg the pardon of the reader for having, whatever the reason, been able to serve him up only something bad. He will never forgive it no matter how one excuses oneself. In my case the incomplete form of the work is not so much to be attributed to careless neglect as it is to intentional omissions. I wanted only to sketch the first strokes of a master plan according to which, as I believe, a construction of not insignificant value could be produced if, under more practiced hands, the parts of the sketch gain greater correctness and the whole a perfect regularity. With this intention it would have been unnecessary to employ too scrupulous a care in painting exactly all the features of *each* particular part since as a

zelnen Stücken alle Züge genau auszumalen, da der Entwurf im Ganzen
allererst das strenge Urtheil der Meister in der Kunst abzuwarten hat.
Ich habe daher öfters nur Beweisthümer angeführt, ohne mich anzumaßen,
daß ich ihre Verknüpfung mit der Folgerung für jetzt deutlich zeigen könnte.
Ich habe bisweilen gemeine Verstandesurtheile angeführt, ohne ihnen durch
logische Kunst die Gestalt der Festigkeit zu geben, die ein Baustück in einem
System haben muß, entweder weil ich es schwer fand, oder weil die Weitläuftigkeit der nöthigen Vorbereitung der Größe, die das Werk haben sollte,
nicht gemäß war, oder auch weil ich mich berechtigt zu sein glaubte, da ich
keine Demonstration ankündige, der Forderung, die man mit Recht an
systematische Verfasser thut, entschlagen zu sein. Ein kleiner Theil derer,
die sich das Urtheil über Werke des Geistes anmaßen, wirft kühne Blicke
auf das Ganze eines Versuchs und betrachtet vornehmlich die Beziehung,
die die Hauptstücke desselben zu einem tüchtigen Bau haben könnten, wenn
man gewisse Mängel ergänzte oder Fehler verbesserte. Diese Art Leser ist
es, deren Urtheil dem menschlichen Erkenntniß vornehmlich nutzbar ist.
Was die übrige anlangt, welche, unvermögend eine Verknüpfung im
Großen zu übersehen, an einem oder andern kleinen Theile grüblerisch ge-
heftet sind, unbekümmert ob der Tadel, den er etwa verdiente, auch den
Werth des Ganzen anfechte, und ob nicht Verbesserungen in einzelnen
Stücken den Hauptplan, der nur in Theilen fehlerhaft ist, erhalten können,
diese, die nur immer bestrebt sind, einen jeden angefangenen Bau in
Trümmer zu verwandeln, können zwar um ihrer Menge willen zu fürchten
sein, allein ihr Urtheil ist, was die Entscheidung des wahren Werthes anlangt, bei Vernünftigen von wenig Bedeutung.

Ich habe mich an einigen Orten vielleicht nicht umständlich genug
erklärt, um denen, die nur eine scheinbare Veranlassung wünschen, auf
eine Schrift den bittern Vorwurf des Irrglaubens zu werfen, alle Gelegenheit dazu zu benehmen, allein welche Behutsamkeit hätte dieses auch
wohl verhindern können; ich glaube indessen für diejenige deutlich genug
geredet zu haben, die nichts anders in einer Schrift finden wollen, als was
des Verfassers Absicht gewesen ist hinein zu legen. Ich habe mich so wenig
wie möglich mit Widerlegungen eingelassen, so sehr auch meine Sätze von
anderer ihren abweichen. Diese Entgegenstellung ist etwas, das ich dem
Nachdenken des Lesers, der beide eingesehen hat, überlasse. Wenn man
die Urtheile der unverstellten Vernunft in verschiedenen denkenden Personen
mit der Aufrichtigkeit eines unbestochenen Sachwalters prüfte, der von

5*

whole the draft has to await the strict judgment of masters of the art. I have, therefore, often only cited proofs [*Beweistümer*]without claiming for now that I could distinctly show their connection with the conclusion. I have occasionally cited judgments of common sense without using the art of logic to give them the solidity that a building block of a system must have, either because I found it difficult, or because the necessary preparation would not have been commensurate with the intended size of the work, or because I felt justified in believing myself excused from the demands which properly are placed upon systematic authors since I am not proclaiming a demonstration here.

A small portion of those who claim to pass judgment upon works of the mind cast bold eyes over the whole of the endeavor, noting principally the relation that the main parts of it could have to a sound structure were certain wants fulfilled or errors corrected. This sort of reader is the one whose judgment is particularly useful for human knowledge. So far as the others are concerned—those who, incapable of taking an overview of the whole nexus, fix with excessive subtlety upon one or another small part, unconcerned with whether the censure that it perhaps earns calls the value of the whole into question, or whether the main plan which is defective only in parts cannot be improved; those who always attempt to reduce any newly begun structure to ruins—these can be feared for their great numbers, to be sure, but their judgment has little significance for sensible people so far as the evaluation of true worth is concerned.

Perhaps I have not expressed myself fully enough in a few places to forestall the objections of those who only want an apparent reason for taking every opportunity to subject writing to the bitter reproach of heresy. Yet what provision could have prevented this? I believe, however, that I have spoken distinctly enough for those who want to read into a work nothing but what the author's intention has been. I have been involved as little as possible with refutations, no matter how much my theses diverge from those of others.[3] This polemic is something which I can leave to the reflection of the reader who has understood both. If one were to test the judgments of honest reason in different thinkers with the sincerity of an uncorrupted

zwei strittigen Theilen die Gründe so abwiegt, daß er sich in Gedanken in die Stelle derer, die sie vorbringen, selbst versetzt, um sie so stark zu finden, als sie nur immer werden können, und dann allererst auszumachen, welchem Theile er sich widmen wolle, so würde viel weniger Uneinigkeit in den Meinungen der Philosophen sein, und eine ungeheuchelte Billigkeit, sich selbst der Sache des Gegentheils in dem Grade anzunehmen, als es möglich ist, würde bald die forschende Köpfe auf einem Wege vereinigen.

In einer schweren Betrachtung, wie die gegenwärtige ist, kann ich mich wohl zum voraus darauf gefaßt machen, daß mancher Satz unrichtig, manche Erläuterung unzulänglich und manche Ausführung gebrechlich und mangelhaft sein werde. Ich mache keine solche Forderung auf eine unbeschränkte Unterzeichnung des Lesers, die ich selbst schwerlich einem Verfasser bewilligen würde. Es wird mir daher nicht fremd sein von andern in manchen Stücken eines bessern belehrt zu werden, auch wird man mich gelehrig finden, solchen Unterricht anzunehmen. Es ist schwer dem An=spruche auf Richtigkeit zu entsagen, den man im Anfange zuversichtlich äußerte, als man Gründe vortrug, allein es ist nicht eben so schwer, wenn dieser Anspruch gelinde, unsicher und bescheiden war. Selbst die feinste Eitelkeit, wenn sie sich wohl versteht, wird bemerken, daß nicht weniger Verdienst dazu gehört sich überzeugen zu lassen als selbst zu überzeugen, und daß jene Handlung vielleicht mehr wahre Ehre macht, in so fern mehr Entsagung und Selbstprüfung dazu als zu der andern erfordert wird. Es könnte scheinen eine Verletzung der Einheit, die man bei der Betrachtung seines Gegenstandes vor Augen haben muß, zu sein, daß hin und wieder ziemlich ausführliche physische Erläuterungen vorkommen; allein da meine Absicht in diesen Fällen vornehmlich auf die Methode, vermittelst der Naturwissenschaft zur Erkenntniß Gottes hinaufzusteigen, gerichtet ist, so habe ich diesen Zweck ohne dergleichen Beispiele nicht wohl erreichen können. Die siebente Betrachtung der zweiten Abtheilung bedarf desfalls etwas mehr Nachsicht, vornehmlich da ihr Inhalt aus einem Buche, welches ich ehedem ohne Nennung meines Namens herausgab,*) gezogen worden, wo

---

*) Der Titel desselben ist: Allgemeine Naturgeschichte und Theorie des Himmels. Königsberg und Leipzig 1755. Diese Schrift, die wenig bekannt geworden, muß unter andern auch nicht zur Kenntniß des berühmten Herrn J. H. Lambert gelangt sein, der sechs Jahre hernach in seinen Kosmologischen Briefen 1761 eben dieselbe Theorie von der systematischen Verfassung des Welt=baues im Großen, der Milchstraße, den Nebelsternen u. s. f. vorgetragen hat, die

lawyer, who so balances the arguments for two competing parties that in thought he puts himself in place of those who bring them forward in order to find the arguments as strong as possible and only then decides which side he will take up, there would be far less divergence in the opinions of philosophers. And an unfeigned fairness in assuming the cause of the contrary side as much as possible would soon unite inquiring minds upon a common path.

In a difficult study such as the present one is, I am certainly prepared in advance for many a proposition to be incorrect, many an explanation insufficient, and many an exposition shaky and still defective. I make no demand for the unlimited endorsement by the reader which I would myself hardly grant an author. Therefore it in no way is strange to me that in many parts I may be shown a better way by others; and I will be found docile enough to accept such instruction. It is difficult to renounce the claim to correctness that one so confidently expressed at the outset in presenting arguments. But this is not so difficult if that claim itself was gentle, tentative, and modest. In fact even the most refined vanity, if it properly understands itself, will notice that no less merit attaches to allowing oneself to be convinced than to be convincing; and perhaps the former deed is the more honorable insofar as it requires greater abnegation and self-examination than the latter.

It might appear an interruption of the unity in treatment, which must always be kept in view, that here and there rather wide-reaching physical considerations appear. However, since my intention in these cases is principally directed toward the method of ascending to knowledge of God through means of natural science, I would not have been able to achieve the goal easily without such examples. The Seventh Observation in the second part of the work, however, requires somewhat more forebearance on that account principally because its content is drawn from a book I previously published anonymously,* where the issues are treated in more detail though in connection

*The title of it is: *Universal Natural History and Theory of the Heavens* (Königsberg and Leipzig, 1755). This work, which has been little noticed, must amongst others also not have come to the attention of the celebrated

hievon ausführlicher, obzwar in Verknüpfung mit verschiedenen etwas gewagten Hypothesen gehandelt ward. Die Verwandtschaft indessen, die zum mindesten die erlaubte Freiheit sich an solche Erklärungen zu wagen mit meiner Hauptabsicht hat, imgleichen der Wunsch, einiges an dieser Hypothese von Kennern beurtheilt zu sehen, haben veranlaßt diese Betrachtung einzumischen, die vielleicht zu kurz ist, um alle Gründe derselben zu verstehen, oder auch zu weitläuftig für diejenige, die hier nichts wie Metaphysik anzutreffen vermuthen, und von denen sie füglich kann überschlagen werden. Es wird vielleicht nöthig sein einige Druckfehler, die den Sinn des Vortrages verändern könnten, und die man am Ende des Werks sieht, vorher zu verbessern, ehe man diese Schrift liest.

Das Werk selber besteht aus drei Abtheilungen, davon die erste den Beweisgrund selber, die zweite den weitläuftigen Nutzen desselben, die dritte aber Gründe vorlegt, um darzuthun, daß kein anderer zu einer Demonstration vom Dasein Gottes möglich sei.

man in meiner gedachten Theorie des Himmels im ersten Theile, imgleichen in der Vorrede daselbst antrifft, und wovon etwas in einem kurzen Abrisse Seite 154 bis 158[1] des gegenwärtigen Werks angezeigt wird. Die Übereinstimmung der Gedanken dieses sinnreichen Mannes mit denen, die ich damals vortrug, welche fast bis auf die kleineren Züge untereinander übereinkommen, vergrößert meine Vermuthung: daß dieser Entwurf in der Folge mehrere Bestätigung erhalten werde.

[1] Der Originalausgabe (1763). Vgl. unten S. 139—141.

with different and somewhat risky hypotheses. To say the least, the affinity of my presumed freedom to venture upon such an explanation with my primary intention here as well as the hope to have something of this hypothesis judged by experts is my excuse for introducing this Observation. It is perhaps too short to understand all its reasons or else too long for those who expect here to encounter nothing except metaphysics, and this Observation may conveniently be omitted by them.

Perhaps it would be necessary to correct a few of those printer's errors which could alter the sense of the essay before beginning to read the essay. They are noted at the back.

The work consists of three sections. The *first* puts forward the ground of proof itself. The *second* shows the extensive utility of this, and the *third* section lays out the reasons by which it will be shown that no other one is possible for a demonstration of the existence of God.

J.H. Lambert, who six years later in his *Cosmological Letters* (1761) [*Cosmological Letters on the Structure of the Universe, Written by J.H. Lambert* (Augsburg, 1761)] presented exactly the same theory of the systematic composition of the universe as a whole, of the Milky Way, and of the nebulae, etc., that is to be found in my proposed theory of the heavens in the first part and likewise in the preface. Something of this is shown in brief outine on pages 190-194 of the present work. The agreement of the reflections of this thoughtful man with those which I announced at that time—an agreement extending almost to the smallest features—strengthens my confidence that this project will in time receive further confirmation.

Erste Abtheilung,

worin der

Beweisgrund zur Demonstration des Daseins Gottes

geliefert wird.

Erste Betrachtung.
Vom Dasein überhaupt.

Die Regel der Gründlichkeit erfordert es nicht allemal, daß selbst im tiefsinnigsten Vortrage ein jeder vorkommende Begriff entwickelt oder er= klärt werde: wenn man nämlich versichert ist, daß der blos klare gemeine Begriff in dem Falle, da er gebraucht wird, keinen Mißverstand veran= lassen könne; so wie der Meßkünstler die geheimsten Eigenschaften und Verhältnisse des Ausgedehnten mit der größten Gewißheit aufdeckt, ob er sich gleich hiebei lediglich des gemeinen Begriffs vom Raum bedient, und wie selbst in der allertiefsinnigsten Wissenschaft das Wort Vorstellung genau genug verstanden und mit Zuversicht gebraucht wird, wiewohl seine Bedeutung niemals durch eine Erklärung kann aufgelöset werden.

Ich würde mich daher in diesen Betrachtungen nicht bis zur Auflösung des sehr einfachen und wohlverstandnen Begriffs des Daseins versteigen, wenn nicht hier gerade der Fall wäre, wo diese Verabsäumung Verwirrung und wichtige Irrthümer veranlassen kann. Es ist sicher, daß er in der übrigen ganzen Weltweisheit so unentwickelt, wie er im gemeinen Gebrauch vorkommt, ohne Bedenken könne angebracht werden, die einzige Frage vom absolut nothwendigen und zufälligen Dasein ausgenommen, denn

PART ONE

In Which the Basis for a Demonstration
of the Existence of God is Provided

OBSERVATION ONE

Existence in General

The rule of thoroughness does not always require that every concept, in even the most profound essay, be developed or defined; particularly if one may be assured that the clear, common concept can cause no misunderstanding where it is used. Thus the geometer reveals, with greatest certainty, the most esoteric properties and relations of the extended though in this he is simply using the common concept of space. Even in the most profound science the term "representation" is precisely understood and employed with confidence, although its meaning can never be analyzed through a definition.

Thus in these observations I would not aspire to analysis of the very simple and well-understood concept of existence, were this not just the case wherein neglect could engender confusion and important errors. Certainly it may be unhesitatingly applied in all the rest of philosophy in the undeveloped form in which it occurs in ordinary use; the single exception is in the question of absolutely necessary and contingent existence. For here more

hier hat eine subtilere Nachforschung aus einem unglücklich gekünstelten, sonst sehr reinen Begriff irrige Schlüsse gezogen, die sich über einen der erhabensten Theile der Weltweisheit verbreitet haben.

Man erwarte nicht, daß ich mit einer förmlichen Erklärung des Daseins den Anfang machen werde. Es wäre zu wünschen, daß man dieses niemals thäte, wo es so unsicher ist, richtig erklärt zu haben, und dieses ist es öfter, als man wohl denkt. Ich werde so verfahren als einer, der die Definition sucht und sich zuvor von demjenigen versichert, was man mit Gewißheit bejahend oder verneinend von dem Gegenstande der Erklärung sagen kann, ob er gleich noch nicht ausmacht, worin der ausführlich bestimmte Begriff desselben bestehe. Lange vorher, ehe man eine Erklärung von seinem Gegenstande wagt, und selbst dann, wenn man sich gar nicht getraut sie zu geben, kann man viel von derselben Sache mit größter Gewißheit sagen. Ich zweifle, daß einer jemals richtig erklärt habe, was der Raum sei. Allein ohne mich damit einzulassen, bin ich gewiß, daß, wo er ist, äußere Beziehungen sein müssen, daß er nicht mehr als drei Abmessungen haben könne, u. s. w. Eine Begierde mag sein, was sie will, so gründet sie sich auf irgend eine Vorstellung, sie setzt eine Lust an dem Begehrten voraus u. s. f. Oft kann aus diesem, was man vor aller Definition von der Sache gewiß weiß, das, was zur Absicht unserer Untersuchung gehört, ganz sicher hergeleitet werden, und man wagt sich alsdann in unnöthige Schwierigkeiten, wenn man sich bis dahin versteigt. Die Methodensucht, die Nachahmung des Mathematikers, der auf einer wohlgebähnten Straße sicher fortschreitet, auf dem schlüpfrigen Boden der Metaphysik hat eine Menge solcher Fehltritte veranlaßt, die man beständig vor Augen sieht, und doch ist wenig Hoffnung, daß man dadurch gewarnt und behutsamer zu sein lernen werde. Diese Methode ist es allein, kraft welcher ich einige Aufklärungen hoffe, die ich vergeblich bei andern gesucht habe; denn was die schmeichelhafte Vorstellung anlangt, die man sich macht, daß man durch größere Scharfsinnigkeit es besser als andre treffen werde, so versteht man wohl, daß jederzeit alle so geredet haben, die uns aus einem fremden Irrthum in den ihrigen haben ziehen wollen.

subtle investigation has drawn false conclusions, from an unfortunately over-refined but otherwise very pure concept, that have spread over one of the most sublime parts of philosophy.

It is not to be expected that I begin with a formal definition[4] of existence. It might be wished that this were never done where it is so uncertain that it has been properly defined and that is more frequent than might be thought. I will proceed as one seeking the definition who first makes sure of what can be affirmed or denied with certainty, even though he cannot yet make out in what the fully determined concept of the thing may consist. A good deal may still be said with great certainty about an object long before one dares a definition of it, and even when one is not entirely confident in giving it, for example, I doubt that anyone has ever properly explained what space is. Still, without getting involved in that, I can be certain that where it is there must be external relations: it cannot have more than three dimensions, etc. A desire may be what it will. Still it is founded on some sort of representation; it presupposes an inclination toward what is desired, etc. What concerns the intention of our investigation can often be derived with complete safety from what is certainly known prior to any definition of a thing, and one ventures into unnecessary difficulties by then aspiring to a definition. On the slippery ground of metaphysics the passion for method, in imitation of the mathematician who strides safely along a well-marked road, has occasioned a host of such missteps, as can constantly be seen. And yet there is little hope that one will be warned by that and thereby learn to be more careful.[5] This method is the only one by virtue of which I hope for a bit of enlightenment, which I have sought in vain in others. As concerns the flattering suggestion that through superior cleverness one will hit upon results denied to others, it must be recognized that this has always been said by those who have wanted to draw us from another error into their own.

1.

Das Dasein ist gar kein Prädicat oder Determination von irgend einem Dinge.

Dieser Satz scheint seltsam und widersinnig, allein er ist ungezweifelt gewiß. Nehmet ein Subject, welches ihr wollt, z. E. den Julius Cäsar. Fasset alle seine erdenkliche Prädicate, selbst die der Zeit und des Orts nicht ausgenommen, in ihm zusammen, so werdet ihr bald begreifen, daß er mit allen diesen Bestimmungen existiren, oder auch nicht existiren kann. Das Wesen, welches dieser Welt und diesem Helden in derselben das Dasein gab, konnte alle diese Prädicate, nicht ein einiges ausgenommen, erkennen und ihn doch als ein blos möglich Ding ansehen, das, seinen Rath-schluß ausgenommen, nicht existirt. Wer kann in Abrede ziehen, daß Millionen von Dingen, die wirklich nicht dasind, nach allen Prädicaten, die sie enthalten würden, wenn sie existirten, blos möglich seien; daß in der Vorstellung, die das höchste Wesen von ihnen hat, nicht eine einzige Bestimmung ermangele, obgleich das Dasein nicht mit darunter ist, denn es erkennt sie nur als mögliche Dinge. Es kann also nicht statt finden, daß, wenn sie existiren, sie ein Prädicat mehr enthielten, denn bei der Möglichkeit eines Dinges nach seiner durchgängigen Bestimmung kann gar kein Prädicat fehlen. Und wenn es Gott gefallen hätte, eine andere Reihe der Dinge, eine andere Welt zu schaffen, so würde sie mit allen den Bestimmungen und keinen mehr existirt haben, die er an ihr doch erkennt, ob sie gleich blos möglich ist.

Gleichwohl bedient man sich des Ausdrucks vom Dasein als eines Prädicats, und man kann dieses auch sicher und ohne besorgliche Irr-thümer thun, so lange man es nicht darauf aussetzt, das Dasein aus blos möglichen Begriffen herleiten zu wollen, wie man zu thun pflegt, wenn man die absolut nothwendige Existenz beweisen will. Denn alsdann sucht man umsonst unter den Prädicaten eines solchen möglichen Wesens, das Dasein findet sich gewiß nicht darunter. Es ist aber das Dasein in den Fällen, da es im gemeinen Redegebrauch als ein Prädicat vorkommt, nicht sowohl ein Prädicat von dem Dinge selbst, als vielmehr von dem Gedanken, den man davon hat. Z. E. dem Seeeinhorn kommt die Existenz zu, dem Landeinhorn nicht. Es will dieses nichts anders sagen, als: die Vorstellung des Seeeinhorns ist ein Erfahrungsbegriff, das ist, die Vorstellung eines existirenden Dinges. Daher man auch, um die Richtigkeit

1.
Existence is not a predicate or determination of any thing.

This proposition seems strange and absurd; yet it is undoubtedly true. Take any subject you like—Julius Caesar, for instance. Combine in him all his conceivable predicates, not even excluding those of time and place, and you will quickly see that with all of these determinations he can exist or not exist. The being who gave existence to the world, and to that hero in it, would know all of these predicates without a single exception and yet regard him as a merely possible thing which would not exist save for his decree. Who can deny that millions of things that are not actually existent would be possible only according to all the predicates that they would contain were they to exist. Not a single determination [6] would be wanting in the idea [*die Vorstellung*] that the supreme being has of them, and yet existence is not amongst them since he knows them as only possible things. Thus it cannot be that if they existed they would contain one more predicate, for in the possibility of a thing according to its thorough determination, absolutley no predicate can be missing. Had it pleased God to create a different series of things, a different world, it would have existed with all the determinations, and no more, that he recognizes in it although it is merely possible.

Nevertheless, the term "existence" is used as a predicate and this can be done safely and without troublesome errors so long as it is not proposed to deduce being from merely possible concepts as one is wont to do in proving absolutely necessary existence. For then one seeks in vain amongst the predicates of such a possible being, because existence certainly is not to be found amongst them. In those instances of ordinary speech where existence is encountered as a predicate it is not so much a predicate of the thing itself as it is of the thought one has of it. For example, existence belongs to a sea unicorn [i.e., a Narwahl], but not to a land unicorn. This is to say nothing other than that the notion of a sea unicorn is a concept of experience, that is a notion of an existent thing.

dieses Satzes von dem Dasein einer solchen Sache darzuthun, nicht in dem
Begriffe des Subjects sucht, denn da findet man nur Prädicate der Mög=
lichkeit, sondern in dem Ursprunge der Erkenntniß, die ich davon habe. Ich
habe, sagt man, es gesehen, oder von denen vernommen, die es gesehen haben.
Es ist daher kein völlig richtiger Ausdruck zu sagen: Ein Seeeinhorn ist ein
existirend Thier, sondern umgekehrt: einem gewissen existirenden Seethiere
kommen die Prädicate zu, die ich an einem Einhorn zusammen gedenke. Nicht:
regelmäßige Sechsecke existiren in der Natur, sondern: gewissen Dingen in
der Natur, wie den Bienenzellen oder dem Bergkrystall, kommen die Prädicate
zu, die in einem Sechsecke beisammen gedacht werden. Eine jede menschliche
Sprache hat von den Zufälligkeiten ihres Ursprungs einige nicht zu ändernde
Unrichtigkeiten, und es würde grüblerisch und unnütz sein, wo in dem ge=
wöhnlichen Gebrauche gar keine Mißdeutungen daraus erfolgen können,
an ihr zu künsteln und einzuschränken, genug daß in den seltnern Fällen
einer höher gesteigerten Betrachtung, wo es nöthig ist, diese Unter=
scheidungen beigefügt werden. Man wird von dem hier Angeführten nur
allererst zureichend urtheilen können, wenn man das folgende wird gelesen
haben.

2.

Das Dasein ist die absolute Position eines Dinges und unter=
scheidet sich dadurch auch von jeglichem Prädicate, welches als
ein solches jederzeit blos beziehungsweise auf ein ander Ding
gesetzt wird.

Der Begriff der Position oder Setzung ist völlig einfach und mit dem
vom Sein überhaupt einerlei. Nun kann etwas als blos beziehungsweise
gesetzt, oder besser blos die Beziehung (respectus logicus) von etwas als
einem Merkmal zu einem Dinge gedacht werden, und dann ist das Sein,
das ist die Position dieser Beziehung, nichts als der Verbindungsbegriff
in einem Urtheile. Wird nicht blos diese Beziehung, sondern die Sache an
und für sich selbst gesetzt betrachtet, so ist dieses Sein so viel als Dasein.

So einfach ist dieser Begriff, daß man nichts zu seiner Auswickelung
sagen kann, als nur die Behutsamkeit anzumerken, daß er nicht mit den
Verhältnissen, die die Dinge zu ihren Merkmalen haben, verwechselt werde.

Wenn man einsieht, daß unsere gesammte Erkenntniß sich doch zuletzt
in unauflöslichen Begriffen endige, so begreift man auch, daß es einige
geben werde, die beinahe unauflöslich sind, das ist, wo die Merkmale nur

Thus in order to demonstrate the truth of this proposition about the existence of such a thing, one seeks not in the concept of the subject, for here only the predicates of possibility can be found, but rather in the origin of the knowledge I have of the subject. One says, "I have seen it," or "I have accepted it from those who have seen it." It is thus not a fully correct expression to say "A sea unicorn is an existent animal," but rather conversely: "The predicates that I think together as a sea unicorn belong to certain existent sea creatures." Not: "Regular hexagons exist in nature," but rather: "The predicates that are thought together in a hexagon belong to certain things in nature, such as honeycombs or rock crystals."

Every human language has a few unalterable inadequacies owing to the accidents of its origin. Where absolutely no misinterpretation can follow from ordinary usage it would be carping and useless to elaborate and limit them. Enough that in the infrequent cases of a more ambitious study these distinctions be appended where they are necessary. It will be possible to judge sufficiently the one cited here only after the following has been read.

2.

Existence is the absolute position of the thing and thus is distinguished from every predicate which as such is always posited merely with respect to some other thing.

The concept of position or positing is totally simple and on the whole identical with the concept of being in general. Now something can be posited as merely relational; or better, be thought merely as the relation (*respectus logicus*) of something as a property of a thing. Then being, that is the position of this relation, is only the copulative concept in a judgment. Should not only this relation but the thing in and for itself be viewed as posited, then this being is the same as existence.

This concept is so simple that nothing can be added to its development except to note the caution that it is not to be confused with the relationship that things have to their properties.

If it be seen that our entire knowledge finally ends in unanalyzable concepts, then it is also clear that there will be some concepts which are nearly unanalyzable, that is, where the

sehr wenig klärer und einfacher sind, als die Sache selbst. Dieses ist der Fall bei unserer Erklärung von der Existenz. Ich gestehe gerne, daß durch dieselbe der Begriff des Erklärten nur in einem sehr kleinen Grade deutlich werde. Allein die Natur des Gegenstandes in Beziehung auf die Vermögen unseres Verstandes verstattet auch keinen höhern Grad.

Wenn ich sage: Gott ist allmächtig, so wird nur diese logische Beziehung zwischen Gott und der Allmacht gedacht, da die letztere ein Merkmal des erstern ist. Weiter wird hier nichts gesetzt. Ob Gott sei, das ist, absolute gesetzt sei oder existire, das ist darin gar nicht enthalten. Daher auch dieses Sein ganz richtig selbst bei den Beziehungen gebraucht wird, die Undinge gegen einander haben. Z. E. Der Gott des Spinoza ist unaufhörlichen Veränderungen unterworfen.

Wenn ich mir vorstelle, Gott spreche über eine mögliche Welt sein allmächtiges Werde, so ertheilt er dem in seinem Verstande vorgestellten Ganzen keine neue Bestimmungen, er setzt nicht ein neues Prädicat hinzu, sondern er setzt diese Reihe der Dinge, in welcher alles sonst nur beziehungsweise auf dieses Ganze gesetzt war, mit allen Prädicaten absolute oder schlechthin. Die Beziehungen aller Prädicate zu ihren Subjecten bezeichnen niemals etwas Existirendes, das Subject müsse denn schon als existirend voraus gesetzt werden. Gott ist allmächtig, muß ein wahrer Satz auch in dem Urtheil desjenigen bleiben, der dessen Dasein nicht erkennt, wenn er mich nur wohl versteht, wie ich den Begriff Gottes nehme. Allein sein Dasein muß unmittelbar zu der Art gehören, wie sein Begriff gesetzt wird, denn in den Prädicaten selber wird es nicht gefunden. Und wenn nicht schon das Subject als existirend vorausgesetzt ist, so bleibt es bei jeglichem Prädicate unbestimmt, ob es zu einem existirenden oder blos möglichen Subjecte gehöre. Das Dasein kann daher selber kein Prädicat sein. Sage ich: Gott ist ein existirend Ding, so scheint es, als wenn ich die Beziehung eines Prädicats zum Subjecte ausdrückte. Allein es liegt auch eine Unrichtigkeit in diesem Ausdruck. Genau gesagt, sollte es heißen: Etwas Existirendes ist Gott, das ist, einem existirenden Dinge kommen diejenigen Prädicate zu, die wir zusammen genommen durch den Ausdruck: Gott, bezeichnen. Diese Prädicate sind beziehungsweise auf dieses Subject gesetzt, allein das Ding selber sammt allen Prädicaten ist schlechthin gesetzt.

Ich besorge durch zu weitläuftige Erläuterung einer so einfachen Idee unvernehmlich zu werden. Ich könnte auch noch befürchten die Zärtlichkeit derer, die vornehmlich über Trockenheit klagen, zu beleidigen. Allein ohne

properties are only very slightly clearer and simpler than the thing itself. This is the case in our definition of existence. I freely admit that thereby the concept of the thing defined is made distinct only to a very slight degree. Still the nature of the subject in relation to the capacity of our understanding permits of no higher degree.

If I say "God is omnipotent," only this logical relation between God and omnipotence is thought since the latter is property of the former. Nothing further is posited here. Whether God is, that is, is absolutely posited or exists, is by no means contained in that. Thus this being [expressed by the copula] is quite properly used even for the relations that non-entities have to one another. For example, Spinoza's God is subject to incessant modifications.

When I think of God as pronouncing his omnipotent *fiat* over a possible world, he imparts no new determinations to the whole represented in his understanding. He adds no new predicate to it; rather, he establishes absolutely and positively this series of things with all the predicates in which otherwise everything was posited only relative to this whole. The relations of all predicates to their subjects never denote anything existent; the subject would then have to be posited as already existent. "God is omnipotent" must remain a true proposition even in the judgment of one who does not acknowledge his existence if only he understands how I take the concept of God. Yet his existence must belong immediately to the way in which his concept is posited, for it is not to be found in the predicates themselves. And if the subject is not assumed to exist, then it remains undetermined for every one of these predicates whether it belongs to an existent or only to a merely possible subject. Thus existence cannot itself be a predicate. If I say, "God is an existent thing," it seems as though I am expressing the relation of a predicate to a subject. However there is an inaccuracy in this expression. Precisely expressed it should read: "Something existent is God," that is, "Those predicates taken together that we signify by the expression 'God' belong to an existent thing." These predicates are posited relative to the subject, but the thing itself together with all its predicates is absolutely posited.

I fear becoming unintelligible by too thorough an exposition of such a simple idea. And indeed I might also fear

diesen Tadel für etwas Geringes zu halten, muß ich mir diesmal hiezu
Erlaubniß ausbitten. Denn ob ich schon an der überfeinen Weisheit der=
jenigen, welche sichere und brauchbare Begriffe in ihrer logischen Schmelz=
küche so lange übertreiben, abziehen und verfeinern, bis sie in Dämpfen
und flüchtigen Salzen verrauchen, so wenig Geschmack als jemand anders
finde, so ist der Gegenstand der Betrachtung, den ich vor mir habe, doch
von der Art, daß man entweder gänzlich es aufgeben muß, eine demon=
strativische Gewißheit davon jemals zu erlangen, oder es sich muß gefallen
lassen, seine Begriffe bis in diese Atomen aufzulösen.

3.

Kann ich wohl sagen, daß im Dasein mehr als in der bloßen Möglichkeit sei?

Diese Frage zu beantworten, merke ich nur zuvor an, daß man unter=
scheiden müsse, was da gesetzt sei, und wie es gesetzt sei. Was das erstere
anlangt, so ist in einem wirklichen Dinge nicht mehr gesetzt als in einem
blos möglichen, denn alle Bestimmungen und Prädicate des wirklichen
können auch bei der bloßen Möglichkeit desselben angetroffen werden, aber
das letztere betreffend, so ist allerdings durch die Wirklichkeit mehr gesetzt.
Denn frage ich: wie ist alles dieses bei der bloßen Möglichkeit gesetzt?, so
werde ich inne, es geschehe nur beziehungsweise auf das Ding selber, d. i.
wenn ein Triangel ist, so sind drei Seiten, ein beschlossener Raum, drei
Winkel u. f. w., oder besser: die Beziehungen dieser Bestimmungen zu
einem solchen Etwas, wie ein Triangel ist, sind bloß gesetzt, aber existirt
er, so ist alles dieses absolute, d. i. die Sache selbst zusammt diesen Be=
ziehungen, mithin mehr gesetzt. Um daher in einer so subtilen Vorstellung
alles zusammen zu fassen, was die Verwirrung verhüten kann, so sage ich:
in einem Existirenden wird nichts mehr gesetzt als in einem blos Mög=
lichen (denn alsdann ist die Rede von den Prädicaten desselben), allein
durch etwas Existirendes wird mehr gesetzt als durch ein blos Mögliches,
denn dieses geht auch auf absolute Position der Sache selbst. Sogar ist in
der bloßen Möglichkeit nicht die Sache selbst, sondern es sind bloße Be=
ziehungen von Etwas zu Etwas nach dem Satze des Widerspruchs gesetzt,
und es bleibt fest, daß das Dasein eigentlich gar kein Prädicat von irgend
einem Dinge sei. Obgleich meine Absicht hier gar nicht ist mit Wider=
legungen mich einzulassen, und meiner Meinung nach, wenn ein Verfasser

to offend the sensibilities of those who complain about tediousness. Still, without seeming to take such censure lightly, I must ask permission for it this time. Though to be sure I have as little taste as anyone else for the super-refined wisdom of those who overcook, abstract, and refine certain and useful concepts in their logic-hearths until they evaporate in vapors and volatile salts, the object of the study that I intend to deal with is of the sort which requires either that the attempt to achieve demonstrative certainty be given up entirely or else that one be willing to analyze its concepts into these atoms.

3.
Can I properly say that there is more in existence than in the merely possible?

To answer this question I note first that one must distinguish here what is posited and how it is posited. What the former comes to is that nothing more is posited in an actual thing than in a merely possible one since all the determinations and predicates of the actual may also be encountered in the mere possibility of it. However, insofar as the latter is concerned, of course, more is posited through actuality. For if I ask "How is all this posited in the merely possible?", I see that it happens only relative to the thing itself. That is, if there is a triangle, then there are three sides, an enclosed space, three angles and so on. Or better, the relations of these determinations are simply posited to something such as a triangle is, but if the triangle exists, then all of this is posited absolutely, that is, the thing itself together with all these relations—and thus more—is posited. To summarize everything then which in such a subtle notion can prevent confusion, I say that: in an existent thing nothing more is posited than in a merely possible one (for then it is a question of the predicates of the thing). However, something more is posited through an existent thing than through a merely possible one, because this concerns the absolute position of the thing itself. So the thing itself is not posited in the mere possibility, but rather merely the relations of something to something else are posited according to the law of contradiction, and it remains true that existence can in no way properly be a predicate of any thing. Although it is not at all my intention here to become involved in refutations since, in my view, if an author has read other reflections with an

mit vorurtheilfreier Denkungsart anderer Gedanken gelesen und durch da=
mit verknüpftes Nachdenken sie sich eigen gemacht hat, er das Urtheil über
seine neue und abweichende Lehrsätze ziemlich sicher dem Leser überlassen
kann, so will ich doch nur mit wenig Worten darauf führen.

Die Wolffische Erklärung des Daseins, daß es eine Ergänzung der
Möglichkeit sei, ist offenbar sehr unbestimmt. Wenn man nicht schon vor=
her weiß, was über die Möglichkeit in einem Dinge kann gedacht werden,
so wird man es durch diese Erklärung nicht lernen. Baumgarten führt
die durchgängige innere Bestimmung, in so fern sie dasjenige ergänzt, was
durch die im Wesen liegende oder daraus fließende Prädicate unbestimmt
gelassen ist, als dasjenige an, was im Dasein mehr als in der bloßen Mög=
lichkeit ist; allein wir haben schon gesehen, daß in der Verbindung eines
Dinges mit allen erdenklichen Prädicaten niemals ein Unterschied desselben
von einem blos Möglichen liege. Überdem kann der Satz, daß ein möglich
Ding, als ein solches betrachtet, in Ansehung vieler Prädicate unbestimmt
sei, wenn er so nach dem Buchstaben genommen wird, eine große Unrichtig=
keit veranlassen. Denn die Regel der Ausschließung eines Mittlern zwischen
zwei widersprechend entgegen Gesetzten verbietet dieses, und es ist daher
z. E. ein Mensch, der nicht eine gewisse Statur, Zeit, Alter, Ort u. d. g.
hätte, unmöglich. Man muß ihn vielmehr in diesem Sinne nehmen: durch
die an einem Dinge zusammengedachte Prädicate sind viele andere ganz
und gar nicht bestimmt, so wie durch dasjenige, was in dem Begriff eines
Menschen als eines solchen zusammengenommen ist, in Ansehung der be=
sondern Merkmale des Alters, Orts u. s. w. nichts ausgemacht wird. Aber
diese Art der Unbestimmtheit ist alsdann eben so wohl bei einem existirenden
als bei einem blos möglichen Dinge anzutreffen, weswegen dieselbe zu kei=
nem Unterschiede beider kann gebraucht werden. Der berühmte Crusius
rechnet das Irgendwo und Irgendwenn zu den untrüglichen Bestimmungen
des Daseins. Allein ohne uns in die Prüfung des Satzes selber, daß alles,
was da ist, irgendwo oder irgendwenn sein müsse, einzulassen, so gehören
diese Prädicate noch immer auch zu blos möglichen Dingen. Denn so
könnte an manchen bestimmten Orten mancher Mensch zu einer gewissen
Zeit existiren, dessen alle Bestimmungen der Allwissende, so wie sie ihm
beiwohnen würden, wenn er existirte, wohl kennt, und der gleichwohl wirk=
lich nicht da ist; und der ewige Jude Ahasverus nach allen Ländern, die
er durchwandern, oder allen Zeiten, die er durchleben soll, ist ohne Zweifel
ein möglicher Mensch. Man wird doch hoffentlich nicht fordern, daß das

unprejudiced mind and through the associated reflection made them his own, he can pretty safely leave to the reader judgment of his new and modified doctrines, I will add only a few words in that direction.

The Wolffian definition of existence as a complement of possibility [7] obviously is very indefinite. If one does not already know what can be thought beyond the possibility of the thing, he will certainly not learn it through this definition. Baumgarten [8] cites thoroughgoing inner determination as that which is the more in existence than in mere possibility, insofar as it supplements whatever is left undetermined through the predicates implicit in or flowing from the essence. But we have already seen that a difference between the thing and a mere possibility never lies in a connection of the thing with all of its conceivable predicates. In addition, the proposition that a possible thing as such is undetermined in respect to many predicates may cause a considerable error if it be taken literally. The rule of the exclusion of a mean between two contradictory opposites forbids this, and thus for example a man who had no certain stature, time, age, place, and the like is impossible. [9] One must, rather, take it [i.e. the proposition regarding the indeterminancy of the merely possibly] in this sense: That through the many predicates which are thought together in a thing many others are left entirely undetermined. Thus that which is taken together in the concept of a man as such constitutes nothing with respect to particular characteristics of age, place and so on. But then this sort of indeterminacy is to be encountered as much in an existent as in a merely possible thing and therefore cannot be used as a distinction between the two. The famous Crusius [10] counts being somewhere and being at some time as the infallible determinations of existence. However without getting involved in an examination of the proposition that whatever exists must be somewhere and somewhen, these predicates still belong to merely possible things. Thus many a man, all of whose determinations the omniscient certainly knows as they would be in him if he existed, could exist in many a determinate place at a given time

Irgendwo und Irgendwenn nur dann ein zureichend Merkmal des Daseins sei, wenn das Ding wirklich da oder alsdann ist, denn da würde man fordern, daß dasjenige schon eingeräumt werde, was man sich anheischig macht, durch ein taugliches Merkmal von selber kenntlich zu machen.

Zweite Betrachtung.
Von der innern Möglichkeit, in so fern sie ein Dasein voraussetzt.

1.
Nöthige Unterscheidung bei dem Begriffe der Möglichkeit.

Alles, was in sich selbst widersprechend ist, ist innerlich unmöglich. Dieses ist ein wahrer Satz, wenn man es gleich dahin gestellt sein läßt, daß es eine wahre Erklärung sei. Bei diesem Widerspruche aber ist klar, daß Etwas mit Etwas im logischen Widerstreit stehen müsse, das ist, dasjenige verneinen müsse, was in eben demselben zugleich bejaht ist. Selbst nach dem Herren Crusius, der diesen Streit nicht blos in einem innern Widerspruche setzt, sondern behauptet, daß er überhaupt durch den Verstand nach einem ihm natürlichen Gesetze wahrgenommen werde, ist im Unmöglichen allemal eine Verknüpfung mit Etwas, was gesetzt, und Etwas, wodurch es zugleich aufgehoben wird. Diese Repugnanz nenne ich das Formale der Undenklichkeit oder Unmöglichkeit; das Materiale, was hiebei gegeben ist, und welches in solchem Streite steht, ist an sich selber etwas und kann gedacht werden. Ein Triangel, der viereckicht wäre, ist schlechterdings unmöglich. Indessen ist gleichwohl ein Triangel, imgleichen etwas Viereckichtes an sich selber Etwas. Diese Unmöglichkeit beruht lediglich auf logischen Beziehungen von einem Denklichen zum andern, da eins nur nicht ein Merkmal des andern sein kann. Eben so muß in jeder Möglichkeit das Etwas, was gedacht wird, und dann die Übereinstimmung desjenigen, was in ihm zugleich gedacht wird, mit dem Satze des Widerspruchs unterschieden werden. Ein Triangel, der einen rechten Winkel hat, ist an sich selber möglich. Der Triangel sowohl, als der rechte Winkel sind die Data oder das Materiale in diesem Möglichen, die Übereinstimmung aber des einen mit dem andern nach dem Satze des Widerspruchs sind das Formale der Möglichkeit. Ich werde dieses letztere auch das Logische in

even although he does not [really] exist. And the eternal Judas Ahaverus [11] is without a doubt a possible man after all the lands he is to wander through or all the times he is to live through. One would not, I should hope, demand that the somewhere and somewhen be an adequate sign of existence only if the thing is actually here or then, for that would require that one already grant what one has pledged to render knowable through a suitable characteristic of it.

OBSERVATION TWO
On Internal Possibility Insofar As It Presupposes An Existence

1.
A necessary distinction in the concept of possibility

Everything that is contradictory in itself is internally impossible. This is a true proposition, even if one allows it to remain undecided whether it is a true definition. In this contradiction, however, it is clear that something must stand in logical conflict with something else. That is, that must be denied which simultaneously is affirmed in the very same thing. Even for Crusius, [12] who does not place this conflict merely in an internal contradiction but rather maintains that in general it is perceived by the understanding according to laws that are natural to it, in impossibility there is always a conjunction of something which is posited and something through which simultaneously it is annulled. This repugnance I term the formal element of inconceivability or impossibility. The material element which is given along with this and which stands in such a conflict is in itself something and can be thought. A triangle which is four-sided is absolutely impossible. Nevertheless, a triangle as well as something four-sided is in itself something. This impossibility rests purely upon logical relations of one conceivable thing to another, since one cannot be a property of the other. Even so, in every possibility there must be distinguished the thing thought and the agreement of that which is thought in it with the principle of contradiction. A triangle that has a right angle is in itself possible. The triangle as well as the right angle are the data or the matter in this possible thing. But the agreement of the one with the other according to the law of contradiction is the formal element of possibility. I shall also call this latter "the logical element of possibility" because the

67

der Möglichkeit nennen, weil die Vergleichung der Prädicate mit ihren Subjecten nach der Regel der Wahrheit nichts anders als eine logiſche Beziehung iſt, das Etwas oder was in dieſer Übereinſtimmung ſteht, wird bisweilen das Reale der Möglichkeit heißen. Übrigens bemerke ich, daß hier jederzeit von keiner andern Möglichkeit oder Unmöglichkeit, als der innern oder ſchlechterdings und abſolute ſo genannten die Rede ſein wird.

2.
Die innere Möglichkeit aller Dinge ſetzt irgend ein Daſein voraus.

Es iſt aus dem anjetzt Angeführten deutlich zu erſehen, daß die Mög= lichkeit wegfalle, nicht allein wenn ein innerer Widerſpruch als das Logiſche der Unmöglichkeit anzutreffen, ſondern auch wenn kein Materiale, kein Datum zu denken da iſt. Denn alsdann iſt nichts Denkliches gegeben alles Mögliche aber iſt etwas, was gedacht werden kann, und dem die logiſche Beziehung gemäß dem Satze des Widerſpruchs zukommt.

Wenn nun alles Daſein aufgehoben wird, ſo iſt nichts ſchlechthin ge= ſetzt, es iſt überhaupt gar nichts gegeben, kein Materiale zu irgend etwas Denklichem, und alle Möglichkeit fällt gänzlich weg. Es iſt zwar kein innerer Widerſpruch in der Verneinung aller Exiſtenz. Denn da hiezu erfordert würde, daß etwas geſetzt und zugleich aufgehoben werden müßte, hier aber überall nichts geſetzt iſt, ſo kann man freilich nicht ſagen, daß dieſe Aufhebung einen innern Widerſpruch enthalte. Allein daß irgend eine Möglichkeit ſei und doch gar nichts Wirkliches, das widerſpricht ſich, weil, wenn nichts exiſtirt, auch nichts gegeben iſt, das da denklich wäre, und man ſich ſelbſt widerſtreitet, wenn man gleichwohl will, daß etwas möglich ſei. Wir haben in der Zergliederung des Begriffs vom Daſein verſtanden, daß das Sein oder ſchlechthin Geſetzt ſein, wenn man dieſe Worte dazu nicht braucht, logiſche Beziehungen der Prädicate zu Subjecten auszudrücken, ganz genau einerlei mit dem Daſein bedeute. Demnach zu ſagen: es exiſtirt nichts, heißt eben ſo viel, als: es iſt ganz und gar nichts; und es widerſpricht ſich offenbar, deſſen ungeachtet hinzuzufügen, es ſei etwas möglich.

comparison of the predicate with its subject according to the rule of truth [*die Regel der Wahrheit*] is nothing more than a logical relation. The thing or what stands in this agreement will now and again be called the "real element of possibility." In any event I shall not here discuss any possibility or impossibility except that which is internal, the so-called unconditional and absolute.[13]

2.
The internal possibility of all things presupposes some existence.

It is clear from what has been adduced up to now that possibility is abolished not only if internal contradiction is encountered, as in logical impossibility, but also when no matter or no datum for thought exists. For thereupon nothing conceivable is given. But every possibility is something which can be conceived and to which the logical relation in accord with the law of contradiction belongs.

Now if all existence be abolished, nothing is absolutely posited; nothing at all is given, no matter of anything conceivable; and all possibility is entirely abolished. There is, to be sure, no internal contradiction in the denial of all existence. For since this would require that something be posited and simultaneously canceled; and since here nothing at all is posited, it certainly cannot be said that this denial contains an internal contradiction. But that there be some possibility and yet absolutely nothing actual contradicts itself. For if nothing exists, nothing conceivable is given and one would contradict himself in nevertheless pretending something to be possible. We have understood in the analysis of the concept of existence that being, or that which is absolutely posited (if one does not use this word to express logical relations of predicates to subjects) means exactly the same as existence. Accordingly to say "Nothing exists" means the same thing as "There is absolutely nothing." It is obviously self-contradictory to add, despite this, that something is possible.

3.

Es ist schlechterdings unmöglich, daß gar nichts existire.

Wodurch alle Möglichkeit überhaupt aufgehoben wird, das ist schlechterdings unmöglich. Denn dieses sind gleichbedeutende Ausdrücke. Nun wird erstlich durch das, was sich selbst widerspricht, das Formale aller Möglichkeit, nämlich die Übereinstimmung mit dem Satze des Wider= spruchs, aufgehoben, daher ist, was in sich selbst widersprechend ist, schlechterdings unmöglich. Dieses ist aber nicht der Fall, in dem wir die gänzliche Beraubung alles Daseins zu betrachten haben. Denn darin liegt, wie erwiesen ist, kein innerer Widerspruch. Allein wodurch das Materiale und die Data zu allem Möglichen aufgehoben werden, dadurch wird auch alle Möglichkeit verneint. Nun geschieht dieses durch die Auf= hebung alles Daseins, also wenn alles Dasein verneint wird, so wird auch alle Möglichkeit aufgehoben. Mithin ist schlechterdings unmöglich, daß gar nichts existire.

4.

Alle Möglichkeit ist in irgend etwas Wirklichem gegeben, entweder in demselben als eine Bestimmung, oder durch dasselbe als eine Folge.

Es ist von aller Möglichkeit insgesammt und von jeder insonderheit darzuthun, daß sie etwas Wirkliches, es sei nun ein Ding oder mehrere, voraussetze. Diese Beziehung aller Möglichkeit auf irgend ein Dasein kann nun zwiefach sein. Entweder das Mögliche ist nur denklich, in so fern es selber wirklich ist, und dann ist die Möglichkeit in dem Wirklichen als eine Bestimmung gegeben; oder es ist möglich darum, weil etwas anders wirklich ist, d. i. seine innere Möglichkeit ist als eine Folge durch ein ander Dasein gegeben. Die erläuternde Beispiele können noch nicht füglich hier herbei geschafft werden. Die Natur desjenigen Subjects, welches das einzige ist, das zu einem Beispiele in dieser Betrachtung dienen kann, soll allererst erwogen werden. Indessen bemerke ich nur noch, daß ich dasjenige Wirkliche, durch welches als einen Grund die innere Möglichkeit anderer gegeben ist, den ersten Realgrund dieser absoluten Möglichkeit nennen werde, so wie der Satz des Widerspruchs der erste logische Grund derselben ist, weil in der Übereinstimmung mit ihm das

3.
It is absolutely impossible that nothing exist.

That through which all possibility is altogether abolished is absolutely impossible. For these are terms meaning the same thing. Now, it is first through what is self-contradictory that the formal element of all possibility, namely agreement with the principle of contradiction, is abolished. Thus what is in itself self-contradictory is absolutely impossible. This is not the case, however, where we have to consider the complete deprivation of all existence. In that, as has been shown, there is no internal contradiction. However, that through which the matter and the data for all possibility are annulled is also that through which all possibility is denied. Now this obtains through the annulment of all existence. Thus if all existence is denied, all possibility is also abolished. Consequently it is absolutely impossible that nothing at all exist.

4.
All possibility is given in something actual; either in it as a determination or through it as a consequence.

It is to be shown that all possibility in sum and each possibility in particular presuppose something actual, be it one thing or many. Now this relation of possibility to some existence can only be two-fold. Either the possible is conceivable only insofar as it is itself actual, and then possibility is given as a determination in the actual; or it is possible because something else is actual; that is, its inner possibility is given as a consequence through another existence. Illuminating examples cannot yet conveniently be produced here. The nature of that subject which is the only one which can serve as an example in this study must first be considered. Meanwhile I will only observe that I call this actuality, through which as ground the internal possibility of an other is given, the ultimate real ground of this absolute possibility: just as the principle of contradiction is the ultimate logical ground of such internal possibility, since the formal element in all possibility lies in conformity with the

Formale der Möglichkeit liegt, so wie jenes die Data und das Materiale im Denklichen liefert.

Ich begreife wohl, daß Sätze von derjenigen Art, als in dieser Betrachtung vorgetragen werden, noch mancher Erläuterung bedürftig sind, um dasjenige Licht zu bekommen, das zur Augenscheinlichkeit erfordert wird. Indessen legt die so sehr abgezogene Natur des Gegenstandes selbst aller Bemühung der größeren Aufklärung Hindernisse, so wie die mikroskopischen Kunstgriffe des Sehens zwar das Bild des Gegenstandes bis zur Unterscheidung sehr kleiner Theile erweitern, aber auch in demselben Maße die Helligkeit und Lebhaftigkeit des Eindrucks vermindern. Gleichwohl will ich so viel, als ich vermag, den Gedanken von dem selbst bei der innren Möglichkeit jederzeit zum Grunde liegenden Dasein in eine etwas größere Naheit zu den gemeinern Begriffen eines gesunden Verstandes zu bringen suchen.

Ihr erkennet, daß ein feuriger Körper, ein listiger Mensch oder dergleichen etwas möglich seien, und wenn ich nichts mehr als die innere Möglichkeit verlange, so werdet ihr gar nicht nöthig finden, daß ein Körper oder Feuer u. s. w. als die Data hiezu existiren müssen, denn sie sind einmal denklich, und das ist genug. Die Zusammenstimmung aber des Prädicats feurig mit dem Subjecte Körper nach dem Grunde des Widerspruchs liegt in diesen Begriffen selber, sie mögen wirkliche oder blos mögliche Dinge sein. Ich räume auch ein, daß weder Körper noch Feuer wirkliche Dinge sein dürfen, und gleichwohl ein feuriger Körper innerlich möglich sei. Allein ich fahre fort zu fragen: ist denn ein Körper selber an sich möglich? Ihr werdet mir, weil ihr hier euch nicht auf Erfahrung berufen müsset, die Data zu seiner Möglichkeit, nämlich Ausdehnung, Undurchdringlichkeit, Kraft und wer weiß was mehr, herzählen und dazu setzen, daß darin kein innerer Widerstreit sei. Ich räume noch alles ein, allein ihr müßt mir Rechenschaft geben, weswegen ihr den Begriff der Ausdehnung als ein Datum so gerade anzunehmen Recht habt, denn gesetzt, er bedeute nichts, so ist eure dafür ausgegebene Möglichkeit des Körpers ein Blendwerk. Es wäre auch sehr unrichtig, sich auf die Erfahrung wegen dieses Dati zu berufen, denn es ist jetzt eben die Frage, ob eine innere Möglichkeit des feurigen Körpers statt findet, wenn gleich gar nichts existirt. Gesetzt daß ihr anjetzt nicht mehr den Begriff der Ausdehnung in einfachere Data zerfällen könnt, um anzuzeigen, daß in ihm nichts Widerstreitendes sei, wie ihr denn nothwendig zuletzt auf etwas, dessen Möglichkeit nicht zergliedert

principle, so the former provides the data and the material element in the conceivable.

I fully understand that theses of the sort that are presented in this study still require a great deal of explication in order to obtain the illumination required to be obvious. Nevertheless, the highly abstract nature of the object itself lays obstacles in the way of attempts at greater enlightenment, just as microscopic techniques of vision extend the image of the object to the discrimination of very minute parts but also to the same extent diminish the brightness and vivacity of the impression. Nevertheless I want to try, so far as I am able, to bring the notions of this existence, which in itself always lies at the base of internal possibility, into a somewhat closer proximity to the more ordinary concepts of common sense.

You know that a fiery body or a crafty man or something of that sort is possible, and if I require nothing more than the internal possibility, you would by no means find it necessary that a body or a fire or so forth must exist as the data for it, for they are simply thinkable and that is enough. The agreement of the predicate "fiery" with the subject "body" according to the law of contradiction lies in these concepts themselves be they possible or actual things. I also grant that neither body nor fire might be actual things and that nevertheless a fiery body might yet be internally possible. But I continue to ask: "Is then a body in itself possible?" Because you must not call upon experience here you will enumerate for me the data of its possibility; namely extension, impenetrability, force, and who knows what else, and add that there is no internal conflict therein. I grant all of this too, and yet you must give me some justification of your right immediately to assume the concept of extension as a datum: for assuming that it denotes nothing, the possibility of the body for which it is datum is an illusion. It would also be quite wrong to appeal to experience for the sake of this datum, for the question is just whether there is an internal possibility of a fiery body even if absolutely nothing exists. Granted that henceforth you cannot analyze the concept of extension into simpler data in order to show that there is no conflict in it, since you must necessarily finally come to something whose possibility cannot be analyzed, then the question here is whether

werden kann, kommen müßt, so ist alsdann hier die Frage, ob Raum oder Ausdehnung leere Wörter sind, oder ob sie etwas bezeichnen. Der Mangel des Widerspruchs macht es hier nicht aus; ein leeres Wort bezeichnet niemals etwas Widersprechendes. Wenn nicht der Raum existirt, oder wenigstens durch etwas Existirendes gegeben ist als eine Folge, so bedeutet das Wort Raum gar nichts. So lange ihr noch die Möglichkeiten durch den Satz des Widerspruchs bewähret, so fußet ihr euch auf dasjenige, was euch in dem Dinge Denkliches gegeben ist, und betrachtet nur die Verknüpfung nach dieser logischen Regel; aber am Ende, wenn ihr bedenket, wie euch denn dieses gegeben sei, könnt ihr euch nimmer worauf anders, als auf ein Dasein berufen.

Allein wir wollen den Fortgang dieser Betrachtungen abwarten. Die Anwendung selber wird einen Begriff faßlicher machen, den, ohne sich selbst zu übersteigen, man kaum für sich allein deutlich machen kann, weil er von dem ersten, was beim Denklichen zum Grunde liegt, selber handelt.

Dritte Betrachtung.
Von dem schlechterdings nothwendigen Dasein.

1.
Begriff der absolut nothwendigen Existenz überhaupt.

Schlechterdings nothwendig ist, dessen Gegentheil an sich selbst unmöglich ist. Dieses ist eine ungezweifelt richtige Nominal=Erklärung. Wenn ich aber frage: worauf kommt es denn an, damit das Nichtsein eines Dinges schlechterdings unmöglich sei?, so ist das, was ich suche, die Realerklärung, die uns allein zu unserm Zwecke etwas nutzen kann. Alle unsere Begriffe von der inneren Nothwendigkeit in den Eigenschaften möglicher Dinge, von welcher Art sie auch sein mögen, laufen darauf hinaus, daß das Gegentheil sich selber widerspricht. Allein wenn es auf eine schlechterdings nothwendige Existenz ankommt, so würde man mit schlechtem Erfolg durch das nämliche Merkmal bei ihr etwas zu verstehen suchen. Das Dasein ist gar kein Prädicat und die Aufhebung des Daseins keine Verneinung eines Prädicats, wodurch etwas in einem Dinge sollte aufgehoben werden und ein innerer Widerspruch entstehen können. Die Aufhebung eines existirenden Dinges ist eine völlige Verneinung alle des=

space and extension are only empty words or whether they denote something. The want of contradiction here does not make it so; an empty word never denotes anything contradictory. If space does not exist, or at least is not given as a consequence of some other existent, then the word "space" denotes nothing at all.

So long as you still demonstrate possibility through the principle of contradiction, you rely upon that which is given you as thinkable in the thing and observe only conjunctions according to this logical rule. However when finally you consider how this may be given, you can never appeal to anything but an existence.

But we want to await the progress of this observation. Application of it will make more comprehensible a concept which can hardly be made clear alone without overextending oneself since it is concerned with the ultimate which lies at the ground of the conceivable itself.

OBSERVATION THREE
On Positively Necessary Existence

1.
The concept of absolutely necessary existence in general.

The contradiction of that which is in itself impossible is absolutely necessary. This is an undeniably correct nominal definition. However if I ask "How does it happen that the non-being of a thing is absolutely impossible?," what I am looking for is the real definition which alone can be of use to us. All of our concepts of the inner necessity in the properties of possible things, of whatever kind they may be, take off from this: that their opposite is self-contradictory. However, when it comes to an absolutely necessary existence [*die Existenz*] one has poor results if he seeks to understand something through the nominal characteristic. Existence [*das Dasein*] is certainly not a predicate and the annulment of existence is not the denial of a predicate through which something in a thing is annulled and an internal contradiction could arise. The annulment of an

jenigen, was schlechthin oder absolute durch sein Dasein gesetzt wurde. Die logische Beziehungen zwischen dem Dinge als einem Möglichen und seinen Prädicaten bleiben gleichwohl. Allein diese sind ganz was anders, als die Position des Dinges zusammt seinen Prädicaten schlechthin, als worin das Dasein besteht. Demnach wird nicht eben dasselbe, was in dem Dinge gesetzt wird, sondern was anders durch das Nichtsein aufgehoben, und ist demnach hierin niemals ein Widerspruch. In der letztern Betrachtung dieses Werks wird alles dieses in dem Falle, da man die absolutnoth=wendige Existenz wirklich vermeint hat durch den Satz des Widerspruchs zu begreifen, durch eine klare Entwickelung dieser Untauglichkeit über=zeugender gemacht werden. Man kann indessen die Nothwendigkeit in den Prädicaten blos möglicher Begriffe die logische Nothwendigkeit nennen. Allein diejenige, deren Hauptgrund ich aufsuche, nämlich die des Daseins, ist die absolute Realnothwendigkeit. Ich finde zuerst: daß, was ich schlechter=dings als nichts und unmöglich ansehen soll, das müsse alles Denkliche vertilgen. Denn bliebe dabei noch etwas zu denken übrig, so wäre es nicht gänzlich undenklich und schlechthin unmöglich.

Wenn ich nun einen Augenblick nachdenke, weswegen dasjenige, was sich widerspricht, schlechterdings nichts und unmöglich sei, so bemerke ich: daß, weil dadurch der Satz des Widerspruchs, der letzte logische Grund alles Denklichen, aufgehoben wird, alle Möglichkeit verschwinde, und nichts dabei mehr zu denken sei. Ich nehme daraus alsbald ab, daß, wenn ich alles Dasein überhaupt aufhebe, und hiedurch der letzte Realgrund alles Denklichen wegfällt, gleichfalls alle Möglichkeit verschwindet, und nichts mehr zu denken bleibt. Demnach kann etwas schlechterdings nothwendig sein, entweder wenn durch sein Gegentheil das Formale alles Denklichen aufgehoben wird, das ist, wenn es sich selbst widerspricht, oder auch wenn sein Nichtsein das Materiale zu allem Denklichen und alle Data dazu auf=hebt. Das erste findet, wie gesagt, niemals beim Dasein statt, und weil kein drittes möglich ist, so ist entweder der Begriff von der schlechterdings nothwendigen Existenz gar ein täuschender und falscher Begriff, oder er muß darin beruhen, daß das Nichtsein eines Dinges zugleich die Ver=neinung von den Datis zu allem Denklichen sei. Daß aber dieser Begriff nicht erdichtet, sondern etwas Wahrhaftes sei, erhellt auf folgende Art.

existent thing is a complete denial of all that would be positively or absolutely posited through its existence. The logical relations between the thing as possible thing and its predicates nevertheless remain. But these are something quite different from the absolute position in which the existence of the thing, together with its predicates, consists. Thus precisely what is posited in the thing is not canceled by its non-being, but rather something else is; and accordingly there is never a contradiction in canceling this. In the final Observation of this work all this will be made more apparent by a clear exposition of this worthlessness in the case where it is really intended to understand absolutely necessary existence through the principle of contradiction. Meantime, necessity in the predicates of merely possible concepts can be called logical necessity. But that whose fundamental basis I am seeking, namely that of existence, is absolute real necessity. I find first that whatever I have to regard as absolutely nothing and absolutely impossible must negative everything thinkable. For if anything remained to be thought it would not be totally inconceivable and absolutely impossible.

Now if I consider for a moment why that which is self contradictory is absolutely nothing and impossible, I see that since through it the law of contradiction, the ultimate logical ground of everything conceivable, is annulled, all possibility disappears and nothing more remains to be thought. From this I immediately conclude that, if I annul all existence in general and if through that the final real ground of all thought is abolished, then likewise all possibility disappears and there is nothing left to be thought. Accordingly, something may be absolutely necessary either when through its opposite the formal element of all conceivability is annulled, that is, when it contradicts itself; or when its non-being annuls the material element for all thought and all data for it. As was said, the former never obtains in existence, and since there is no third possibility either the concept of absolutely necessary existence is an entirely misleading and false notion, or else it must rest upon the fact that the non-being of a thing would be the negation of the data for all thought as well. That this concept is not fictitious but something true will be shown in the following manner.

2.
Es existirt ein schlechterdings nothwendiges Wesen.

Alle Möglichkeit setzt etwas Wirkliches voraus, worin und wodurch alles Denkliche gegeben ist. Demnach ist eine gewisse Wirklichkeit, deren Aufhebung selbst alle innere Möglichkeit überhaupt aufheben würde. Dasjenige aber, dessen Aufhebung oder Verneinung alle Möglichkeit vertilgt, ist schlechterdings nothwendig. Demnach existirt etwas absolut nothwendiger Weise. Bis dahin erhellt, daß ein Dasein eines oder mehrerer Dinge selbst aller Möglichkeit zum Grunde liege, und daß dieses Dasein an sich selbst nothwendig sei. Man kann hieraus auch leichtlich den Begriff der Zufälligkeit abnehmen. Zufällig ist nach der Worterklärung, dessen Gegentheil möglich ist. Um aber die Sacherklärung davon zu finden, so muß man auf folgende Art unterscheiden. Im logischen Verstande ist dasjenige als ein Prädicat an einem Subjecte zufällig, dessen Gegentheil demselben nicht widerspricht. Z. E. Einem Triangel überhaupt ist es zufällig, daß er rechtwinklicht sei. Diese Zufälligkeit findet lediglich bei der Beziehung der Prädicate zu ihren Subjecten statt und leidet, weil das Dasein kein Prädicat ist, auch gar keine Anwendung auf die Existenz. Dagegen ist im Realverstande zufällig dasjenige, dessen Nichtsein zu denken ist, das ist, dessen Aufhebung nicht alles Denkliche aufhebt. Wenn demnach die innere Möglichkeit der Dinge ein gewisses Dasein nicht voraussetzt, so ist dieses zufällig, weil sein Gegentheil die Möglichkeit nicht aufhebt. Oder: Dasjenige Dasein, wodurch nicht das Materiale zu allem Denklichen gegeben ist, ohne welches also noch etwas zu denken, das ist, möglich ist, dessen Gegentheil ist im Realverstande möglich, und das ist in eben demselben Verstande auch zufällig.

3.
Das nothwendige Wesen ist einig.

Weil das nothwendige Wesen den letzten Realgrund aller andern Möglichkeit enthält, so wird ein jedes andere Ding nur möglich sein, in so fern es durch ihn als einen Grund gegeben ist. Demnach kann ein jedes andere Ding nur als eine Folge von ihm statt finden und ist also aller andern Dinge Möglichkeit und Dasein von ihm abhängend. Etwas aber, was selbst abhängend ist, enthält nicht den letzten Realgrund aller Mög-

6*

2.
There exists an absolutely necessary being.

All possibility presupposes something actual in which and ▬ through which everything conceivable is given. Accordingly ▬ there is a certain actuality whose annulment itself would totally annul all internal possibility. But that whose annulment or negation eradicates all possibility is absolutely necessary. Accordingly something exists in an absolutely necessary fashion. From this much it is obvious that the existence of one or more things lies at the base of possibility itself, and that this existence is in itself necessary. The concept of contingency can easily be derived from this. According to the nominal definition, a thing is contingent whose opposite is possible. But in order to find a material definition distinctions must be made in the following way. In the logical sense, that whose opposite does not contradict the subject is contingently the predicate of a subject. For example, it is contingent that any triangle as such be right-angled. This contingency occurs simply in the relation of the predicates to their subjects, and since existence (*das Dasein*) is not a predicate it suffers absolutely no application to existence (*die Existenz*). One the other hand, in the real sense a thing is contingent if its non-being may be thought, that is, if its annulment does not annul everything conceivable. Accordingly, when the internal possibility of things does not presuppose a certain existent, this existent is contingent because its opposite does not annul possibility. Or again, that existence through which the material for all thought is not given, that therefore without which there is still something to be thought, is possible. This is a thing whose opposite is possible in the real sense, and it is contingent in exactly the same sense.

3.
The necessary being is unitary.

Because the necessary being contains the ultimate ground of the possibility of all other beings, every other thing is possible only insofar as it is given through it as a ground. Accordingly, every other thing can occur only as a consequence of it, and the possibility and existence of all other things are dependent upon it. But something which is itself dependent

lichkeit und ist demnach nicht schlechterdings nothwendig. Mithin können nicht mehrere Dinge absolut nothwendig sein.

Setzet, A sei ein nothwendiges Wesen und B ein anderes. So ist vermöge der Erklärung B nur in so fern möglich, als es durch einen andern Grund A als die Folge desselben gegeben ist. Weil aber vermöge der Voraussetzung B selber nothwendig ist, so ist seine Möglichkeit in ihm als ein Prädicat und nicht als eine Folge aus einem andern und doch nur als eine Folge laut dem vorigen gegeben, welches sich widerspricht.

4.
Das nothwendige Wesen ist einfach.

Daß kein Zusammengesetztes aus viel Substanzen ein schlechterdings nothwendiges Wesen sein könne, erhellt auf folgende Art. Setzet, es sei nur eins seiner Theile schlechterdings nothwendig, so sind die andern nur insgesammt als Folgen durch ihn möglich und gehören nicht zu ihm als Nebentheile. Gedenket euch, es wären mehrere oder alle nothwendig, so widerspricht dieses der vorigen Nummer. Es bleibt demnach nichts übrig, als sie müssen ein jedes besonders zufällig, alle aber zusammen schlechterdings nothwendig existiren. Nun ist dieses aber unmöglich, weil ein Aggregat von Substanzen nicht mehr Nothwendigkeit im Dasein haben kann, als den Theilen zukommt, und da diesen gar keine zukommt, sondern ihre Existenz zufällig ist, so würde auch die des Ganzen zufällig sein. Wenn man gedächte, sich auf die Erklärung des nothwendigen Wesens berufen zu können, so daß man sagte, in jeglichem der Theile wären die letzten Data einiger innern Möglichkeit, in allen zusammen alles Mögliche gegeben, so würde man etwas ganz Ungereimtes nur auf eine verborgene Art vorgestellt haben. Denn wenn man sich alsdann die innere Möglichkeit so gedenkt, daß einige können aufgehoben werden, doch so, daß übrigens, was durch die andere Theile noch Denkliches gegeben worden, bliebe, so müßte man sich vorstellen, es sei an sich möglich, daß die innere Möglichkeit verneint oder aufgehoben werde. Es ist aber gänzlich undenklich und widersprechend, daß etwas nichts sei, und dieses will so viel sagen: eine innere Möglichkeit aufheben, ist alles Denkliche vertilgen, woraus erhellt, daß die Data zu jedem Denklichen in demjenigen Dinge müssen gegeben sein, dessen Aufhebung auch das Gegentheil aller Möglichkeit ist, daß also, was den letzten Grund von einer innern Möglichkeit enthält, ihn auch von

does not contain the ultimate ground of all possibility, and is accordingly not absolutely necessary. Thus several things cannot be absolutely necessary.

Suppose that A is a necessary being and B another. Now by definition B is possible only insofar as it is given through another ground, A, as a consequence of A. But since, according to the assumption, B itself is necessary, its possibility is in itself as a predicate and not as the consequence of another. Yet the preceding maintains it is only as a consequence that it is given, and this is self-contradictory.

4.
The necessary being is simple.

That no composite of many substances could be an absolutely necessary being is obvious from the following. Suppose that only one of its parts is absolutely necessary so that the others, one and all, are consequences possible only through it and do not belong to it as secondary parts. Remember that if several—or all—of them were necessary this would contradict the previous paragraph. Accordingly nothing remains except that each particular must exist as contingent and yet that all of them together exist as absolutely necessary. But this is impossible. For an aggregate of substances cannot have more necessity in existence than belongs to its parts; and since none inheres in these, for their existence is contingent, so also would the existence of the whole be contingent. If one thought to appeal to the definition of the necessary being, so that one said the ultimate data of their own internal possibilities were in each of the parts and that in these together everything possible was given, something quite discordant would be surreptitiously introduced. If one conceives internal possibility so that some may be annulled and yet, for the rest, what is given through other parts still remains conceivable, one would have to imagine that it is in itself possible for internal possibility to be negated or annulled. But it is totally unthinkable and contradictory that something be nothing. That is, annulment of internal possibility is the negation of everything thinkable. It is clear from that that the data for everything conceivable must be given in that thing whose annulment is also the opposite of all possibility, and therefore that that which contains the ultimate ground of an internal possibility also contains it for all things in general and

aller überhaupt enthalte, mithin dieser Grund nicht in verschiedenen Sub=
stanzen vertheilt sein könne.

5.

Das nothwendige Wesen ist unveränderlich und ewig.

Weil selbst seine eigene Möglichkeit und jede andere dieses Dasein
voraussetzt, so ist keine andere Art der Existenz desselben möglich, das
heißt, es kann das nothwendige Wesen nicht auf vielerlei Art existiren.
Nämlich alles, was da ist, ist durchgängig bestimmt; da dieses Wesen nun
lediglich darum möglich ist, weil es existirt, so findet keine Möglichkeit
desselben statt, außer in so fern es in der That da ist; es ist also auf keine
andere Art möglich, als wie es wirklich ist. Demnach kann es nicht auf
andere Art bestimmt oder verändert werden. Sein Nichtsein ist schlechter=
dings unmöglich, mithin auch sein Ursprung und Untergang, demnach ist
es ewig.

6.

Das nothwendige Wesen enthält die höchste Realität.

Da die Data zu aller Möglichkeit in ihm anzutreffen sein müssen, ent=
weder als Bestimmungen desselben, oder als Folgen, die durch ihn als den
ersten Realgrund gegeben sind, so sieht man, daß alle Realität auf eine
oder andere Art durch ihn begriffen sei. Allein eben dieselbe Bestimmungen,
durch die dieses Wesen der höchste Grund ist von aller möglichen Realität,
setzen in ihm selber den größten Grad realer Eigenschaften, der nur immer
einem Dinge beiwohnen kann. Weil ein solches Wesen also das realste
unter allen möglichen ist, indem sogar alle andere nur durch dasselbe mög=
lich sind, so ist dieses nicht so zu verstehen, daß alle mögliche Realität zu
seinen Bestimmungen gehöre. Dieses ist eine Vermengung der Begriffe,
die bis dahin ungemein geherrscht hat. Man ertheilt alle Realitäten Gott
oder dem nothwendigen Wesen ohne Unterschied als Prädicate, ohne wahr=
zunehmen, daß sie nimmermehr in einem einzigen Subject als Bestimmungen
neben einander können statt finden. Die Undurchdringlichkeit der Körper,
die Ausdehnung u. d. g. können nicht Eigenschaften von demjenigen sein,
der da Verstand und Willen hat. Es ist auch umsonst eine Ausflucht
darin zu suchen, daß man die gedachte Beschaffenheiten nicht für wahre
Realität halte. Es ist ohne allen Zweifel der Stoß eines Körpers oder
die Kraft des Zusammenhanges etwas wahrhaftig Positives. Eben so ist

accordingly the ground cannot be distributed in different substances.

5.

The necessary being is immutable and eternal.

Because this existence presupposes both its own possibility and every other possibility, no other mode of existence is possible for it; that is, the necessary being cannot exist in multiple modes. That is to say, everything that is, is thoroughly determined. Since this being is purely possible solely because it exists, there is no possibility of it at all except insofar as it in fact exists. Thus it is not possible for it to be in any way other than it actually is, nor can it be determined in any other way or changed. Its non-existence is absolutely impossible, thus also its generation and decay; accordingly it is eternal.

6.

The necessary being contains the highest reality.

Because the data for all possibility must be met within it, either as determinations of the being itself or as consequences that are given through it as the first real ground, it is apparent that in one way or the other all reality is to be understood through it. But those same determinations through which this being is the ultimate ground of all[15] possible reality presuppose in it the maximum degree of real properties that can ever belong to a thing. Because such a being thus is the most real of all possible ones, and since all the others are possible only through it, it is not to be understood that all possible reality belongs to its determinations. This is a confusion of the concepts which hitherto have very much dominated. All realities are accorded to God or to the necessary being as predicates without differentiation, without noting that they could never occur with each other as determinations in a single subject. The impenetrability of bodies, extension, and the like could not be properties of that which has understanding and will. It is also vain to seek an escape by holding that the character [thus] conceived is not a true reality. Without a doubt, the thrust of a body or the power of composition is something truly positive.

der Schmerz in den Empfindungen eines Geistes nimmermehr eine bloße
Beraubung. Ein irriger Gedanke hat eine solche Vorstellung dem Scheine
nach gerechtfertigt. Es heißt: Realität und Realität widersprechen ein=
ander niemals, weil beides wahre Bejahungen sind; demnach widerstreiten
sie auch einander nicht in einem Subjecte. Ob ich nun gleich einräume,
daß hier kein logischer Widerstreit sei, so ist dadurch doch nicht die Real=
repugnanz gehoben. Diese findet jederzeit statt, wenn etwas als ein Grund
die Folge von etwas anderm durch eine reale Entgegensetzung vernichtigt.
Die Bewegungskraft eines Körpers nach einer Direction und die Tendenz
mit gleichem Grade in entgegengesetzter stehen nicht im Widerspruche. Sie
sind auch wirklich zugleich in einem Körper möglich. Aber eine vernichtigt
die Realfolge aus der andern, und da sonst von jeder insbesondere die
Folge eine wirkliche Bewegung sein würde, so ist sie jetzt von beiden zu=
sammen in einem Subjecte O, das ist, die Folge von diesen entgegen ge=
setzten Bewegungskräften ist die Ruhe. Die Ruhe aber ist ohne Zweifel
möglich, woraus man denn auch sieht, daß die Realrepugnanz ganz was
anders sei als die logische oder der Widerspruch; denn das, was daraus
folgt, ist schlechterdings unmöglich. Nun kann aber in dem allerrealsten
Wesen keine Realrepugnanz oder positiver Widerstreit seiner eigenen Be=
stimmungen sein, weil die Folge davon eine Beraubung oder Mangel sein
würde, welches seiner höchsten Realität widerspricht, und da, wenn alle
Realitäten in demselben als Bestimmungen lägen, ein solcher Widerstreit
entstehen müßte, so können sie nicht insgesammt als Prädicate in ihm
sein, mithin weil sie doch alle durch ihn gegeben sind, so werden sie ent=
weder zu seinen Bestimmungen oder Folgen gehören.

Es könnte auch beim ersten Anblick scheinen zu folgen: daß, weil das
nothwendige Wesen den letzten Realgrund aller andern Möglichkeit ent=
hält, in ihm auch der Grund der Mängel und Verneinungen der Wesen
der Dinge liegen müsse, welches, wenn es zugelassen würde, auch den
Schluß veranlassen dürfte, daß es selbst Negationen unter seinen Prädi=
caten haben müsse und nimmermehr nichts als Realität. Allein man richte
nur seine Augen auf den einmal festgesetzten Begriff desselben. In seinem
Dasein ist seine eigene Möglichkeit ursprünglich gegeben. Dadurch, daß
es nun andere Möglichkeiten sind, wovon es den Realgrund enthält, folgt
nach dem Satze des Widerspruchs, daß es nicht die Möglichkeit des realsten
Wesens selber und daher solche Möglichkeiten, welche Verneinungen und
Mängel enthalten, sein müssen.

Likewise, pain in the sensations of mind is never a simple privation. A false consideration has the appearance of justifying such a suggestion. It is that reality and reality can never contradict each other because both are true affirmations and accordingly can never conflict with each other in a subject. Though I quite admit that there is no logical conflict, still real repugnance is not thereby avoided. This obtains anytime something, as ground, obliterates the consequence of another thing in a genuine conflict. The motive force of a body in one direction and the tendency to move in the opposite one with equal force do not stand in contradiction. They are also actually possible simultaneously in a body. But the one negates the real consequence of the other; and whereas otherwise the consequence of each alone would be an actual motion, the consequence of both together in one subject is 0; that is, the consequence of these opposing motive forces is rest. But rest is without a doubt possible, from which it is also seen that real repugnance is something quite different from logical repugnance or contradiction, for what follows from that is absolutely impossible. But now, in the most real being, there can be no real repugnance or positive conflict of its own determinations, since the consequence of that would be a privation or want, which would contradict its maximum reality. Real conflict would arise if all realities were to reside in it as determinations, so that they cannot be in it collectively as predicates. Thus, since they are all given through it, they will belong either to its determinations or to its consequences.

It might also seem on first blush to follow that because the necessary being contains the ultimate ground of the possibility of all other beings, the ground of privation and negation of the being of things must lie in it, which if admitted would also permit the conclusion that it must have negations amongst its predicates—and no longer only reality. Yet one need only attend to the previously established concept itself. In its existence its own possibility is originally given. Now, in this way, since there are other possibilities of which it contains the real ground, it follows according to the law of contradiction that it is not the possibility of the most real being itself which contains privation and negation, and hence privation and negation must be contained by such other possibilities.

Demnach beruht die Möglichkeit aller andern Dinge in Ansehung dessen, was in ihnen real ist, auf dem nothwendigen Wesen als einem Realgrunde, die Mängel aber darauf, weil es andere Dinge und nicht das Urwesen selber sind, als einem logischen Grunde. Die Möglichkeit des Körpers, in so fern er Ausdehnung, Kräfte u. d. g. hat, ist in dem obersten aller Wesen gegründet; in so fern ihm die Kraft zu denken gebricht, so liegt diese Verneinung in ihm selbst nach dem Satz des Widerspruchs.

In der That sind Verneinungen an sich selbst nicht Etwas, oder denklich, welches man sich leichtlich auf folgende Art faßlich machen kann. Setzet nichts als Negationen, so ist gar nichts gegeben und kein Etwas, das zu denken wäre. Verneinungen sind also nur durch die entgegengesetzte Positionen denklich, oder vielmehr, es sind Positionen möglich, die nicht die größte sind. Und hierin liegen schon nach dem Satze der Identität die Verneinungen selber. Es fällt auch leicht in die Augen, daß alle den Möglichkeiten anderer Dinge beiwohnende Verneinungen keinen Realgrund (weil sie nichts Positives sind), mithin lediglich einen logischen Grund voraussetzen.

Vierte Betrachtung.
Beweisgrund zu einer Demonstration des Daseins Gottes.

1.
Das nothwendige Wesen ist ein Geist.

Es ist oben bewiesen, daß das nothwendige Wesen eine einfache Substanz sei, imgleichen daß nicht allein alle andere Realität durch dasselbe als einen Grund gegeben sei, sondern auch die größt mögliche, die in einem Wesen als Bestimmung kann enthalten sein, ihm beiwohne. Nun können verschiedene Beweise geführt werden, daß hiezu auch die Eigenschaften des Verstandes und Willens gehören. Denn erstlich, beides ist wahre Realität, und beides kann mit der größt möglichen in einem Dinge beisammen bestehn, welches letztere man durch ein unmittelbares Urtheil des Verstandes einzuräumen sich gedrungen sieht, ob es zwar nicht füglich zu derjenigen Deutlichkeit gebracht werden kann, welche logisch vollkommene Beweise erfordern.

Zweitens sind die Eigenschaften eines Geistes, Verstand und Willen, von der Art, daß wir uns keine Realität denken können, die in Ermangelung

Thus the possibility of all other things in respect to what is real in them rests upon the necessary being as a real ground. Privations, however, have their logical ground in the fact that there are other things, and not solely the original being itself. The possibility of body insofar as it has extension, power, and the like is grounded in the highest of all beings. Insofar as it lacks the power to think, this negation lies in body itself according to the principle of contradiction.

In fact negations are not in themselves something or conceivable, as can be made comprehensible easily in the following way. If only negations be posited, absolutely nothing is given and there would be nothing to think. Negations are conceivable only through contrary positions or rather through possible positions which are not the maximum. And according to the law of identity, the negations derive from this. It is apparent that all negations inherent in the possibilities of other things presuppose no real ground (because they are nothing positive), but simply a logical ground.

OBSERVATION FOUR
The Argument [*der Beweisgrund*] for a
Demonstration of the Existence of God

1.
The necessary being is a spirit.

It has been proved above that the necessary being is a simple substance in that not only are all other realities given through it as a ground, but also since the maximum possible that may be contained in a being as determinations inheres in it. Now different proofs may be adduced that the properties of understanding and will also belong to it. For first, both are true realities and both may subsist together with the maximum possible in a thing. One is compelled to admit this latter by an immediate judgment of understanding, although to be sure it cannot suitably be brought to such distinctness as is demanded by logically·perfect proofs.

Second, the properties of a spirit, understanding and will, are of the sort that we can conceive no reality that could be

derselben einem Wesen eine Ersetzung thun könnte, welche dem Abgang derselben gleich wäre. Und da diese Eigenschaften also diejenige sind, welche der höchsten Grade der Realität fähig sind, gleichwohl aber unter die möglichen gehören, so müßte durch das nothwendige Wesen, als einen Grund, Verstand und Wille und alle Realität der geistigen Natur an andern möglich sein, die gleichwohl in ihm selbst nicht als eine Bestimmung angetroffen würde. Es würde demnach die Folge größer sein als selbst der Grund. Denn es ist gewiß, daß, wenn das höchste Wesen nicht selbst Ver= stand und Willen hat, ein jedes andere, welches durch es mit diesen Eigen= schaften gesetzt werde, unerachtet es abhängend wäre und mancherlei andere Mängel der Macht u. s. w. hätte, gleichwohl in Ansehung dieser Eigen= schaften von der höchsten Art jenem in Realität vorgehen müßte. Weil nun die Folge den Grund nicht übertreffen kann, so müssen Verstand und Wille der nothwendigen einfachen Substanz als Eigenschaften beiwohnen, das ist, sie ist ein Geist.

Drittens, Ordnung, Schönheit, Vollkommenheit in allem, was mög= lich ist, setzen ein Wesen voraus, in dessen Eigenschaften entweder diese Beziehungen gegründet sind, oder doch wenigstens durch welches Wesen die Dinge diesen Beziehungen gemäß als aus einem Hauptgrunde möglich sind. Nun ist das nothwendige Wesen der hinlängliche Realgrund alles andern, was außer ihm möglich ist, folglich wird in ihm auch diejenige Eigenschaft, durch welche diesen Beziehungen gemäß alles außer ihm wirk= lich werden kann, anzutreffen sein. Es scheint aber, daß der Grund der äußern Möglichkeit, der Ordnung, Schönheit und Vollkommenheit nicht zureichend ist, wofern nicht ein dem Verstande gemäßer Wille voraus ge= setzt ist. Also werden diese Eigenschaften dem obersten Wesen müssen bei= gemessen werden.

Jedermann erkennt, daß ungeachtet aller Gründe der Hervorbringung von Pflanzen und Bäumen dennoch regelmäßige Blumenstücke, Alleen u. d. g. nur durch einen Verstand, der sie entwirft, und durch einen Willen, der sie ausführt, möglich sind. Alle Macht oder Hervorbringungskraft, imgleichen alle andere Data zur Möglichkeit ohne einen Verstand sind un= zulänglich die Möglichkeit solcher Ordnung vollständig zu machen.

Aus einem dieser hier angeführten Gründe, oder aus ihnen ins= gesammt wird der Beweis, daß das nothwendige Wesen Willen und Ver= stand haben, mithin ein Geist sein müsse, hergeleitet werden können. Ich

substituted to make up the deficiency in a being which lacked them. And since these properties are capable of the maximum degree of reality but still belong amongst the possible ones, understanding and will and all reality of a spiritual nature would have to be possible in another through the necessary being as a ground while nevertheless not encountered in that being itself as a determination. But then the consequent would be greater than the ground itself. For it is certain that if the necessary being had not understanding and will itself, any other being posited through it with these properties—regardless of its dependence and diverse other defects of power and so forth that it had—nevertheless would have to exceed that in reality with respect to these properties of the highest kind. But because the consequences cannot outstrip their ground, understanding and will must inhere in the necessary simple substance as properties. That is, it is a spirit.

Third, order, excellence, and perfection in everything that is possible presuppose either a being in whose properties these relations are grounded, or at least a being through which, as a main ground, the things that conform to these relations are possible. Now the necessary being is the sufficient real ground of everything else that is possible in addition to it. Consequently the property through which everything besides it can become actual in accord with these relations is to be found in it. But it seems that the ground of external possibility of order, excellence, and perfection is not sufficient if a will conformable to the understanding is not presupposed. Thus these properties must be attributed to the highest being.

Everyone knows that regardless of all grounds for the generation of plants and trees, the regular organization of floral pieces, avenues, and the like are possible only through an understanding which plans and a will which executes them. All the might or power of generation as well as all other data for possibility are insufficient without an understanding to make complete the possibility of such order.

From one of the reasons cited here, or from all of them together, it may be deduced that the necessary being has will and understanding; thus that it must be a spirit. I will be

begnüge mich blos, den Beweisgrund vollständig zu machen. Meine Ab=
sicht ist nicht eine förmliche Demonstration darzulegen.

2.

Es ist ein Gott.

Es existirt etwas schlechterdings nothwendig. Dieses ist einig in
seinem Wesen, einfach in seiner Substanz, ein Geist nach seiner Natur,
ewig in seiner Dauer, unveränderlich in seiner Beschaffenheit, allgenug=
sam in Ansehung alles Möglichen und Wirklichen. Es ist ein Gott. Ich
gebe hier keine bestimmte Erklärung von dem Begriffe von Gott. Ich
müßte dieses thun, wenn ich meinen Gegenstand systematisch betrachten
wollte. Was ich hier darlege, soll die Analyse sein, dadurch man sich zur
förmlichen Lehrverfassung tüchtig machen kann. Die Erklärung des Be=
griffs der Gottheit mag indessen angeordnet werden, wie man es für gut
findet, so bin ich doch gewiß, daß dasjenige Wesen, dessen Dasein wir nur
eben bewiesen haben, eben dasjenige göttliche Wesen sei, dessen Unter=
scheidungszeichen man auf eine oder die andere Art in die kürzeste Be=
nennung bringen wird.

3.

Anmerkung.

Weil aus der dritten Betrachtung nichts mehr erhellt, als daß alle
Realität entweder in dem nothwendigen Wesen als eine Bestimmung oder
durch dasselbe als einen Grund müsse gegeben sein, so würde bis dahin
unentschieden bleiben, ob die Eigenschaften des Verstandes und Willens
in dem obersten Wesen als ihm beiwohnende Bestimmungen anzutreffen
seien, oder blos durch dasselbe an anderen Dingen als Folgen anzusehen
wären. Wäre das letztere, so würde unerachtet aller Vorzüge, die von
diesem Urwesen aus der Zulänglichkeit, Einheit und Unabhängigkeit seines
Daseins als eines großen Grundes in die Augen leuchten, doch seine Natur
derjenigen weit nachstehen, die man sich denken muß, wenn man einen
Gott denkt. Denn selber ohne Erkenntniß und Entschließung, würde es ein
blindlings nothwendiger Grund anderer Dinge und sogar anderer Geister
sein und sich von dem ewigen Schicksale einiger Alten in nichts unter=
scheiden, als daß es begreiflicher beschrieben wäre. Dies ist die Ursache,
weswegen in jeglicher Lehrverfassung auf diesen Umstand besonders ge=

satisfied simply with making complete the basis for a proof. My intention is not to present a formal demonstration.

2.
It is a God.

There exists something positively necessary. This is an entity which is unitary in its essence, simple in its substance, a spirit in its nature, eternal in its duration, immutable in its constitution, and sufficient in respect to everything possible and actual. It is a God. I am not giving a definite definition of the concept of God here. I would need to do that if I wanted to study my object systematically. What I present here will be the analysis through which one can qualify himself for the formal treatise. The definition of the concept of divinity meanwhile may be arranged as one finds apt. But I am certain that that being whose existence we have just demonstrated is precisely the divine being whose defining characteristics will quickly be designated in one way or the other.

3.
Note.

Because nothing more is evident from the Third Observation than that all reality is either in the necessary being as a determination or else must be given through that being as a ground, it would remain undecided up to this point whether the properties of understanding and will are to be met with in it as inherent determinations or merely to be regarded as consequences of it in other things. Were it the latter, despite the advantages that are obvious in this primordial being owing to its sufficiency, unity, and the independence of its existence as an eminent cause, its nature would remain far from what one must think if one thinks of God. For surely without knowledge and purpose it would be only a blind necessary ground of other things and even of other minds, distinguished not at all from the eternal fate of some of the ancients except that it would be described more comprehensibly. This is the reason why every

sehen werden muß, und warum wir ihn nicht haben aus den Augen setzen können.

Ich habe in dem ganzen Zusammenhange aller bisher vorgetragenen zu meinem Beweise gehörigen Gründe nirgend des Ausdrucks von Vollkommenheit gedacht. Nicht als wenn ich dafür hielte, alle Realität sei schon so viel wie alle Vollkommenheit, oder auch die größte Zusammenstimmung zu Einem mache sie aus. Ich habe wichtige Ursachen von diesem Urtheile vieler andern sehr abzugehen. Nachdem ich lange Zeit über den Begriff der Vollkommenheit insgemein oder insbesondere sorgfältige Untersuchungen angestellt habe, so bin ich belehrt worden, daß in einer genauern Kenntniß derselben überaus viel verborgen liege, was die Natur eines Geistes, unser eigen Gefühl und selbst die ersten Begriffe der praktischen Weltweisheit aufklären kann.

Ich bin inne geworden, daß der Ausdruck der Vollkommenheit zwar in einigen Fällen, nach der Unsicherheit jeder Sprache Ausartungen von dem eigenthümlichen Sinne leide, die ziemlich weit abweichen, daß er aber in der Bedeutung, darauf hauptsächlich jedermann selbst bei jenen Abirrungen acht hat, allemal eine Beziehung auf ein Wesen, welches Erkenntniß und Begierde hat, voraussetze. Da es nun viel zu weitläuftig geworden sein würde, den Beweisgrund von Gott, und der ihm beiwohnenden Realität bis zu dieser Beziehung hindurch zu führen, ob es zwar vermöge dessen, was zum Grunde liegt, gar wohl thunlich gewesen wäre, so habe ich es der Absicht dieser Blätter nicht gemäß befunden, durch die Herbeiziehung dieses Begriffs Anlaß zu einer allzugroßen Weitläuftigkeit zu geben.

4.

Beschluß.

Ein jeder wird sehr leicht nach dem wie gedacht geführten Beweise so offenbare Folgerungen hinzufügen können, als da sind: Ich, der ich denke, bin kein so schlechterdings nothwendiges Wesen, denn ich bin nicht der Grund aller Realität, ich bin veränderlich; kein ander Wesen, dessen Nichtsein möglich ist, das ist, dessen Aufhebung nicht zugleich alle Möglichkeit aufhebt, kein veränderliches Ding oder in welchem Schranken sind, mithin auch nicht die Welt ist von einer solchen Natur; die Welt ist nicht ein Accidens der Gottheit, weil in ihr Widerstreit, Mängel, Veränderlichkeit, alles Gegentheile der Bestimmungen einer Gottheit angetroffen werden;

treatise must pay particular attention to the situation and why we have not been able to ignore it.

I have not thought of the term "perfection" in the entire complex of reasons belonging to the proof I have given. [It is] not as though I held all reality is already one with all perfection or even that the greatest harmonization into a one would constitute it such. I have important reasons for departing greatly from this judgment of many others. Having for a long time employed careful investigations of the concept of perfection in general or in particular I am convinced that in more precise knowledge of it a great deal lies concealed that can clarify the nature of mind, our own sensation, and even the ultimate notions of practical philosophy.

I am convinced that the term "perfection"—though to be sure it may deviate rather widely from the proper sense in some cases because of the uncertainty of every language—always presupposes a relation to a being that has intelligence and desire and that one always intends this even in those deviant uses. But since it would have been too prolix to carry the argument for God and the reality inherent in him up to this relation—though to be sure it would have been quite possible through that which is at the base—I did not find it commensurate with the intent of these pages to give occasion to an all-too-extensive prolixity through the inclusion of this notion.

4.
Conclusion.

According to the proof thought to be adduced here everyone will very easily be able to add obvious conclusions such as: I whom I think am not such an absolutely necessary being, for I am not the ground of all reality; I am mutable. No other being whose non-being is possible, that is, whose annulment does not simultaneously annul all possibilty, no mutable thing or one in which there are limits, and thus also the world, is of this nature. The world is not an accident of divinity, for in it conflict, privation, and alteration, all contraries of the determinations of divinity, are encountered. God is not the only substance which exists, and all others are only dependent upon him. And so on forth.

Gott ist nicht die einige Substanz, die da existirt, und alle andre sind nur abhängend von ihm da u. s. w.

Ich bemerke hier nur noch folgendes. Der Beweisgrund von dem Dasein Gottes, den wir geben, ist lediglich darauf erbauet, weil etwas möglich ist. Demnach ist er ein Beweis, der vollkommen a priori geführt werden kann. Es wird weder meine Existenz noch die von andern Geistern noch die von der körperlichen Welt vorausgesetzt. Er ist in der That von dem innern Kennzeichen der absoluten Nothwendigkeit hergenommen. Man erkennt auf diese Weise das Dasein dieses Wesens aus demjenigen, was wirklich die absolute Nothwendigkeit desselben ausmacht, also recht genetisch.

Alle Beweise, die sonst von den Wirkungen dieses Wesens auf sein, als einer Ursache, Dasein geführt werden möchten, gesetzt daß sie auch so strenge beweisen möchten, als sie es nicht thun, können doch niemals die Natur dieser Nothwendigkeit begreiflich machen. Blos daraus, daß etwas schlechterdings nothwendig existirt, ist es möglich, daß etwas eine erste Ursache von anderem sei, aber daraus daß etwas eine erste, das ist, unab= hängige Ursache ist, folgt nur, daß, wenn die Wirkungen da sind, sie auch existiren müsse, nicht aber daß sie schlechterdings nothwendiger Weise da sei.

Weil nun ferner aus dem angepriesnen Beweisgrunde erhellt, daß alle Wesen anderer Dinge und das Reale aller Möglichkeit in diesem einigen Wesen gegründet seien, in welchem die größte Grade des Verstan= des und eines Willens, der der größt mögliche Grund ist, anzutreffen, und weil in einem solchen alles in der äußerst möglichen Übereinstimmung sein muß, so wird daraus schon zum voraus abzunehmen sein, daß, da ein Wille jederzeit die innere Möglichkeit der Sache selbst voraussetzt, der Grund der Möglichkeit, das ist, das Wesen Gottes, mit seinem Willen in der größten Zusammenstimmung sein werde, nicht als wenn Gott durch seinen Willen der Grund der inneren Möglichkeit wäre, sondern weil eben dieselbe unendliche Natur, die die Beziehung eines Grundes auf alle Wesen der Dinge hat, zugleich die Beziehung der höchsten Begierde auf die da= durch gegebene größte Folgen hat, und die letztere nur durch die Voraus= setzung der erstern fruchtbar sein kann. Demnach werden die Möglichkeiten der Dinge selbst, die durch die göttliche Natur gegeben sind, mit seiner großen Begierde zusammenstimmen. In dieser Zusammenstimmung aber besteht das Gute und die Vollkommenheit. Und weil sie mit einem über=

encountered. God is not the only substance which exists, and all others are only dependent upon him. And so on forth.

I note only the following here: the ground of proof we give for the existence of God is built simply upon [the fact] that something is possible. Thus it is a proof which may be adduced completely a priori. Neither my existence nor that of other minds nor that of the corporeal world is presupposed. In fact it is deduced from the internal mark of absolute necessity. In this way the existence of this being is known from what really constitutes its absolute necessity and thus entirely genetically.

All proofs that would pretend to lead from the effects of this entity to its being as a cause, and also pretend to demonstrate strictly (which they do not) can never make the nature of this necessity conceivable. Simply because a positively necessary being exists it is possible that something is a first cause of other things. But because something is a first, that is an independent, cause it follows only that if the effects exist the cause must also exist; but not that it would exist necessarily.

Because from the recommended argument [*der Beweisgrund*] it follows further that the essence of all other things and the real element of all possibility are grounded in this single being in which the maximum degree of understanding and will is to be found, and because in such a being everything must be harmonized to the greatest possible extent, it may be concluded in advance that, since a will always presupposes the internal possibility of the thing itself, the ground of possibility that is the essence of God will be in greatest possible harmony with his will. [It is] not as though God were the ground of internal possibility through his will, but rather because the same infinite nature which has the relation of ground to the essence of all things simultaneously has a relation of maximum desire for the greatest consequences given through it, and the latter can be fruitful only on the assumption of the former. Thus the possibilities of things that are themselves given through the divine nature harmonize with his great desire. But good and perfection consist of this harmonization. And because they

einstimmen, so wird selbst in den Möglichkeiten der Dinge Einheit, Har=
monie und Ordnung anzutreffen sein.

Wenn wir aber auch durch eine reife Beurtheilung der wesentlichen
Eigenschaften der Dinge, die uns durch Erfahrung bekannt werden, selbst
in den nothwendigen Bestimmungen ihrer innern Möglichkeit eine Ein=
heit im Mannigfaltigen und Wohlgereimtheit in dem Getrennten wahr=
nehmen, so werden wir durch den Erkenntnißweg a posteriori auf ein
einiges Principium aller Möglichkeit zurückschließen können und uns zu=
letzt bei demselben Grundbegriffe des schlechterdings nothwendigen Daseins
befinden, von dem wir durch den Weg a priori anfänglich ausgegangen
waren. Nunmehr soll unsere Absicht darauf gerichtet sein, zu sehen, ob
selbst in der innern Möglichkeit der Dinge eine nothwendige Beziehung
auf Ordnung und Harmonie und in diesem unermeßlichen Mannigfaltigen
Einheit anzutreffen sei, damit wir daraus urtheilen können, ob die Wesen
der Dinge selbst einen obersten gemeinschaftlichen Grund erkennen.

harmonize with one single, principle [17] unity, harmony and order are to be met in the very possibilities of things.

But if through a considered judgment of the essential properties of things that are known to us through experience we perceive even in the necessary determinations of their inner possibility a unity in the manifold and a coherence in separated things we will be able to infer back to a single principle of all possibility through the a posteriori method of knowledge and finally find ourselves with the same basic concept of an absolutely necessary existence from which we had begun through the a priori way. From here on our attention will be directed toward seeing whether in the internal possibility of things a necessary relation to order and harmony and a unity in this immeasurable manifold is to be found from which we may judge whether the essences of things themselves reveals a supreme common ground.

Zweite Abtheilung

von dem

weitläuftigen Nutzen, der dieser Beweisart besonders eigen ist.

Erste Betrachtung,

Worin aus der wahrgenommenen Einheit in den Wesen der Dinge auf das Dasein Gottes a posteriori geschlossen wird.

1.

Die Einheit in dem Mannigfaltigen der Wesen der Dinge gewiesen an den Eigenschaften des Raums.

Die nothwendige Bestimmungen des Raums verschaffen dem Meß=
künstler ein nicht gemeines Vergnügen durch die Augenscheinlichkeit in der
Überzeugung und durch die Genauigkeit in der Ausführung, imgleichen
durch den weiten Umfang der Anwendung, wogegen das gesammte mensch=
liche Erkenntniß nichts aufzuzeigen hat, das ihm beikäme, vielweniger es
überträfe. Ich betrachte aber anjetzt den nämlichen Gegenstand in einem
ganz andern Gesichtspunkte. Ich sehe ihn mit einem philosophischen Auge
an und werde gewahr: daß bei so nothwendigen Bestimmungen Ordnung
und Harmonie und in einem ungeheuren Mannigfaltigen Zusammen=
passung und Einheit herrsche. Ich will z. E., daß ein Raum durch die
Bewegung einer geraden Linie um einen festen Punkt umgrenzt werde.
Ich begreife gar leicht, daß ich dadurch einen Kreis habe, der in allen
seinen Punkten von dem gedachten festen Punkt gleiche Entfernungen hat.

PART TWO

The Extensive Utility Peculiar to
This Mode of Proof

OBSERVATION ONE
In Which the Existence of God is Concluded
A Posteriori From The Perceived Unity
In The Essence Of Things

1.
*Unity in the manifold of the essence of things shown in the
properties of space*

The necessary properties of space provide the geometer an uncommon pleasure through obviousness of conviction and through exactitude of execution, as well as by the wide range of their application, in comparison with which nothing that the whole of human knowledge can show would even approach, much less exceed. From here on, however, I will study the aforementioned object from a completely different perspective. I will look at it philosophically and note that, with such necessary determinations, order and harmony, and unity and coherence in an immense manifold, dominate. For example, I want to enclose a space by the motion of a straight line around a fixed point. I quite easily understand that thereby I have a circle whose points all are equidistant from the imagined fixed point.

Allein ich finde gar keine Veranlassung unter einer so einfältigen Construction sehr viel Mannigfaltiges zu vermuthen, das eben dadurch großen Regeln der Ordnung unterworfen sei. Indessen entdecke ich, daß alle gerade Linien, die einander aus einem beliebigen Punkt innerhalb dem Cirkel durchkreuzen, indem sie an den Umkreis stoßen, jederzeit in geometrischer Proportion geschnitten sind; imgleichen daß alle diejenige, die von einem Punkt außerhalb dem Kreise diesen durchschneiden, jederzeit in solche Stücke zerlegt werden, die sich umgekehrt verhalten wie ihre Ganzen. Wenn man bedenkt, wie unendlich viel verschiedene Lagen diese Linien annehmen können, indem sie den Cirkel wie gedacht durchschneiden, und wahrnimmt, wie sie gleichwohl beständig unter dem nämlichen Gesetze stehen, von dem sie nicht abweichen können, so ist es unerachtet dessen, daß die Wahrheit davon leicht begriffen wird, dennoch etwas Unerwartetes, daß so wenig Anstalt in der Beschreibung dieser Figur und gleichwohl so viel Ordnung und in dem Mannigfaltigen eine so vollkommene Einheit daraus erfolgt.

Wenn aufgegeben wäre, daß schiefe Flächen in verschiedenen Neigungen gegen den Horizont, doch von solcher Länge angeordnet würden, damit frei herabrollende Körper darauf gerade in gleicher Zeit herab kämen, so wird ein jeder, der die mechanische Gesetze versteht, einsehen, daß hiezu mancherlei Veranstaltung gehöre. Nun findet sich aber diese Einrichtung im Cirkel von selber mit unendlich viel Abwechselung der Stellungen und doch in jedem Falle mit der größten Richtigkeit. Denn alle Sehnen, die an den Vertikaldurchmesser stoßen, sie mögen von dessen obersten oder untersten Punkte ausgehen, nach welchen Neigungen man auch will, haben insgesammt das gemein: daß der freie Fall durch dieselbe in gleichen Zeiten geschieht. Ich erinnere mich, daß ein verständiger Lehrling, als ihm dieser Satz mit seinem Beweise von mir vorgetragen wurde, nachdem er alles wohl verstand, dadurch nicht weniger, wie durch ein Naturwunder gerührt wurde. Und in der That wird man durch eine so sonderbare Vereinigung vom Mannigfaltigen nach so fruchtbaren Regeln in einer so schlecht und einfältig scheinenden Sache, als ein Cirkelkreis ist, überrascht und mit Recht in Bewunderung gesetzt. Es ist auch kein Wunder der Natur, welches durch die Schönheit oder Ordnung, die darin herrscht, mehr Ursache zum Erstaunen gäbe, es müßte denn sein, daß es deswegen geschähe, weil die Ursache derselben da nicht so deutlich einzusehen ist, und die Bewunderung eine Tochter der Unwissenheit ist.

But I find absolutely no reason in such a simple construction to assume a complex manifold which is thereby subject to the great rules of order. However, I discover that all straight lines which intersect each other from a random point inside the circle are always cut in geometric proportion as they strike the circumference. And likewise all the lines which intersect the circle from a point outside of it can always be divided into parts which are inversely proportional to their whole extent. One can consider how infinitely many places these lines might occupy while still intersecting the circle, and how they would nevertheless all constantly stand under the aforementioned law from which they cannot deviate. Despite being able to grasp this truth, it is somewhat unexpected that from so little arrangement in the construction of this figure so much order and such perfect unity in the manifold nevertheless result.

Should it be proposed that inclined planes be arranged with different slopes toward the horizon yet with such lengths that freely falling bodies reach the bottom of each one in the same time, anyone who understood mechanical laws at all would realize that a good many provisions are involved. Now the same contrivance may be found in the circle itself with infinitely many changes of position and with the greatest accuracy in this case. Any chords that cut through the vertical axis of the circle—whether from the highest or from the lowest point and from whatever slope one likes—together have in common that free fall through them occurs in the same time. I recall that a bright student for whom I had proved this law, having understood everything well, was stirred by it no less than by a miracle. And in fact one is surprised and justifiably marvels at the remarkable unity of the manifold according to such productive rules in a thing as base and seemingly so simple as a circle. But there is no miracle of nature which would give more reason for astonishment, owing to the beauty or order which rules in it. It must be then that this [astonishment] obtains because the cause [of such extensive unity] is not so distinctly discerned, and wonder is a daughter of ignorance.

Das Feld, darauf ich Denkwürdigkeiten sammle, ist davon so voll, daß, ohne einen Fuß weiter setzen zu dürfen, sich auf derselben Stelle, da wir uns befinden, noch unzählige Schönheiten darbieten. Es giebt Auflösungen der Geometrie, wo dasjenige, was nur durch weitläuftige Veranstaltung scheint möglich zu sein, sich gleichsam ohne alle Kunst in der Sache selbst darlegt. Diese werden von jedermann als artig empfunden und dieses um desto mehr, je weniger man selbst dabei zu thun hat, und je verwickelter gleichwohl die Auflösung zu sein scheint. Der Cirkelring zwischen zwei Kreisen, die einen gemeinschaftlichen Mittelpunkt haben, hat eine von einer Cirkelfläche sehr verschiedene Gestalt, und es kommt jedermann anfänglich als mühsam und künstlich vor, ihn in diese Figur zu verwandeln. Allein so bald ich einsehe, daß die den inwendigen Cirkel berührende Linie, so weit gezogen, bis sie zu beiden Seiten den Umkreis des größern schneidet, der Durchmesser dieses Cirkels sei, dessen Fläche dem Inhalt des Cirkelringes gerade gleich ist, so kann ich nicht umhin einige Befremdung über die einfältige Art zu äußern, wie das Gesuchte in der Natur der Sache selbst sich so leicht offenbart, und meiner Bemühung hiebei fast nichts beizumessen ist.

Wir haben, um in den nothwendigen Eigenschaften des Raums Einheit bei der größten Mannigfaltigkeit und Zusammenhang in dem, was eine von dem andern ganz abgesonderte Nothwendigkeit zu haben scheint, zu bemerken, nur blos unsere Augen auf die Cirkelfigur gerichtet, welche deren noch unendliche hat, davon ein kleiner Theil bekannt ist. Hieraus läßt sich abnehmen, welche Unermeßlichkeit solcher harmonischen Beziehungen sonst in den Eigenschaften des Raums liege, deren viele die höhere Geometrie in den Verwandtschaften der verschiedenen Geschlechter der krummen Linien darlegt, und alle außer der Übung des Verstandes durch die denkliche Einsicht derselben das Gefühl auf eine ähnliche oder erhabnere Art wie die zufällige Schönheiten der Natur rühren.

Wenn man bei dergleichen Anordnungen der Natur berechtigt ist nach einem Grunde einer so weit erstreckten Übereinstimmung des Mannigfaltigen zu fragen, soll man es denn weniger sein bei Wahrnehmung des Ebenmaßes und der Einheit in den unendlich vielfältigen Bestimmungen des Raums? Ist diese Harmonie darum weniger befremdlich, weil sie nothwendig ist? Ich halte dafür, sie sei es darum nur desto mehr. Und weil dasjenige Viele, davon jedes seine besondere und unabhängige Nothwendigkeit hätte, nimmermehr Ordnung, Wohlgereimtheit und Einheit in

The field in which I assemble items of interest for reflection is so full of them that without being allowed to step a foot farther innumerable beauties are presented in the very place where we are. There are solutions in geometry where what appears possible only through extensive arrangement emerges in the matter itself as it were, without the least contrivance. These are felt by anyone to be charming and the more so the less one must do with them and the more complicated and difficult the solution appears to be. The ring between the two circles which have a common center is very different in form from a circular surface, and initially it seems laborious and artificial for anyone to transform it into this figure. Yet as soon as I see that the lines tangential to the interior circle, extended to intersect both sides of the larger circle, are the diameter of the circle whose area is exactly equivalent to the content of the ring, I cannot refrain from expressing some surprise at the simple way in which the object of inquiry is easily revealed in the nature of the thing. Almost nothing here is due to my effort.

We have directed our attention only to the circular figure in order to mark the unity of the necessary properties of space in the face of the greatest multiplicity and interconnections where one thing seems to have an entirely separate necessity from another. This circular figure has infinite necessary properties of which only a small portion are known. From this may be assumed the immeasurability of such harmonious relations which yet lie in the properties of space. Higher geometry may demonstrate many of these in the relationships of the various species of curved lines. All of them, besides exercising the understanding through their rational comprehension, arouse a feeling analogous to, or more sublime than, the sort the contingent excellences of nature stimulate.

If with these same structures of nature one be justified in inquiring after the ground of the far-reaching harmony of the manifold, is he any less so justified with the perception of the symmetry and unity in the infinitely manifold determinations of space? I hold that it is even more so. Indeed, since that multiplicity in which each would have its particular and independent necessity could never have order, harmonious adaptation [*die Wohlgereimtheit*]18 and unity in opposing

den gegenseitigen Beziehungen haben könnte, wird man dadurch nicht eben
sowohl, wie durch die Harmonie in den zufälligen Anstalten der Natur
auf die Vermuthung eines obersten Grundes selbst der Wesen der Dinge
geführt, da die Einheit des Grundes auch Einheit in dem Umfange aller
Folgen veranlaßt?

2.

**Die Einheit im Mannigfaltigen der Wesen der Dinge,
gewiesen an demjenigen, was in den Bewegungsgesetzen
nothwendig ist.**

Wenn man in der Natur eine Anordnung entdeckt, die um eines be=
sondern Zwecks willen scheint getroffen zu sein, indem sie sich nicht blos
nach den allgemeinen Eigenschaften der Materie würde dargeboten haben,
so sehen wir diese Anstalt als zufällig und als die Folge einer Wahl an.
Zeigen sich nun neue Übereinstimmung, Ordnung und Nutzen und beson=
ders dazu abgerichtete Mittelursachen, so beurtheilen wir dieselbe auf die
ähnliche Art; dieser Zusammenhang ist der Natur der Sachen ganz fremd,
und blos weil es jemand beliebt hat sie so zu verknüpfen, stehen sie in
dieser Harmonie. Man kann keine allgemeine Ursache angeben, weswegen
die Klauen der Katze, des Löwen u. a. m. so gebauet sind, daß sie sporen,
das ist, sich zurücklegen können, als weil irgend ein Urheber sie zu dem
Zwecke, um vor dem Abschleifen gesichert zu sein, so angeordnet hat, indem
diese Thiere geschickte Werkzeuge haben müssen, ihren Raub zu ergreifen
und zu halten. Allein wenn gewisse allgemeinere Beschaffenheiten, die
der Materie beiwohnen, außer einem Vortheile, den sie schaffen, und um
dessen willen man sich vorstellen kann, daß sie so geordnet worden, ohne
die mindeste neue Vorkehrung gleichwohl eine besondere Tauglichkeit zu
noch mehr Übereinstimmung zeigen, wenn ein einfältiges Gesetz, das jeder=
mann um eines gewissen Guten willen allein schon nöthig finden würde,
gleichwohl eine ausgebreitete Fruchtbarkeit an noch viel mehrerem zeigt,
wenn die übrigen Nutzen und Wohlgereimtheiten daraus ohne Kunst,
sondern vielmehr nothwendiger Weise fließen, wenn endlich dieses sich
durch die ganze materiale Natur so befindet: so liegen offenbar selbst in
den Wesen der Dinge durchgängige Beziehungen zur Einheit und zum Zu=
sammenhange, und eine allgemeine Harmonie breitet sich über das Reich
der Möglichkeit selber aus. Dieses veranlaßt eine Bewunderung über so
viel Schicklichkeit und natürliche Zusammenpassung, die, indem sie die

relations, is one not as much led to the assumption of a first ground of the very essence of things by that as by harmony in the contingent structures of nature, since unity of the ground also provides unity in the domain of all consequences?

2.
Unity in the manifold of the essences of things shown in what is necessary in the laws of motion.

If in nature a structure be discovered that seems to be good for the sake of a special purpose, while it would not have emerged according to the general properties of matter alone, we regard this provision as contingent and the consequence of a choice. If new coherences or utilities and the special mediating causes necessary to effect them appear, we judge them in an analogous way. This coherence is quite foreign to the nature of the thing, and it is simply because somebody has wished to join them in this way that they stand in such harmony. No universal cause can be given as to why the claws of cats, lions, and many others are built so as to be spurred, that is, so they may be retracted, except that some creator has ordered it for the purpose of protecting them against dullness since these animals must have adequate tools in order to grasp and to hold their prey. But if certain more universal properties inhering in matter, without the slightest new provision—save for the advantage they provide and for whose sake one may suppose they were so arranged—nevertheless show a particular fitness for still more coherence; if a simple law which everyone would find necessary for the sake of a certain good nevertheless shows an extensive productivity for still many others; if the remaining utilities and harmonious adaptations flow without artifice but rather necessarily from it; and if finally all of this takes place throughout the whole of material nature; then obviously the thoroughgoing relations of unity and coherence lie in the very essences of things and univeral harmony extends over the realm of possibility itself. This prompts wonder at so much elegance and natural coherence which, while they likewise obviate

peinliche und erzwungene Kunst entbehrlich macht, gleichwohl selber nimmermehr dem Ungefähr beigemessen werden kann, sondern eine in den Möglichkeiten selbst liegende Einheit und die gemeinschaftliche Abhängigkeit selbst der Wesen aller Dinge von einem einigen großen Grunde anzeigt. Ich werde diese sehr große Merkwürdigkeit durch einige leichte Beispiele deutlich zu machen suchen, indem ich die Methode sorgfältig befolge, aus dem, was durch Beobachtung unmittelbar gewiß ist, zu dem allgemeinern Urtheile langsam hinauf zu steigen.

Man kann einen Nutzen unter tausend wählen, weswegen man es als nöthig ansehen kann, daß ein Luftkreis sei, wenn man durchaus einen Zweck zum Grunde zu haben verlangt, wodurch eine Anstalt in der Natur zuerst veranlaßt worden. Ich räume also dieses ein und nenne etwa das Athmen der Menschen und Thiere als die Endabsicht dieser Veranstaltung. Nun giebt diese Luft durch die nämliche Eigenschaften und keine mehr, die sie zum Athemholen allein bedürfte, zugleich Anlaß zu einer Unendlichkeit von schönen Folgen, die damit nothwendiger Weise begleitet sind und nicht dürfen durch besondere Anlagen befördert werden. Eben dieselbe elastische Kraft und Gewicht der Luft macht das Saugen möglich, ohne welches junge Thiere der Nahrung entbehren müßten, und die Möglichkeit der Pumpwerke ist davon eine nothwendige Folge. Durch sie geschieht es, daß Feuchtigkeit in Dünsten hinaufgezogen wird, welche sich oben in Wolken verdicken, die den Tag verschönern, öfters die übermäßige Hitze der Sonne mildern, vornehmlich aber dazu dienen, die trockene Gegenden der Erdfläche durch den Raub von den Wasserbetten der niedrigen milde zu befeuchten. Die Dämmerung, die den Tag verlängert und dem Auge durch allmählige Zwischengrade den Überschritt von der Nacht zum Tage unschädlich macht, und vornehmlich die Winde sind ganz natürliche und ungezwungene Folgen derselben.

Stellet euch vor, ein Mensch mache sich einen Entwurf, wie die Küsten der Länder des heißen Weltstrichs, die sonst heißer sein müßten als die tiefer im Lande liegende Gegenden, eine etwas erträglichere Wärme sollten genießen können, so wird er am natürlichsten auf einen Seewind verfallen, der zu dieser Absicht in den heißesten Tagesstunden wehen müßte. Weil aber, da es zur Nachtzeit über der See viel geschwinder kalt wird als über dem Lande, nicht zuträglich sein dürfte, daß derselbe Wind immer wehte, so würde er wünschen, daß es der Vorsehung gefallen hätte es so zu veranstalten, damit in den mittlern Stunden der Nacht der Wind

painstaking and unnatural art, can themselves never be attributed to mere chance. Rather they indicate a unity lying in the possibilities themselves and the common dependence of the essences of all things upon a single great ground. I shall try to make this remarkable fact apparent through a few simple examples, while carefully following the method of ascending slowly through observation from what is immediately certain to the more general judgment.

Any one of a thousand uses may be chosen, on account of which an atmosphere may be regarded as being necessary, if one really demands a purpose as the reason for which a structure in nature initially was provided. I grant this and perhaps I call the breathing of men and animals the ultimate intention of this provision. Now, through precisely those properties which it requires just for respiration and no more, air also simultaneously gives rise to an infinity of excellent consequences which have accompanied it necessarily and need not be advanced through special structures. The very same elasticity and weight of air makes suckling possible—without which young animals would have to do without their nourishment—and the possibility of a pumping apparatus is a necessary consequence of this. Through them [i.e., elasticity and weight] it happens that moisture is taken up in vapors, thickening at some height into clouds which beautify the day and often moderate the excessive heat of the sun. But above all else they serve liberally to moisten the dry areas of the globe by preying upon the water tables of the lower areas. The twilight which lengthens the day and makes the change from night to day harmless for our eyes by [its] gradual intermediate degrees, and above all, the wind, are all completely natural and regular consequences of the same thing.

Suppose that one were to devise a plan by which the coasts of lands in the tropical zones of the earth, which would otherwise be hotter than regions deeper in the interior, could enjoy a somewhat more bearable heat. For this purpose he would most naturally fall back upon a sea breeze that would have to blow during the hot hours of the day. But, since at night it becomes cold over the sea much more quickly than over land,

vom Lande wieder zurück kehrte, welches auch viel andern Nutzen mit
befördern könnte. Nun würde nur die Frage sein, durch welche Mechanik
und künstliche Anordnung dieser Windeswechsel zu erhalten wäre, und
hiebei würde man noch große Ursache haben zu besorgen: daß, da der
Mensch nicht verlangen kann, daß alle Naturgesetze sich zu seiner Bequem-
lichkeit anschicken sollen, dieses Mittel zwar möglich, aber mit den übrigen
nöthigen Anstalten so übel zusammenpassend sein dürfte, daß die oberste
Weisheit es darum nicht zu verordnen gut fände. Alles dieses Bedenken
ist indessen unnöthig. Was eine nach überlegter Wahl getroffene Anordnung thun würde, verrichtet hier die Luft nach den allgemeinen Bewegungsgesetzen, und eben dasselbe einfache Principium ihrer anderweitigen Nutzbarkeit bringt auch diese ohne neue und besondere Anstalten hervor. Die
von der Tageshitze verdünnte Luft über dem brennenden Boden eines
solchen Landes weicht nothwendiger Weise der dichtern und schwerern über
dem kühlen Meere und verursacht den Seewind, der um deswillen von den
heißesten Tagesstunden an bis spät in den Abend weht, und die Seeluft,
die aus den nämlichen Ursachen am Tage so stark nicht erhitzt worden
war, als die über dem Lande, verkühlt des Nachts geschwinder, zieht sich
zusammen und veranlaßt den Rückzug der Landluft zur Nachtzeit. Jedermann weiß: daß alle Küsten des heißen Welttheils diesen Wechselwind
genießen.

Ich habe, um die Beziehungen, welche einfache und sehr allgemeine
Bewegungsgesetze durch die Nothwendigkeit ihres Wesens auf Ordnung
und Wohlgereimtheit haben, zu zeigen, nur meinen Blick auf einen kleinen
Theil der Natur, nämlich auf die Wirkungen der Luft, geworfen. Man
wird leicht gewahr werden, daß die ganze unermeßliche Strecke der großen
Naturordnung in eben demselben Betracht vor mir offen liege. Ich be-
halte mir vor, noch etwas in dem Folgenden zu Erweiterung dieser schönen
Aussicht beizufügen. Anjetzt würde ich etwas Wesentliches aus der acht
lassen, wenn ich nicht der wichtigen Entdeckung des Herrn v. Maupertuis
gedächte, die er in Ansehung der Wohlgereimtheit der nothwendigen und
allgemeinsten Bewegungsgesetze gemacht hat.

Das, was wir zum Beweise angeführt haben, betrifft zwar weit ausgebreitete und nothwendige Gesetze, allein nur von einer besondern Art der
Materien der Welt. Der Herr v. Maupertuis bewies dagegen: daß selbst
die allgemeinsten Gesetze, wornach die Materie überhaupt wirkt, sowohl
im Gleichgewichte als beim Stoße, sowohl der elastischen als unelastischen

it would not do for the same wind always to blow. Thus he would wish that it had pleased providence to arrange things so that in the middle of the night the land winds returned. And this can further many other uses too. Then it would be only a question of through which mechanism and ingenious structure this change of winds was to be effected. Here one would have good reason for concern, for man should not demand that all natural laws be designed to issue in his comfort. Perhaps the means, although possible, so ill accord with the remainder of the necessary causes that supreme wisdom would not find it good to order it. However all this caution is unnecessary. What good provision would order upon considered choice, the air performs according the universal laws of motion. And the very same simple principle of its other extensive utilities also produced this without new and special causes. The air, thinned by the heat of the day over the scorching earth of such a country, necessarily yields to more dense and heavier air from the cooler sea, thus causing the sea breeze which for this reason blows from the hottest hours of the day until the late evening. And the sea air, which for the same reasons was not as strongly heated as that over the land, is quickly cooled by the evening, contracts and occasions the return of the wind from the land by night. It is well known that all coasts of the hot regions of the world enjoy this change of winds.

In order to show the relations between simple and very general laws of motion to order and harmonious adaptation through the necessity of their essence, I have been concentrating my attention on only a small part of nature, namely the effects of air. It will be easily seen that exactly the same treatment of the immeasurable extent of the natural order lies open to me. In what follows I shall be limiting myself to appending something that enlarges this happy prospect. Something essential would be omitted were I not to consider the important discovery Maupertuis has made concerning the harmonious adaptation of the necessary and most general laws of motion.[19]

What has been cited in this proof concerns, to be sure, widespread and necessary laws, yet only those of a particular

Körper, bei dem Anziehen des Lichts in der Brechung eben so gut, als beim Zurückstoßen desselben in der Abprallung, einer herrschenden Regel unterworfen sind, nach welcher die größte Sparsamkeit in der Handlung jederzeit beobachtet ist. Durch diese Entdeckung sind die Wirkungen der Materie ungeachtet der großen Verschiedenheiten, die sie an sich haben mögen, unter eine allgemeine Formel gebracht, die eine Beziehung auf Anständigkeit, Schönheit und Wohlgereimtheit ausdrückt. Gleichwohl sind die Gesetze der Bewegung selber so bewandt, daß sich nimmermehr eine Materie ohne sie denken läßt, und sie sind so nothwendig, daß sie auch ohne die mindeste Versuche aus der allgemeinen und wesentlichen Beschaffenheit aller Materie mit größter Deutlichkeit können hergeleitet werden. Der gedachte scharfsinnige Gelehrte empfand alsbald, daß, indem dadurch in dem unendlichen Mannigfaltigen des Universum Einheit und in dem blindlings Nothwendigen Ordnung verursacht wird, irgend ein oberstes Principium sein müsse, wovon alles dieses seine Harmonie und Anständigkeit her haben kann. Er glaubte mit Recht, daß ein so allgemeiner Zusammenhang in den einfachsten Naturen der Dinge einen weit tauglichern Grund an die Hand gebe, irgend in einem vollkommenen Urwesen die letzte Ursache von allem in der Welt mit Gewißheit anzutreffen, als alle Wahrnehmung verschiedener zufälligen und veränderlichen Anordnung nach besondern Gesetzen. Nunmehr kam es darauf an, welchen Gebrauch die höhere Weltweisheit von dieser wichtigen neuen Einsicht würde machen können, und ich glaube in der Muthmaßung nicht zu fehlen, wenn ich dafür halte, daß die königliche Akademie der Wissenschaften in Berlin dieses zur Absicht der Preisfrage gehabt habe: ob die Bewegungsgesetze nothwendig oder zufällig seien, und welche niemand der Erwartung gemäß beantwortet hat.

Wenn die Zufälligkeit im Realverstande genommen wird, daß sie in der Abhängigkeit des Materialen der Möglichkeit von einem andern besteht, so ist augenscheinlich, daß die Bewegungsgesetze und die allgemeine Eigenschaften der Materie, die ihnen gehorchen, irgend von einem großen gemeinschaftlichen Urwesen, dem Grunde der Ordnung und Wohlgereimtheit, abhängen müssen. Denn wer wollte dafür halten: daß in einem weitläuftigen Mannigfaltigen, worin jedes einzelne seine eigene völlig unabhängige Natur hätte, gleichwohl durch ein befremdlich Ungefähr sich alles sollte gerade so schicken, daß es wohl mit einander reimte und im Ganzen Einheit sich hervorfände. Allein daß dieses gemeinschaftliche Principium

7*

sort of material in the world. Maupertuis on the contrary shows that even the most universal laws according to which matter in general operates, in equilibrium and in stress, in elastic and inelastic bodies, in the bending of light in refraction as well as in its rebound in reflection, are subject to a dominant rule according to which the greatest economy in action is always observed. Through this discovery, the various effects of matter are brought into a universal formula expressing a relationship to fittingness, beauty, and harmonious adaptation in spite of the great diversity that they have among themselves. Yet these laws of motion are such that no material can ever be conceived without them, and they are so necessary that they can be derived with no experiments at all and with the greatest certainty from the universal and essential constitution of matter. The clear-minded scholar just mentioned discovered then that since unity is caused through them in the infinite manifold of the universe, and order results in blind necessity, there must be some sort of supreme principle from which everything has harmony and fittingness. He rightly believes that such a universal coherence in the simplest nature of things immediately gives a far more suitable reason for somehow locating with certainty the ultimate cause of everything in the world in a perfect primordial being than [does] the perception of different contingent and mutable structures according to separate laws. And now it was a matter of the great use which higher philosophy might make of this insight, and I do not believe the conjecture mistaken when I suggest that this is the issue the Royal Academy of Sciences in Berlin was intending to raise when it put the question for its essay contest: "Whether the laws of motion are necessary or contingent,"[20] which nobody has answered according to that expectation.

If contingency be taken in the real sense, that it consists in the dependence of the matter of possibility upon another, then it is obvious that the laws of motion and the most universal properties of matter which obey them must somehow depend upon a great common primordial being as the ground of order and harmonious adaptation. For who would want to hold that in an extensive manifold where every particular had its own fully independent nature that nevertheless through an

nicht blos auf das Daſein dieſer Materie und der ihr ertheilten Eigen=
ſchaften gehen müſſe, ſondern ſelbſt auf die Möglichkeit einer Materie über=
haupt und auf das Weſen ſelbſt, leuchtet dadurch deutlich in die Augen,
weil das, was einen Raum erfüllen ſoll, was der Bewegung des Stoßes
und Druckes ſoll fähig ſein, gar nicht unter andern Bedingungen kann
gedacht werden, als diejenige ſind, woraus die genannten Geſetze noth=
wendiger Weiſe herfließen. Auf dieſen Fuß ſieht man ein: daß dieſe Bewe=
gungsgeſetze der Materie ſchlechterdings nothwendig ſeien, das iſt, wenn
die Möglichkeit der Materie voraus geſetzt wird, es ihr widerſpreche, nach
andern Geſetzen zu wirken, welches eine logiſche Nothwendigkeit von der
oberſten Art iſt, daß gleichwohl die innere Möglichkeit der Materie ſelbſt,
nämlich die Data und das Reale, was dieſem Denklichen zum Grunde
liegt, nicht unabhängig oder für ſich ſelbſt gegeben ſei, ſondern durch
irgend ein Principium, in welchem das Mannigfaltige Einheit und das
Verſchiedene Verknüpfung bekommt, geſetzt ſei, welches die Zufälligkeit
der Bewegungsgeſetze im Realverſtande beweiſet.

Zweite Betrachtung.

Unterſcheidung der Abhängigkeit aller Dinge von Gott in die moraliſche und unmoraliſche.

Ich nenne diejenige Abhängigkeit eines Dinges von Gott, da er ein
Grund deſſelben durch ſeinen Willen iſt, moraliſch, alle übrige aber iſt
unmoraliſch. Wenn ich demnach behaupte, Gott enthalte den letzten
Grund ſelbſt der innern Möglichkeit der Dinge, ſo wird ein jeder leicht
verſtehen, daß dieſe Abhängigkeit nur unmoraliſch ſein kann; denn der
Wille macht nichts möglich, ſondern beſchließt nur, was als möglich ſchon
vorausgeſetzt iſt. In ſo fern Gott den Grund von dem Daſein der Dinge
enthält, ſo geſtehe ich, daß dieſe Abhängigkeit jederzeit moraliſch ſei, daß
iſt, daß ſie darum exiſtiren, weil er gewollt hat, daß ſie ſein ſollten.

Es bietet nämlich die innere Möglichkeit der Dinge demjenigen, der
ihr Daſein beſchloß, Materialien dar, die eine ungemeine Tauglichkeit zur
Übereinſtimmung und eine in ihrem Weſen liegende Zuſammenpaſſung
zu einem auf vielfältige Art ordentlichen und ſchönen Ganzen enthalten.
Daß ein Luftkreis exiſtirt, kann um der daraus zu erreichenden Zwecke
willen Gott als einem moraliſchen Grunde beigemeſſen werden. Allein

astonishing accident all things conform so completely that they square precisely with everything else and that a unity is found in the whole. That this common principle cannot be laid merely to the existence of this matter or to that of its imparted properties but rather to the possibility of matter in general and to essence itself is apparent from the fact that whatever fills space and whatever is capable of stress and resistance can be thought under no conditions save those from which the above-mentioned laws necessarily flow. In this way it can be seen that these laws of the motion *of matter* are absolutely necessary. That is if the possibility of matter be presupposed it would be contradictory for it to operate according to other laws. And this is a logical necessity of the highest sort. Nevertheless the inner possibility of matter itself, namely the data and the real element which lies at the base of this conceivable thing, cannot be given independently and for itself but rather through some presupposed principle in which the manifold receives unity and the diverse receives connection. This proves the contingence of laws of motion in the real sense.

OBSERVATION TWO
Distinction of the Dependence of All Things Upon God into the Moral and Non-Moral

I call that dependence of a thing upon God where he is the ground of it through his will, *moral*. All other [dependence] is non-moral. Thus when I maintain that God contains the ultimate ground of the internal possibility of things, it will be seen clearly that this dependence can only be non-moral, for will makes nothing possible. Rather it only decides upon what already is presupposed as possible. Insofar as God contains the ground of the existence of things, I confess that this dependence is always moral. That is, they exist because he has willed that they should be.

Of course the internal possibility of things provides to whatever decides upon their existence materials containing an uncommon propensity for accord and a coherence, lying in the essence of things, for an excellent, complexly ordered whole.

daß eine so große Fruchtbarkeit in dem Wesen eines einzigen, so einfachen Grundes liegt, so viel schon in seiner Möglichkeit liegende Schicklichkeit und Harmonie, welche nicht neuer Vorkehrungen bedarf, um mit andern möglichen Dingen einer Welt mannigfaltigen Regeln der Ordnung gemäß sich zusammen zu schicken, das kann gewiß nicht wiederum einer freien Wahl beigemessen werden; weil aller Entschluß eines Willens die Erkenntniß der Möglichkeit des zu Beschließenden voraus setzt.

Alles dasjenige, dessen Grund in einer freien Wahl gesucht werden soll, muß in so fern auch zufällig sein. Nun ist die Vereinigung vieler und mannigfaltiger Folgen unter einander, die nothwendig aus einem einzigen Grunde fließen, nicht eine zufällige Vereinigung; mithin kann diese nicht einer freiwilligen Bestimmung zugeschrieben werden. So haben wir oben gesehn, daß die Möglichkeit der Pumpwerke, des Athmens, die Erhebung der flüssigen Materien, wenn welche da sind, in Dünste, die Winde ꝛc. von einander unzertrennlich sind, weil sie alle aus einem einzigen Grunde nämlich der Elasticität und Schwere der Luft, abhängen, und diese Übereinstimmung des Mannigfaltigen in Einem ist daher keinesweges zufällig und also nicht einem moralischen Grunde beizumessen.

Ich gehe hier nur immer auf die Beziehung, die das Wesen der Luft, oder eines jeden andern Dinges zu der möglichen Hervorbringung so vieler schönen Folgen hat, das ist, ich betrachte nur die Tauglichkeit ihrer Natur zu so viel Zwecken, und da ist die Einheit wegen der Übereinstimmung eines einigen Grundes zu so viel möglichen Folgen gewiß nothwendig, und diese mögliche Folgen sind in so fern von einander und von dem Dinge selbst unzertrennlich. Was die wirkliche Hervorbringung dieser Nutzen anlangt, so ist sie in so fern zufällig, als eins von den Dingen, darauf sich das Ding bezieht, fehlen, oder eine fremde Kraft die Wirkung hindern kann.

In den Eigenschaften des Raums liegen schöne Verhältnisse und in dem unermeßlich Mannigfaltigen seiner Bestimmungen eine bewundernswürdige Einheit. Das Dasein aller dieser Wohlgereimtheit, in so fern Materie den Raum erfüllen sollte, ist mit allen ihren Folgen der Willkür der ersten Ursache beizumessen; allein was die Vereinbarung so vieler Folgen, die alle mit den Dingen in der Welt in so großer Harmonie stehen, unter einander anlangt, so würde es ungereimt sein, sie wiederum in einem Willen zu suchen. Unter andern nothwendigen Folgen aus der

That an atmosphere exists may be attributed to God as a moral ground owing to the goals to be achieved through it. But such a great fecundity lies in the essence of a single, simple ground that just in its possibility alone there is an elegance and harmony which require no new provisions in order, along with other possible things, to comprise a world consistent with the manifold rules of order certainly cannot be attributed to a free choice. For all decision of will presupposes knowledge of the possibility of what is to be concluded.

Anything whose ground must be sought in free choice must also be contingent in that degree. But the union with each other of those many and manifold consequences which necessarily follow from a single ground is not a contingent union. Thus it can not be ascribed to a voluntary determination. We have seen above that the possibility of a pumping apparatus, of breathing, of the evaporation of fluid matter in vapors when such matter is present, of the wind, and so on are all inseparable from one another because they depend upon one and the same ground, namely the elasticity and weight of air. This unison of the manifold into one is in no way contingent and cannot be attributed to a moral ground.

I am concerned here only with the relation that the essence of air, or of any other thing, has to the *possible* production of so many excellent consequences. That is, I am studying only the *suitability* of its nature for so many ends; and, since the unity is certainly necessary on account of the agreement of one single ground with so many possible consequences, these possible consequences are in this degree inseparable from each other and from the thing itself. Whatever applies to the actual production of these utilities is contingent to the extent that its actualization may be hindered if one of the things to which it is related be missing or be some extraneous force.

Excellent relations lie in the properties of space, and [there is] a remarkable unity in the immeasurable manifold of its determinations. The existence of all these harmonious adaptations, insofar as matter fills space, together with all the consequences of this harmonious adaptation, is to be attributed to a free choice of a first cause. But so far as what is concerned

Natur der Luft ist auch diejenige zu zählen, da durch sie den darin be=
wegten Materien Widerstand geleistet wird. Die Regentropfen, indem sie
von ungemeiner Höhe herabfallen, werden durch sie aufgehalten und
kommen mit mäßiger Schnelligkeit herab, da sie ohne diese Verzögerung
eine sehr verderbliche Gewalt im Herabstürzen von solcher Höhe würden
erworben haben. Dieses ist ein Vortheil, der, weil ohne ihn die Luft
nicht möglich ist, nicht durch einen besondern Rathschluß mit den übrigen
Eigenschaften derselben verbunden worden. Der Zusammenhang der
Theile der Materie mag nun z. E. bei dem Wasser eine nothwendige Folge
von der Möglichkeit der Materie überhaupt, oder eine besonders veran=
staltete Anordnung sein, so ist die unmittelbare Wirkung davon die runde
Figur kleiner Theile derselben, als der Regentropfen. Dadurch aber wird
der schöne farbichte Bogen nach sehr allgemeinen Bewegungsgesetzen mög=
lich, der mit einer rührenden Pracht und Regelmäßigkeit über dem Ge=
sichtskreise steht, wenn die unverdeckte Sonne in die gegenüber herab=
fallende Regentropfen strahlt. Daß flüssige Materien und schwere Körper
da sind, kann nur dem Begehren dieses mächtigen Urhebers beigemessen
werden, daß aber ein Weltkörper in seinem flüssigen Zustande ganz noth=
wendiger Weise so allgemeinen Gesetzen zu Folge eine Kugelgestalt anzu=
nehmen bestrebt ist, welche nachher besser, wie irgend eine andere mögliche
mit den übrigen Zwecken des Universum zusammenstimmt, indem z. E.
eine solche Oberfläche der gleichförmigsten Vertheilung des Lichts fähig
ist, das liegt in dem Wesen der Sache selbst.

Der Zusammenhang der Materie und der Widerstand, den die Theile
mit ihrer Trennbarkeit verbinden, macht die Reibung nothwendig, welche
von so großem Nutzen ist und so wohl mit der Ordnung in allen mannig=
faltigen Naturveränderungen zusammenstimmt, als irgend etwas, was
nicht aus so allgemeinen Gründen geflossen wäre, sondern durch eine be=
sondere Anstalt wäre hinzu gekommen. Wenn Reibung die Bewegungen
nicht verzögerte, so würde die Aufbehaltung der einmal hervorgebrachten
Kräfte durch die Mittheilung an andere, die Zurückschlagung und immer
fortgesetzte Anstöße und Erschütterungen alles zuletzt in Verwirrung
bringen. Die Flächen, worauf Körper liegen, müßten jederzeit vollkommen
wagerecht sein (welches sie nur selten sein können), sonst würden diese
jederzeit glitschen. Alle gedrehte Stricke halten nur durch Reibung. Denn
die Fäden, welche nicht die ganze Länge des Stricks haben, würden mit
der mindesten Kraft auseinandergezogen werden, wenn nicht die der Kraft,

with the union amongst themselves of so many consequences that stand in great harmony with the things of the world is concerned: it would be incoherent to seek them in a will. Among the other necessary consequences following from the nature of air is that resistance is provided matter moving therein. The raindrops that fall from a considerable height are thereby retarded and come down with more moderate speed, whereas without this retardation they would have gained very dangerous power in the fall from such an altitude. This is an advantage which cannot be tied up with the remaining properties of air by a special decree since air is impossible without it. The aggregation of the parts of matter, water for example, may be a necessary consequence of the possibility of matter in general or of a specially arranged structure. The immediate effect of it is the round figuration of small parts of water such as the raindrops. But because of this the beautifully colored rainbow, which rises over the horizon with splendid glory and regularity whenever the unclouded sun shines through raindrops, is possible according to very general laws of motion. That fluid matter and heavy bodies exist can be attributed only to the desire of a powerful creator. But that a heavenly body in its fluid state is quite necessarily constrained to take on globular shape as a consequence of universal laws, a shape which then better accords with the remaining goals of nature than any other possible one—for example, that such a surface is capable of the most uniform division of light—this is due to the essence of the thing itself.

The cohesion of matter and resistance binding together the parts with their separability renders friction necessary. This is of great utility and conforms as well to the order of all manifold natural variations as something which did not follow from such universal grounds but was added by a special arrangement. Were motion not retarded by friction, the retention of a force once effected by communication to others—the recoil and perpetually continued thrusts and concussions—would finally result in total confusion. The surfaces upon which bodies lay would have to be perfectly level at all times (which they seldom can be) or otherwise they would always be sliding. All woven

womit sie durch das Winden an einander gepreßt sind, gemäße Reibung sie zurück hielte.

Ich führe hier darum so wenig geachtete und gemeine Folgen aus den einfältigsten und allgemeinsten Naturgesetzen an, damit man daraus sowohl die große und unendlich weit ausgebreitete Zusammenstimmung, die die Wesen der Dinge überhaupt untereinander haben, und die große Folgen, die derselben beizumessen sind, auch in den Fällen abnehme, wo man nicht geschickt genug ist, manche Naturordnung bis auf solche einfältige und allgemeine Gründe zurück zu führen, als auch damit man das Widersinnige empfinde, was darin liegt, wenn man bei dergleichen Übereinstimmungen die Weisheit Gottes als den besondern Grund derselben nennt. Daß Dinge da sind, die so viel schöne Beziehung haben, ist der weisen Wahl desjenigen, der sie um dieser Harmonie willen hervorbrachte, beizumessen, daß aber ein jedes derselben eine so ausgebreitete Schicklichkeit zu vielfältiger Übereinstimmung durch einfache Gründe enthielte, und dadurch eine bewundersmürdige Einheit im Ganzen konnte erhalten werden, liegt selbst in der Möglichkeit der Dinge, und da hier das Zufällige, was bei jeder Wahl voraus gesetzt werden muß, verschwindet, so kann der Grund dieser Einheit zwar in einem weisen Wesen, aber nicht vermittelst seiner Weisheit gesucht werden.

Dritte Betrachtung.

Von der Abhängigkeit der Dinge der Welt von Gott vermittelst der Ordnung der Natur, oder ohne dieselbe.

1.

Eintheilung der Weltbegebenheiten, in so fern sie unter der Ordnung der Natur stehen oder nicht.

Es steht etwas unter der Ordnung der Natur, in so fern sein Dasein oder seine Veränderung in den Kräften der Natur zureichend gegründet ist. Hiezu wird erfordert erstlich, daß die Kraft der Natur davon die wirkende Ursache sei; zweitens, daß die Art, wie sie auf die Hervorbringung dieser Wirkung gerichtet ist, selbst in einer Regel der natürlichen Wirkungsgesetze hinreichend gegründet sei. Dergleichen Begebenheiten heißen auch schlechthin natürliche Weltbegebenheiten. Dagegen wo dieses nicht ist, so

ropes are maintained only through friction. For the threads which are not as long as the entire rope would pull away from each other if the force through which they are pressed into each other by winding did not restrain them in accordance with friction.

I cite here little-noted and common conclusions from the most simple and most general laws of nature in order that the great and infinitely extensive harmony which the essences of things at large have with each other, and the great consequences attributed to this, may be learnt even in the cases where one is not adept enough to trace much natural order back to simple universal grounds. Also, what is absurd when the wisdom of God is termed the special ground of this agreement may thus be sensed. That things exist which have many excellent relations is attributable to the wise choice of one who wills them in order to produce this harmony. But that each of them contains such an extensive suitability for multiple concurrence through a simple ground, and through this that such a remarkable unity may be contained in the whole, is due to the possibility of the things. And since that contingency which must be presupposed by every choice vanishes here, the ground of this unity can be sought in a wise being, but not by way of his wisdom.

OBSERVATION THREE
The Dependence of Things in the World Upon God by Means of the Order of Nature or Without It

1.

Division of cosmic events insofar as they stand under the law of nature or not.

A thing stands under the order of nature insofar as its existence or its alteration is sufficiently grounded in the forces of nature. For this it is requiste first, that the force of nature be the efficient cause, and second, that the way in which the force of nature is directed toward production of this effect is itself sufficiently grounded in a rule of natural efficacy. Such events are also called absolutely *natural* cosmic events. On the other

ift der Fall, der unter folchem Grunde nicht ſteht, etwas Übernatürliches, und dieſes findet ſtatt, entweder in ſo fern die nächſte wirkende Urſache außer der Natur iſt, das iſt, in ſo fern die göttliche Kraft ſie unmittelbar hervorbringt, oder zweitens wenn auch nur die Art, wie die Kräfte der Natur auf dieſen Fall gerichtet worden, nicht unter einer Regel der Natur enthalten iſt. Im erſtern Fall nenne ich die Begebenheit **materialiter**, im andern **formaliter** übernatürlich. Da blos der letzte Fall einige Erläuterung zu bedürfen ſcheint, indem das übrige für ſich klar iſt, ſo will ich davon Beiſpiele anführen. Es ſind viele Kräfte in der Natur, die das Vermögen haben, einzelne Menſchen, oder Staaten, oder das ganze menſchliche Geſchlecht zu verderben: Erdbeben, Sturmwinde, Meers=bewegungen, Kometen ꝛc. Es iſt auch nach einem allgemeinen Geſetze genugſam in der Verfaſſung der Natur gegründet, daß einiges von dieſen bisweilen geſchieht. Allein unter den Geſetzen, wornach es geſchieht, ſind die Laſter und das moraliſche Verderben der Menſchengeſchlechter gar keine natürliche Gründe, die damit in Verbindung ſtänden. Die Miſſe=thaten einer Stadt haben keinen Einfluß auf das verborgene Feuer der Erde, und die Üppigkeiten der erſten Welt gehörten nicht zu den wirkenden Urſachen, welche die Kometen in ihren Bahnen zu ſich herab ziehen konnten. Und wenn ſich ein ſolcher Fall ereignet, man mißt ihn aber einem natür=lichen Geſetze bei, ſo will man damit ſagen, daß es ein Unglück, nicht aber daß es eine Strafe ſei, indem das moraliſche Verhalten der Menſchen kein Grund der Erdbeben nach einem natürlichen Geſetze ſein kann, weil hier keine Verknüpfung von Urſachen und Wirkungen ſtatt findet. Z. E. Wenn das Erdbeben die Stadt Port Royal in Jamaica umkehrt,*) ſo wird derjenige, der dieſes eine natürliche Begebenheit nennt, darunter verſtehen: daß, ob zwar die Laſterthaten der Einwohner nach dem Zeugniß ihres Predigers eine ſolche Verwüſtung wohl als ein Strafgericht verdient hätten, dennoch dieſer Fall als einer von vielen anzuſehen ſei, der ſich bis=weilen nach einem allgemeinern Geſetze der Natur zuträgt, da Gegenden der Erde und unter dieſen bisweilen Städte und unter dieſen dann und wann auch ſehr laſterhafte Städte erſchüttert werden. Soll es dagegen als eine Strafe betrachtet werden, ſo müſſen dieſe Kräfte der Natur, da ſie nach einem natürlichen Geſetze den Zuſammenhang mit der Führung der Menſchen nicht haben können, auf jeden ſolchen einzelnen Fall durch

---

*) Siehe Raj von der Welt Anfang, Veränd. und Untergang.

hand, where this is not so, a case which does not stand on such basis is something supernatural. This happens either insofar as the proximate efficient cause is outside nature, that is, insofar as divine power immediately produces it; or when the way in which the forces of nature are directed in this instance is not contained in a rule of nature. In the former case I term the event *materially* and in the latter *formally supernatural*. Since only the latter case seems to require some explication—whilst the rest is clear in itself—I will cite a few examples of it.

There are many forces in nature that have the ability to destroy individual men, states, or the entire human race: earthquakes, gales, rough seas, comets, and so on. That some of these should happen from time to time is also sufficiently grounded in the constitution of nature according to natural law. Among the laws according to which these events obtain, the vices and moral depravity of the human race are in no wise *natural* reasons standing in relation to the events. The misdeeds of a city have no influence on hidden fires of the earth, and the sensuality of the early world was not among the efficient causes which could have pulled down the comets from their orbits upon it. When such a case occurs, one still attributes it to natural causes and means that it is a misfortune, not a punishment, because the moral behavior of man can be no reason for earthquakes, which occur according to natural law. No connection of cause and effect obtains here. For example, when the earthquake shook the city of Port Royal in Jamaica,* those who term it a natural event will understand by this that, although according to the testimony of their ministers the vices of the inhabitants may well have earned such destruction as punishment, yet the event is seen as one among many which happen from time to time according to natural law, where now and again areas of the earth and among these cities, and of these now and then vice-ridden ones, are strongly shaken. If, on the other hand, this is regarded as punishment, then these powers of nature—since they can have no connection to the affairs of men according to natural law—would be specially directed by the supreme being in every such singular case. Then

*See: Ray, *On the Origin, Alteration and Decay of the World.*

das höchste Wesen besonders gerichtet sein; alsdann aber ist die Begeben=
heit im formalen Verstande übernatürlich, obgleich die Mittelursache eine
Kraft der Natur war. Und wenn auch durch eine lange Reihe von Vor=
bereitungen, die dazu besonders in die wirksamen Kräfte der Welt ange=
legt waren, diese Begebenheit endlich als ein Strafgericht zu Stande kam,
wenn man gleich annehmen wollte, daß schon bei der Schöpfung Gott alle
Anstalten dazu gemacht hätte, daß sie nachher durch die darauf in der
Natur gerichteten Kräfte zur rechten Zeit geschehen sollte (wie man dieses
in Whistons Theorie von der Sündfluth, in so fern sie vom Kometen her=
rühren soll, sich so gedenken kann), so ist das übernatürliche dadurch gar
nicht verringert, sondern nur weit bis in die Schöpfung hinaus verschoben
und dadurch unbeschreiblich vermehrt worden. Denn diese ganze Reihen=
folge, in so fern die Art ihrer Anordnung sich auf den Ausgang bezog,
indem sie in Ansehung desselben gar nicht als eine Folge aus allgemeinern
Naturgesetzen anzusehen war, bezeichnet eine unmittelbare, noch größere
göttliche Sorgfalt, die auf eine so lange Kette von Folgen gerichtet war,
um auch den Hindernissen auszuweichen, die die genaue Erreichung der
gesuchten Wirkungen konnten verfehlen machen.

Hingegen giebt es Strafen und Belohnungen nach der Ordnung der
Natur, darum weil das moralische Verhalten der Menschen mit ihnen
nach den Gesetzen der Ursachen und Wirkungen in Verknüpfung steht.
Wilde Wollust und Unmäßigkeit endigen sich in einem siechen und marter=
vollen Leben. Ränke und Arglist scheitern zuletzt, und Ehrlichkeit ist doch
am Ende die beste Politik. In allen diesem geschieht die Verknüpfung der
Folgen nach den Gesetzen der Natur. So viel aber auch immer derjenigen
Strafen oder Belohnungen oder jeder anderen Begebenheiten in der Welt
sein mögen, davon die Richtung der Naturkräfte jederzeit außerordentlich
auf jeden einzelnen Fall hat geschehen müssen, wenn gleich eine gewisse
Einförmigkeit unter vielen derselben herrscht, so sind sie zwar einem
unmittelbaren göttlichen Gesetze, nämlich demjenigen seiner Weisheit, aber
keinem Naturgesetze untergeordnet.

the event is supernatural in the formal sense although the mediate cause was a force of nature. And even if through a long series of preparations specially applied to the efficient powers of the world this event finally came about as a punishment, and if it be assumed that at the time of creation God had made all the arrangements so that it occurred subsequently at the proper time through the forces nature set up for its production (as can be conceived in Whiston's theory of the flood insofar as it was to follow from the comets) [21] the supernatural is by no means thereby decreased but rather only shifted far back to the creation and so vastly increased. For this whole series indicates an immediate and even greater divine care directed toward the long chain of consequences in order to obviate any hindrances which could prevent the exact achievement of the effect sought, insofar as its kind of structure had a bearing upon its outcome while this outcome was not at all regarded as a consequence of more [22] universal laws.

On the other hand there are rewards and punishments according to the order of nature because the moral behavior of men is connected to them according to the laws of cause and effect. Unbridled lust and immoderation end in a painful and sickly life. Deceit and cunning undo themselves ultimately, and honesty is still in the end the best policy. In all of this the conjunction of the consequences occurs according to the laws of nature. However many of those punishments or rewards or other events there may be in the world in which the direction of natural powers would always have to obtain extraordinarily in every single case, they are certainly arranged under immediate and divine law, namely that of God's wisdom, even if a certain uniformity predominates amongst many of them. But they are not ordered by natural law.

2.

Eintheilung der natürlichen Begebenheiten, in so fern sie unter der nothwendigen oder zufälligen Ordnung der Natur stehen.

Alle Dinge der Natur sind zufällig in ihrem Dasein. Die Ver=
knüpfung verschiedener Arten von Dingen, z. E. der Luft, der Erde, des
Wassers, ist gleichfalls ohne Zweifel zufällig und in so fern blos der Will=
kür des obersten Urhebers beizumessen. Allein obgleich die Naturgesetze
in so fern keine Nothwendigkeit zu haben scheinen, als die Dinge selbst,
davon sie es sind, imgleichen die Verknüpfungen, darin sie ausgeübt werden
können, zufällig sind, so bleibt gleichwohl eine Art der Nothwendigkeit
übrig, die sehr merkwürdig ist. Es giebt nämlich viele Naturgesetze, deren
Einheit nothwendig ist, das ist, wo eben derselbe Grund der Überein=
stimmung zu einem Gesetze auch andere Gesetze nothwendig macht.
Z. E. eben dieselbe elastische Kraft und Schwere der Luft, die ein Grund
ist der Gesetze des Athemholens, ist nothwendiger Weise zugleich ein Grund
von der Möglichkeit der Pumpwerke, von der Möglichkeit der zu erzeugen=
den Wolken, der Unterhaltung des Feuers, der Winde rc. Es ist noth=
wendig, daß zu den übrigen der Grund anzutreffen sei, so bald auch nur
zu einem einzigen derselben Grund da ist. Dagegen wenn der Grund
einer gewissen Art ähnlicher Wirkungen nach einem Gesetze nicht zugleich
der Grund einer andern Art Wirkungen nach einem andern Gesetze in
demselben Wesen ist, so ist die Vereinbarung dieser Gesetze zufällig, oder
es herrscht in diesen Gesetzen zufällige Einheit, und was sich darnach in
dem Dinge zuträgt, geschieht nach einer zufälligen Naturordnung. Der
Mensch sieht, hört, riecht, schmeckt u. s. w., aber nicht eben dieselbe Eigen=
schaften, die die Gründe des Sehens sind, sind auch die des Schmeckens.
Er muß andere Organen zum Hören wie zum Schmecken haben. Die
Vereinbarung so verschiedener Vermögen ist zufällig und, da sie zur Voll=
kommenheit abzielt, künstlich. Bei jedem Organe ist wiederum künstliche
Einheit. In dem Auge ist der Theil, der Licht einfallen läßt, ein anderer
als der, so es bricht, noch ein anderer, so das Bild auffängt. Dagegen
sind es nicht andere Ursachen, die der Erde die Kugelrundung verschaffen,
noch andere, die wider den Drehungsschwung die Körper der Erde zurück
halten, noch eine andere, die den Mond im Kreise erhält, sondern die ein=
zige Schwere ist eine Ursache, die nothwendiger Weise zu allem diesem

2.
Division of natural events insofar as they stand under necessary or contingent order of nature.

All natural things are contingent in their existence. Likewise, the conjunction of different sorts of things, for example, air, earth and water, is without a doubt contingent and in that degree attributed simply to the discretion of the prime creator. But although the laws of nature seem to have no more necessity in them than the things themselves of which they are the laws, and while the conjunctions in which they can be exercised are contingent, there remains nevertheless a very remarkable mode of necessity. That is to say there are many laws of nature whose unity is necessary, i.e., where the very same ground of agreement with one law makes other laws necessary. For example, that very same elasticity and weight of air which is a reason for the laws of respiration is simultaneously a necessary ground of the possibility of a pumping apparatus, of clouds' being productive, of the maintenance of fire, wind, and so on. It is necessary that the reason for the remainder be encountered as soon as the ground for even a single one exists. On the other hand, if the ground for certain kinds of analogous effects is not at the same time the ground of other kinds of effects in the same being according to another law, then the conjunction of these laws is contingent. Contingent unity dominates in these laws and what happens in the things according to them obtains as a result of contingent natural order. Man sees, hears, smells, tastes, and so on, but the very same properties which are the basis of vision are not those of taste. One must have different organs to hear and to taste. The union of such different faculties is contingent and, since it tends towards perfection, ingenious. In each organ there is again an ingenious unity. In the eye there is a part which admits light, a different part where it falls, and still another which collects the image. On the other hand there are not different causes which provide the earth with a round figuration and others which hold bodies on the earth against its rotation, and still another that keeps the moon in its orbit; rather gravity alone is a cause which in a necessary way suffices for all these.

zureicht. Nun ist es ohne Zweifel eine Vollkommenheit, daß zu allen diesen Wirkungen Gründe in der Natur angetroffen werden, und wenn der nämliche Grund, der die eine bestimmt, auch zu den andern hinreichend ist, um desto mehr Einheit wächst dadurch dem Ganzen zu. Diese Einheit aber und mit ihr die Vollkommenheit ist in dem hier angeführten Falle nothwendig und klebt dem Wesen der Sache an, und alle Wohlgereimtheit, Fruchtbarkeit und Schönheit, die ihr in so fern zu verdanken ist, hängt von Gott vermittelst der wesentlichen Ordnung der Natur ab, oder vermittelst desjenigen, was in der Ordnung der Natur nothwendig ist. Man wird mich hoffentlich schon verstehen, daß ich diese Nothwendigkeit nicht auf das Dasein dieser Dinge selber, sondern lediglich auf die in ihrer Möglichkeit liegende Übereinstimmung und Einheit als einen nothwendigen Grund einer so überaus großen Tauglichkeit und Fruchtbarkeit erstreckt wissen will. Die Geschöpfe des Pflanzen= und Thierreichs bieten durchgängig die bewundernswürdigste Beispiele einer zufälligen, aber mit großer Weisheit übereinstimmenden Einheit dar. Gefäße, die Saft saugen, Gefäße, die Luft saugen, diejenige, so den Saft ausarbeiten, und die, so ihn ausdünsten ꝛc., ein großes Mannigfaltige, davon jedes einzeln keine Tauglichkeit zu den Wirkungen des andern hat, und wo die Vereinbarung derselben zur gesammten Vollkommenheit künstlich ist, so daß die Pflanze selbst mit ihren Beziehungen auf so verschiedene Zwecke ein zufälliges und willkürliches Eine ausmacht.

Dagegen liefert vornehmlich die unorganische Natur unaussprechlich viel Beweisthümer einer nothwendigen Einheit in der Beziehung eines einfachen Grundes auf viele anständige Folgen, dermaßen daß man auch bewogen wird, zu vermuthen, daß vielleicht da, wo selbst in der organischen Natur manche Vollkommenheit scheinen kann ihre besondere Anstalt zu Grunde zu haben, sie wohl eine nothwendige Folge aus eben demselben Grunde sein mag, welcher sie mit vielen andern schönen Wirkungen schon in seiner wesentlichen Fruchtbarkeit verknüpft, so daß auch sogar in diesen Naturreichen mehr nothwendige Einheit sein mag als man wohl denkt.

Weil nun die Kräfte der Natur und ihre Wirkungsgesetze den Grund einer Ordnung der Natur enthalten, welche, in so fern sie mannigfaltige Harmonie in einer nothwendigen Einheit zusammenfaßt, veranlaßt, daß die Verknüpfung vieler Vollkommenheit in einem Grunde zum Gesetze wird, so hat man verschiedene Naturwirkungen in Ansehung ihrer Schönheit und Nützlichkeit unter der wesentlichen Naturordnung und vermittelst

Now without a doubt it is a perfection that the grounds of all these effects may be encountered in nature. And when the same ground which determines the one is also sufficient for the others, that much more unity thereby accrues to the whole. This unity, however, and with it perfection, is necessary in the cases cited and attaches to the essence of the thing. All harmonious adaptation, fecundity, and excellence which is due to it depends upon God, mediated by the essential order of nature, or mediated by what is necessary in the order of nature. It will, I hope, be understood that I do not regard this unity as extended to the existence of the things themselves, but rather as [extending] purely to the agreement and unity which lies in their possibility as a necessary ground of such an extremely great suitability and fertility. The creatures of the plant and animal kingdoms everywhere provide the most remarkable examples of a contingent unity which still agrees with a great unifying wisdom. Vessels that draw sap, vessels that draw air, those which work up the sap, and those which exhale it, are a great manifold in which each particular part has nothing to do with the efficacy of the others. The unity of these in a common perfection is artificial so that the plants themselves together with their relations to such diverse goals constitute a contingent and an arbitrary unity.

On the other hand, inorganic nature in particular provides so unspeakably many proofs of necessary unity in the relation of a simple ground to many regular consequences to such a degree that one is moved to conjecture that perhaps even in organic nature, where many a perfection may seem to have a special preparation as its basis, it may still be a necessary consequence from that same ground which already unites this perfection with many other excellent effects in its essential productivity so that even in this [inorganic] realm of nature there may be more necessary unity than might be thought.

Now, because the forces of nature and their laws of efficacy contain the ground of an order of nature which, insofar as it conjoins manifold harmonies into a necessary unity, causes the union of many perfections in *one* ground to become a law, diverse natural effects have to be observed with respect to their

derselben unter Gott zu betrachten. Dagegen da auch manche Vollkommen=
heiten in einem Ganzen nicht durch die Fruchtbarkeit eines einzigen
Grundes möglich sind, sondern verschiedene willkürlich zu dieser Absicht
vereinbarte Gründe erheischen, so wird wiederum manche künstliche An=
ordnung die Ursache eines Gesetzes sein, und die Wirkungen, die darnach
geschehen, stehen unter der zufälligen und künstlichen Ordnung der Natur,
vermittelst ihrer aber unter Gott.

Vierte Betrachtung.
Gebrauch unseres Beweisgrundes in Beurtheilung der Voll= kommenheit einer Welt nach dem Laufe der Natur.

1.
Was aus unserm Beweisgrunde zum Vorzuge der Ordnung der Natur vor dem übernatürlichen kann geschlossen werden.

Es ist eine bekannte Regel der Weltweisen oder vielmehr der gesunden
Vernunft überhaupt: daß man ohne die erheblichste Ursache nichts für ein
Wunder, oder eine übernatürliche Begebenheit halten solle. Diese Regel
enthält erstlich, daß Wunder selten seien, zweitens, daß die gesammte
Vollkommenheit des Universum 'auch ohne viele übernatürliche Einflüsse
dem göttlichen Willen gemäß nach den Gesetzen der Natur erreicht werde;
denn jedermann erkennt: daß, wenn ohne häufige Wunder die Welt des
Zwecks ihres Daseins verfehlte, übernatürliche Begebenheiten etwas Ge=
wöhnliches sein müßten. Einige stehen in der Meinung, daß das Formale
der natürlichen Verknüpfung der Folgen mit ihren Gründen an sich selbst
eine Vollkommenheit wäre, welcher allenfalls ein besserer Erfolg, wenn
er nicht anders als übernatürlicher Weise zu erhalten stände, hintangesetzt
werden müßte. Sie setzen in dem Natürlichen als einem solchen unmittel=
bar einen Vorzug, weil ihnen alles Übernatürliche als eine Unterbrechung
einer Ordnung an sich selber scheint einen Übelstand zu erregen. Allein
diese Schwierigkeit ist nur eingebildet. Das Gute steckt nur in Erreichung
des Zweckes und wird den Mitteln nur um seinetwillen zugeeignet. Die
natürliche Ordnung, wenn nach ihr nicht vollkommene Folgen entspringen,
hat unmittelbar keinen Grund eines Vorzugs in sich, weil sie nur nach

excellence and utility under essential natural order and by means of this as under God. On the other hand, since many perfections in a whole are not possible as the product of one single ground but rather require diverse grounds arbitrarily tied to this intention, many an artificial arrangement in turn will be the cause of a law, and the effects that obtain in accord with it will stand under contingent and artificial order of nature, and through that under God.

OBSERVATION FOUR
The Use of Our Proof for Judging the Perfection of a World in Conformity with the Course of Nature

1.

What may be concluded from our proof about the superiority of the order of nature over the supernatural.

It is an acknowledged rule of philosophers and even more of common sense at large that something is not to be regarded as being a miracle or a supernatural event without the most compelling reason. This rule entails: first that there are seldom any miracles; and second, that the collective perfection of the universe can be achieved in accordance with divine will by the laws of nature alone without many supernatural influences. Everyone realizes that were the world to miss the goal of its existence without frequent miracles, supernatural events would have to be something quite common. Some are of the opinion that the form of the natural conjunction of consequences with their grounds is itself a perfection below which a superior result would have to be ranked were it to be maintained only supernaturally. They posit an immediate superiority in the natural as such because everything supernatural, as an interruption of an order, seems to them in itself to produce a bad state. But this problem is only imagined. The good lies in the achievement of an end, and is attributed to the means only for its sake. The natural order has no immediate basis of excellence in itself if perfect consequences do not develop

der Art eines Mittels kann betrachtet werden, welches keine eigene, sondern nur eine von der Größe des dadurch erreichten Zwecks entlehnte Schätzung verſtattet. Die Vorſtellung der Mühſamkeit, welche die Menſchen bei ihren unmittelbaren Ausübungen empfinden, mengt ſich hier ingeheim mit unter und giebt demjenigen, was man fremden Kräften anvertrauen kann, einen Vorzug, ſelbſt da wo in dem Erfolg etwas von dem abge= zweckten Nutzen vermißt würde. Indeſſen wenn ohne größere Beſchwerde der, ſo das Holz an einer Schneidemühle anlegt, es eben ſo wohl unmittel= bar in Bretter verwandeln könnte, ſo wäre alle Kunſt dieſer Maſchine nur ein Spielwerk, weil der ganze Werth derſelben nur an ihr als einem Mittel zu dieſem Zwecke ſtattfinden kann. Demnach iſt etwas nicht darum gut, weil es nach dem Laufe der Natur geſchieht, ſondern der Lauf der Natur iſt gut, in ſo fern das, was daraus fließt, gut iſt. Und da Gott eine Welt in ſeinem Rathſchluſſe begriff, in der alles mehrentheils durch einen natür= lichen Zuſammenhang die Regel des Beſten erfüllte: ſo würdigte er ſie ſeiner Wahl, nicht weil darin, daß es natürlich zuſammenhing, das Gute beſtand, ſondern weil durch dieſen natürlichen Zuſammenhang ohne viele Wunder die vollkommenen Zwecke am richtigſten erreicht wurden.

Und nun entſteht die Frage: wie mag es zugehen, daß die allgemeine Geſetze der Natur dem Willen des Höchſten in dem Verlauf der Begeben= heiten der Welt, die nach ihnen geſchehen, ſo ſchön entſprechen, und welchen Grund hat man ihnen dieſe Schicklichkeit zuzutrauen, daß man nicht öfter, als man wahrnimmt, geheime übernatürliche Vorkehrungen zugeben müßte, die ihren Gebrechen unaufhörlich zu Hülfe kämen?*) Hier leiſtet uns unſer Begriff von der Abhängigkeit ſelbſt der Weſen aller Dinge von Gott einen noch ausgebreitetern Nutzen, als der iſt, den man in dieſer Frage erwartet. Die Dinge der Natur tragen ſogar in den nothwendigſten Be= ſtimmungen ihrer innern Möglichkeit das Merkmal der Abhängigkeit von

---

*) Dieſe Frage iſt dadurch noch lange nicht genugſam beantwortet, wenn man ſich auf die weiſe Wahl Gottes beruft, die den Lauf der Natur einmal ſchon ſo wohl eingerichtet hätte, daß öftere Ausbeſſerungen unnöthig waren. Denn die größte Schwierigkeit beſteht darin, wie es auch nur hat möglich ſein können in einer Verbindung der Weltbegebenheiten nach allgemeinen Geſetzen ſo große Voll= kommenheit zu vereinbaren, vornehmlich wenn man die Menge der Naturdinge und die unermeßlich lange Reihe ihrer Veränderungen betrachtet, wie da nach all= gemeinen Regeln ihrer gegenſeitigen Wirkſamkeit eine Harmonie hat entſpringen können, die keiner öftern übernatürlichen Einflüſſe bedürfe.

immediately from it, for it can be seen only as a kind of means; and this permits no value of its own, but only one borrowed from the magnitude of the ends achieved through it. The suggestion of difficulty which people feel with the immediate execution [of ends] is surreptitiously included and accords preference to what can be entrusted to extrinsic forces even where something of the intended utility is missing in the result. However, if without greater difficulties, whoever put the wood into a sawmill could just as well immediately turn it into lumber, all the artifice of the machine would be only a toy, for its entire value can occur only as a means to achieving the stated goal. Accordingly a thing is not good because it obtains according to the course of nature, but rather the course of nature is good insofar as what follows from it is good. And since in his decision God conceived a world in which everything for the most part is fulfilled in natural accord with the principle of the best, he deemed it worthy of his choice, not because it came about naturally that there was good, but rather because through this natural coordination perfect ends were most infallibly achieved without many miracles.

Now the question arises: how does it happen that the universal laws of nature conform so well to the will of the divine in the course of events in the world which happen according to them? And what reason has one for crediting them with this fitness so that secret supernatural provisions which constantly come to the aid of their frailty need not be conceded more often than they are?* Our notion of the dependence of the very essence of all things upon God affords a still more extensive utility than would be expected in this question. The things of nature bear, even in the most necessary determinations of their

*This question is by no means sufficiently answered if one invokes the wise choice of God which once and for all so well adjusted the course of nature that more frequent improvements were unnecessary. The most important difficulty consists in how it can even have been possible to unite cosmic events with perfection in one nexus according to natural laws, particularly where the vast number of natural events and the immeasurably long series of their changes is considered, and how a harmony which requires no more frequent supernatural influence can have arisen according to universal rules from the reciprocal efficacy of natural events.

demjenigen Wesen an sich, in welchem alles mit den Eigenschaften der
Weisheit und Güte zusammenstimmt. Man kann von ihnen Überein=
stimmung und schöne Verknüpfung erwarten und eine nothwendige Ein=
heit in den mancherlei vortheilhaften Beziehungen, die ein einziger Grund
zu viel anständigen Gesetzen hat. Es wird nicht nöthig sein, daß daselbst,
wo die Natur nach nothwendigen Gesetzen wirkt, unmittelbare göttliche
Ausbesserungen dazwischen kommen, weil, in so fern die Folgen nach der
Ordnung der Natur nothwendig sind, nimmermehr selbst nach den allge=
meinsten Gesetzen sich was Gott Mißfälliges eräugnen kann. Denn wie
sollten doch die Folgen der Dinge, deren zufällige Verknüpfung von dem
Willen Gottes abhängt, ihre wesentliche Beziehungen aber als die Gründe
des Nothwendigen in der Naturordnung von demjenigen in Gott herrühren,
was mit seinen Eigenschaften überhaupt in der größten Harmonie steht,
wie können diese, sage ich, seinem Willen entgegen sein? Und so müssen
alle die Veränderungen der Welt, die mechanisch, mithin aus den Be=
wegungsgesetzen nothwendig sind, jederzeit darum gut sein, weil sie natür=
licher Weise nothwendig sind, und es ist zu erwarten, daß die Folge un=
verbesserlich sein werde, so bald sie nach der Ordnung der Natur unaus=
bleiblich ist.*) Ich bemerke aber, damit aller Mißverstand verhütet
werde: daß die Veränderungen in der Welt entweder aus der ersten An=
ordnung des Universum und den allgemeinen und besondern Gesetzen der
Natur nothwendig sind, dergleichen alles dasjenige ist, was in der körper=
lichen Welt mechanisch vorgeht, oder daß sie gleichwohl bei allem diesem
eine nicht genugsam begriffene Zufälligkeit haben, wie die Handlungen
aus der Freiheit, deren Natur nicht gehörig eingesehen wird. Die letztere
Art der Weltveränderungen, in so fern sie scheinen eine Ungebundenheit
in Ansehung bestimmender Gründe und nothwendiger Gesetze an sich zu
haben, enthalten in so weit eine Möglichkeit in sich von der allgemeinen

---

*) Wenn es ein nothwendiger Ausgang der Natur ist, wie Newton vermeint,
daß ein Weltsystem, wie dasjenige von unserer Sonne, endlich zum völligen Still=
stand und allgemeiner Ruhe gelange, so würde ich nicht mit ihm hinzusetzen: daß
es nöthig sei, daß Gott es durch ein Wunder wieder herstelle. Denn weil es ein
Erfolg ist, darauf die Natur nach ihren wesentlichsten Gesetzen nothwendiger Weise
bestimmt ist, so vermuthe ich hieraus, daß er auch gut sei. Es darf uns dieses
nicht als ein bedauernswürdiger Verlust vorkommen, denn wir wissen nicht, welche
Unermeßlichkeit die sich immerfort in andern Himmelsgegenden bildende Natur
habe, um durch große Fruchtbarkeit diesen Abgang des Universum anderwärts
reichlich zu ersetzen.

internal possibility, the mark of their dependence on that being in which everything is coordinated with the properties of wisdom and goodness. Coordination and excellent conjunction may be expected from them, and a necessary unity in the many advantageous relations that a single ground has to many suitable laws. Where nature works according to necessary laws immediate divine intervention is unnecessary for improvement; for insofar as the consequences are necessary in the order of nature, nothing displeasing to God can obtain according to even the most general laws. How can the consequences of things whose contingent connection depends upon God's will, but whose essential relations follow from God as the grounds of necessity in the natural order—how can these consequences follow from that in God which stands in the greatest harmony with his attributes in general and still be contrary to his will? Thus all of the alterations of the world which are mechanical and therefore necessary according to the laws of motion must always be good because they are necessary in a natural way. And it is to be expected that the consequences will not be able to be improved if they are inevitable in the order of nature.* But to avoid any misunderstanding I note that either the alterations in the world are necessary from the primal ordering of the universe and from the general and special laws of nature—as everything is which proceeds mechanically in the corporeal world—or else despite all this they have a contingency which is not sufficiently understood, such as acts from freedom whose nature has not been sufficiently grasped. The latter sort of alterations of the world as such entail the possibility of divergence from the

*If, as Newton believes, it is a necessary issue of nature for a cosmic system such as our sun finally to come to a complete stop and for universal rest to succeed, I would not add with him that it is necessary for God to produce it again through a miracle. Since this result is a consequence determined necessarily by the most essential laws of nature, I will conjecture that it must also be good. This should not appear to us as a deplorable loss, for we do not know what vast capacity nature—which is continually a-building in different regions of the heavens—may have through great fertility for elsewhere richly replacing the decline of the universe.

Abzielung der Naturdinge zur Vollkommenheit abzuweichen. Und um deswillen kann man erwarten, daß übernatürliche Ergänzungen nöthig sein dürften, weil es möglich ist, daß in diesem Betracht der Lauf der Natur mit dem Willen Gottes bisweilen widerstreitend sein könne. Indessen da selbst die Kräfte frei handlender Wesen in der Verknüpfung mit dem Übrigen des Universum nicht ganz allen Gesetzen entzogen sind, sondern immer, wenn gleich nicht nöthigenden Gründen, dennoch solchen, die nach den Regeln der Willkür die Ausübung auf eine andere Art gewiß machen, unterworfen sind, so ist die allgemeine Abhängigkeit der Wesen der Dinge von Gott auch hier noch jederzeit ein großer Grund, die Folgen, die selbst unter dieser Art von Dingen nach dem Laufe der Natur sich zutragen, (ohne daß die scheinbare Abweichung in einzelnen Fällen uns irre machen darf) im Ganzen für anständig und der Regel des Besten gemäß einzusehen: so daß nur selten die Ordnung der Natur einer unmittelbarn übernatürlichen Verbesserung oder Ergänzung benöthigt ist, wie denn auch die Offenbarung derselben nur in Ansehung gewisser Zeiten und gewisser Völker Erwähnung thut. Die Erfahrung stimmt auch mit dieser Abhängigkeit sogar der freiesten Handlungen von einer großen natürlichen Regel überein. Denn so zufällig wie auch immer die Entschließung zum Heirathen sein mag, so findet man doch in eben demselben Lande, daß das Verhältniß der Ehen zu der Zahl der Lebenden ziemlich beständig sei, wenn man große Zahlen nimmt, und daß z. E. unter 110 Menschen beiderlei Geschlechts sich ein Ehepaar findet. Jedermann weiß, wie viel die Freiheit der Menschen zu Verlängerung oder Verkürzung des Lebens beitrage. Gleichwohl müssen selbst diese freie Handlungen einer großen Ordnung unterworfen sein, weil im Durchschnitte, wenn man große Mengen nimmt, die Zahl der Sterbenden gegen die Lebenden sehr genau immer in eben demselben Verhältniß steht. Ich begnüge mich mit diesen wenigen Beweisthümern, um es einigermaßen verständlich zu machen, daß selbst die Gesetze der Freiheit keine solche Ungebundenheit in Ansehung der Regeln einer allgemeinen Naturordnung mit sich führen, daß nicht eben derselbe Grund, der in der übrigen Natur schon in den Wesen der Dinge selbst eine unausbleibliche Beziehung auf Vollkommenheit und Wohlgereimtheit befestigt, auch in dem natürlichen Laufe des freien Verhaltens wenigstens eine größere Lenkung auf ein Wohlgefallen des höchsten Wesens ohne vielfältige Wunder verursachen sollte. Mein Augenmerk ist aber mehr auf den Verlauf der Naturveränderungen ge-

general aim of natural things towards perfection insofar as they seem themselves to be dissociated from determinate grounds and necessary laws. And for this reason it may be expected that supernatural supplements may be necessary because it is possible in this account that the course of nature could from time to time conflict with the will of God. However, since even the forces of freely acting beings in conjunction with the rest of the universe are not deprived of all law but rather are alwas subject to laws which, even if they are not necessary grounds, still make the exercise sure in another way through the rules of choice, the universal dependence of the essence of things upon God here is thus still always a good reason for regarding the consequences even of the kind of things that obtain according to the course of nature, as on the whole regular and conformable to the rule of the best (without falling into error because of the apparent deviations in particular cases). So it is only seldom that the order of nature requires an immediate improvement or supplementation and the revelation of it is noted only with respect to certain times and certain peoples. Experience certainly agrees with the dependence of even the freest deed to a general [gross] natural rule. No matter how contingent the decision to marry may be, it is found that within a given country the relation of married couples to living people is roughly constant if one takes a large sample. For example, amongst 110 people of both sexes, there is certain to be a married couple.[23] Everyone knows how much the freedom of man contributes to the lengthening or shortening of human life. Nevertheless even these free activities must be subject to a general [gross] order because on the average if a large group be taken the number of those dying very nearly always stands in the same proportion to those living. I am content with these few bits of evidence in order to make it understandable to some extent that even the laws of freedom carry with them no dissolution in respect to the rules of a universal order of nature such that the same ground which strengthens an unavoidable relation to perfection and harmonious adaptation in the very essence of things in the rest of nature should not also cause at least a greater tendency toward the pleasure of the supreme being without multiple miracles in the natural course of free

richtet, in so fern sie durch eingepflanzte Gesetze nothwendig sind. Wunder werden in einer solchen Ordnung entweder gar nicht oder nur selten nöthig sein, weil es nicht füglich sein kann, daß sich solche Unvollkommenheiten natürlicher Weise hervorfänden, die ihrer bedürftig wären.

Wenn ich mir den Begriff von den Dingen der Natur machte, den man gemeiniglich von ihnen hat, daß ihre innere Möglichkeit für sich un= abhängig und ohne einen fremden Grund sei, so würde ich es gar nicht unerwartet finden, wenn man sagte, eine Welt von einiger Vollkommen= heit sei ohne viele übernatürliche Wirkungen unmöglich. Ich würde es vielmehr seltsam und unbegreiflich finden, wie ohne eine beständige Reihe von Wundern etwas Taugliches durch einen natürlichen großen Zusammen= hang in ihr sollte geleistet werden können. Denn es müßte ein befremd= liches Ungefähr sein: daß die Wesen der Dinge, die jegliches für sich seine abgesonderte Nothwendigkeit hätten, sich so sollten zusammenschicken, daß selbst die höchste Weisheit aus ihnen ein großes Ganze vereinbaren könnte, in welchem bei so vielfältiger Abhängigkeit dennoch nach allgemeinen Ge= setzen unverbesserliche Harmonie und Schönheit hervorleuchtete. Dagegen da ich belehrt bin, daß darum nur, weil ein Gott ist, etwas anders mög= lich sei, so erwarte ich selbst von den Möglichkeiten der Dinge eine Zu= sammenstimmung, die ihrem großen Principium gemäß ist, und eine Schicklichkeit durch allgemeine Anordnungen zu einem Ganzen zusammen zu passen, das mit der Weisheit eben desselben Wesens richtig harmonirt, von dem sie ihren Grund entlehnen, und ich finde es sogar wunderbar: daß, so fern etwas nach dem Laufe der Natur gemäß allgemeinen Gesetzen geschieht, oder geschehen würde, es Gott mißfällig und eines Wunders zur Ausbesserung bedürftig sein sollte; und wenn es geschieht, so gehört selbst die Veranlassung dazu zu den Dingen, die sich bisweilen zutragen, von uns aber nimmermehr können begriffen werden.

Man wird es auch ohne Schwierigkeit verstehen, daß, wenn man den wesentlichen Grund einsieht, weswegen Wunder zur Vollkommenheit der Welt selten nöthig sein können, dieses auch von denjenigen gelte, die wir in der vorigen Betrachtung übernatürliche Begebenheiten im formalen Verstande genannt haben, und die man in gemeinen Urtheilen darum sehr häufig einräumt, weil man durch einen verkehrten Begriff darin etwas Natürliches zu finden glaubt.

conduct. My attention, however, is directed more to the course of natural alterations insofar as they are necessary through implanted laws. In such an order miracles are either not at all or only seldom necessary, because it is not fitting that such imperfections as require them should appear.

If I formed the concept of the things of nature which one usually has—that their internal possibility is independent in itself and without an external basis—I would not find it at all strange were it maintained that a world of some perfection is impossible without many supernatural actions. I would find it far stranger and much more incomprehensible how something good could be accomplished through natural conjunction without a constant series of miracles in it. For it would have to be a strange coincidence that the essence of things, each of which had its own separate necessity, could fit so well together that even supreme wisdom might unify them into a whole in which, though there be so much independence, still a harmony and an excellence which cannot be improved upon shines forth according to natural laws. On the contrary, since I am convinced that only because God exists is something else possible, I expect an accord, even from the possibilities of things, which is consistent with their great principle, and a fitness of the whole, coordinated through universal structure, which properly harmonizes with the wisdom of that same being from which they derive their ground. And I even find it wonderful when in the course of nature something happens or might happen which is conformable to universal laws yet could displease God and require a miracle to be put right. When this does happen the cause of it belongs to those things we can never understand that take place from time to time.

If the essential reason why miracles can seldom be necessary for the perfection of the world is clearly seen, it can be understood without difficulty that that will also be true for those which, in the preceding Observation, we have termed supernatural events in the formal sense which ordinary judgment very frequently admits since by some preposterous notion one hopes to find something natural in them.
natural in them.

2.

Was aus unferm Beweisgrunde zum Vorzuge einer oder anderer Naturordnung geschlossen werden kann.

In dem Verfahren der gereinigten Weltweisheit herrscht eine Regel, die, wenn sie gleich nicht förmlich gesagt, dennoch in der Ausübung jeder= zeit beobachtet wird: daß in aller Nachforschung der Ursachen zu gewissen Wirkungen man eine große Aufmerksamkeit bezeigen müsse, die Einheit der Natur so sehr wie möglich zu erhalten, das ist, vielerlei Wirkungen aus einem einzigen, schon bekannten Grunde herzuleiten und nicht zu ver= schiedenen Wirkungen wegen einiger scheinbaren größeren Unähnlichkeit sogleich neue und verschiedene wirkende Ursachen anzunehmen. Man prä= sumirt demnach, daß in der Natur große Einheit sei in Ansehung der Zu= länglichkeit eines einigen Grundes zu mancherlei Art Folgen, und glaubt Ursache zu haben, die Vereinigung einer Art Erscheinungen mit denen von anderer Art mehrentheils als etwas Nothwendiges und nicht als eine Wirkung einer künstlichen und zufälligen Ordnung anzusehen. Wie vieler= lei Wirkungen werden nicht aus der einigen Kraft der Schwere hergeleitet, dazu man ehedem verschiedene Ursachen glaubte nöthig zu finden: das Steigen einiger Körper und das Fallen anderer. Die Wirbel, um die Himmelskörper in Kreisen zu erhalten, sind abgestellt, so bald man die Ursache derselben in jener einfachen Naturkraft gefunden hat. Man prä= sumirt mit großem Grunde: daß die Ausdehnung der Körper durch die Wärme, das Licht, die elektrische Kraft, die Gewitter, vielleicht auch die magnetische Kraft vielerlei Erscheinungen einer und eben derselben wirk= samen Materie, die in allen Räumen ausgebreitet ist, nämlich des Äthers, sei, und man ist überhaupt unzufrieden, wenn man sich genöthigt sieht ein neues Principium zu einer Art Wirkungen anzunehmen. Selbst da, wo ein sehr genaues Ebenmaß eine besondere künstliche Anordnung zu erheischen scheint, ist man geneigt sie dem nothwendigen Erfolg aus all= gemeinern Gesetzen beizumessen und noch immer die Regel der Einheit zu beobachten, ehe man eine künstliche Verfügung zum Grunde setze. Die Schneefiguren sind so regelmäßig und so weit über alles Plumpe, das der blinde Zufall zuwege bringen kann, zierlich, daß man fast ein Mißtrauen in die Aufrichtigkeit derer setzen sollte, die uns Abzeichnungen davon ge= geben haben, wenn nicht ein jeder Winter unzählige Gelegenheit gäbe einen jeden durch eigene Erfahrung davon zu versichern. Man wird wenig

8

2.
What may be concluded from our proof about the superiority of one or another natural order

In the procedure of a purified philosophy a rule dominates—which, even if it is not formally stated, is still constantly observed in practice—that in research into the causes of given effects great attention must be paid to maintaining as far as possible the unity of nature. That is, many effects are to be derived from a single ground which is already known, and new and different efficient causes are not immediately to be assumed for different effects because of a few apparently important dissimilarities. Accordingly one presumes that in nature there is great unity in respect to the sufficiency of one single ground for many different sorts of consequences and one believes one has cause for regarding the conjunction of one kind of appearances with those of another sort as for the most part necessary and not as the effect of an artificial and contingent order. How many effects are seen as following from the force of gravity, for which it previously had been believed necessary to find different causes—the ascent of some bodies and the fall of others, for example. The vortices keeping heavenly bodies in circular orbit are abandoned as soon as the cause of such motion is seen in that simple force of nature. It is assumed with good reason that the expansion of bodies through heat, light, electrical force, thunder, and perhaps even magnetic force are diverse manifestations of one and the same effective matter which is distributed throughout spaces, namely the ether. And one is generally uneasy when he finds himself constrained to assume a new principle for one sort of effect. Even where an exact symmetry seems to require an especially ingenious arrangement, one is inclined to attribute it to the necessary consequence of more general laws and to observe the rule of unity before assuming an artificial arrangement as its basis. Snowflakes are so regular and so much more delicate than anything crude which could be effected by blind contingency that one could almost mistrust the veracity of those who have given us sketches of them if each winter did not provide everyone innumerable opportunities for making certain of this

Blumen antreffen, welche, so viel man äußerlich wahrnehmen kann, mehr
Nettigkeit und Proportion zeigten, und man sieht gar nichts, was die
Kunst hervorbringen kann, das da mehr Richtigkeit enthielte, als diese
Erzeugungen, die die Natur mit so viel Verschwendung über die Erdfläche
ausstreuet. Und gleichwohl hat sich niemand in den Sinn kommen lassen
sie von einem besonderen Schneesamen herzuleiten und eine künstliche
Ordnung der Natur zu ersinnen, sondern man mißt sie als eine Neben=
folge allgemeineren Gesetzen bei, welche die Bildung dieses Products mit
nothwendiger Einheit zugleich unter sich befassen.*)

Gleichwohl ist die Natur reich an einer gewissen andern Art von Her=
vorbringungen, wo alle Weltweisheit, die über ihre Entstehungsart nach=
sinnt, sich genöthigt sieht, diesen Weg zu verlassen. Große Kunst und
eine zufällige Vereinbarung durch freie Wahl gewissen Absichten gemäß
ist daselbst augenscheinlich und wird zugleich der Grund eines besondern
Naturgesetzes, welches zur künstlichen Naturordnung gehört. Der Bau
der Pflanzen und Thiere zeigt eine solche Anstalt, wozu die allgemeine und
nothwendige Naturgesetze unzulänglich sind. Da es nun ungereimt sein
würde die erste Erzeugung einer Pflanze oder Thiers als eine mechanische
Nebenfolge aus allgemeinen Naturgesetzen zu betrachten, so bleibt gleich=
wohl noch eine doppelte Frage übrig, die aus dem angeführten Grunde
unentschieden ist: ob nämlich ein jedes Individuum derselben unmittel=
bar von Gott gebauet und also übernatürlichen Ursprungs sei, und nur
die Fortpflanzung, das ist, der Übergang von Zeit zu Zeit zur Auswicke=
lung einem natürlichen Gesetze anvertrauet sei, oder ob einige Individuen
des Pflanzen= und Thierreichs zwar unmittelbar göttlichen Ursprungs
seien, jedoch mit einem uns nicht begreiflichen Vermögen, nach einem
ordentlichen Naturgesetze ihres gleichen zu erzeugen und nicht blos auszu=
wickeln. Von beiden Seiten zeigen sich Schwierigkeiten. Es ist vielleicht
unmöglich auszumachen, welche die größte sei; allein was uns hier an=
geht, ist nur das Übergewicht der Gründe, in so fern sie metaphysisch sind
zu bemerken. Wie z. E. ein Baum durch eine innere mechanische Ver=
fassung soll vermögend sein den Nahrungssaft so zu formen und zu modeln,

---

*) Die den Gewächsen ähnliche Figur des Schimmels hatte viele bewogen
denselben unter die Producte des Pflanzenreichs zu zählen. Indessen ist es nach
andern Beobachtungen viel wahrscheinlicher, daß die anscheinende Regelmäßigkeit
desselben nicht hindern könne, ihn so wie den Baum der Diane als eine Folge
aus den gemeinen Gesetzen der Sublimirung anzusehen.

through his own experience. Few flowers will be found that, so far as can be observed externally, could show more neatness and proportion, and one can imagine absolutely nothing that art could produce which would contain more regularity than these products which nature so liberally strews over the earth's surface. Nevertheless it will occur to nobody to derive these from a special snow-seed and to fancy an artificial arrangement of nature. Rather they are attributed to derivative consequences of more general laws which are involved with the formulation of these products in a necessary unity.*

Nevertheless nature is rich in another certain kind of generation where all philosophy, in reflecting on its origins, sees it necessary to abandon this way. Great art and a contingent conjunction through free choice in accord with a certain intent is apparent in these cases and is simultaneously the basis of a natural law belonging to an artificial order of nature. The structure of plants and animals shows such a form for which universal and necessary laws of nature are insufficient. Because it would be incoherent to regard the initial generation of plants or animals as a mechanical by-product of universal law, a double question remains which is unresolved on the basis cited above—namely, whether each individual is immediately made by God and therefore of supernatural origin so that only perpetuation, that is the transition from one time to another in evolution, is entrusted to natural law; or whether there are some individuals of the plant and animal kingdoms which, despite their immediate divine origin, have the capacity, which we do not understand, of actually generating their own kind according to an ordinary natural law and not merely [the capacity] of evolving.[25] Difficulties appear on both sides. It is perhaps impossible to determine which are the greatest. What concerns us here is only the preponderance of the reasons insofar as they are to be treated metaphysically. For example, it is impossible in

---

*The resemblance of plants which the shape of mould shows has induced many to count this amongst the products of the plant kingdom. However, according to other observations it is much more probable that the apparent regularity of this cannot prevent regarding it, like the Tree of Diana,[24] as a consequence of the general law of sublimation.

daß in dem Auge der Blätter oder seinem Samen etwas entstände, das einen ähnlichen Baum im kleinen, oder woraus doch ein solcher werden könnte, enthielte, ist nach allen unsern Kenntnissen auf keine Weise einzusehen. Die innerliche Formen des Herrn von Buffon und die Elemente organischer Materie, die sich zu Folge ihrer Erinnerungen den Gesetzen der Begierden und des Abscheues gemäß nach der Meinung des Herrn von Maupertuis zusammenfügen, sind entweder eben so unverständlich als die Sache selbst, oder ganz willkürlich erdacht. Allein ohne sich an dergleichen Theorien zu kehren, muß man denn darum selbst eine andere dafür aufwerfen, die eben so willkürlich ist, nämlich daß alle diese Individuen übernatürlichen Ursprungs seien, weil man ihre natürliche Entstehungsart gar nicht begreift? Hat wohl jemals einer das Vermögen des Hefens seines gleichen zu erzeugen mechanisch begreiflich gemacht? und gleichwohl bezieht man sich desfalls nicht auf einen übernatürlichen Grund.

Da in diesem Falle der Ursprung aller solcher organischen Producte als völlig übernatürlich angesehen wird, so glaubt man dennoch etwas für den Naturalphilosophen übrig zu lassen, wenn man ihn mit der Art der allmähligen Fortpflanzung spielen läßt. Allein man bedenke wohl: daß man dadurch das Übernatürliche nicht vermindert, denn es mag diese übernatürliche Erzeugung zur Zeit der Schöpfung oder nach und nach in verschiedenen Zeitpunkten geschehen, so ist in dem letzteren Falle nicht mehr Übernatürliches als im ersten, denn der ganze Unterschied läuft nicht auf den Grad der unmittelbaren göttlichen Handlung, sondern lediglich auf das Wenn hinaus. Was aber jene natürliche Ordnung der Auswickelung anlangt, so ist sie nicht eine Regel der Fruchtbarkeit der Natur, sondern eine Methode eines unnützen Umschweifs. Denn es wird dadurch nicht der mindeste Grad einer unmittelbaren göttlichen Handlung bespart. Demnach scheint es unvermeidlich: entweder bei jeder Begattung die Bildung der Frucht unmittelbar einer göttlichen Handlung beizumessen, oder der ersten göttlichen Anordnung der Pflanzen und Thiere eine Tauglichkeit zuzulassen, ihres Gleichen in der Folge nach einem natürlichen Gesetze nicht blos zu entwickeln, sondern wahrhaftig zu erzeugen.

Meine gegenwärtige Absicht ist nur hiedurch zu zeigen, daß man den Naturdingen eine größere Möglichkeit nach allgemeinen Gesetzen ihre Folgen hervorzubringen einräumen müsse, als man es gemeiniglich thut.

8*

and shape its nourishment through its internal mechanical any way for our knowledge to grasp how a tree is able to form constitution so that in the buds of leaves or in their stems something develops which contains an analogous tree in miniature or something from which such can develop. The internal forms of Buffon[26] and the elements of organic nature which conjoin themselves in a succession according to their recollections of the laws of desire and aversion, according to Maupertuis,[27] are either as totally incomprehensible as the things themselves or else they are entirely arbitrarily conceived. Without turning to these theories themselves, must not still another theory be raised which is just as arbitrary, namely that these individuals are of supernatural origin because their natural mode of generation has not fully been grasped? Has the ability of a yeast to reproduce its own kind yet been made understandable mechanically? Nevertheless one does not, for this reason, resort to a supernatural cause.

Because in this case the origin of all such organic products is regarded as being entirely supernatural, it is believed that there is still something left for natural philosophers if they are allowed to play with the mode of gradual perpetuation. But it should be noted that in this way the supernatural is not diminished, for this supernatural production may be allowed to happen at the time of creation or from time to time in different epochs. The latter instance is no less supernatural than the former, for the difference is not in the degree of divine action but merely *when* it obtains. But so far as the natural order of evolution is concerned, this is not a rule of the fecundity of nature, but a method of useless diversion. Through it not the slightest degree of immediate divine treatment is spared. Thus it seems unavoidable that either the formation of the fruit of every mating is to be at once attributed to divine action, or else the initial divine arrangement of plants and animals permitted them an ability not merely to evolve but really to generate their kind in conformity with natural law.

My present intention is only to show through this that one must grant natural things a greater possibility of bringing forth their progeny according to natural law than is commonly done.

Fünfte Betrachtung,

Worin die Unzulänglichkeit der gewöhnlichen Methode der Physikotheologie gewiesen wird.

1.
Von der Physikotheologie überhaupt.

Alle Arten, das Dasein Gottes aus den Wirkungen desselben zu er= kennen, lassen sich auf die drei folgende bringen. Entweder man gelangt zu dieser Erkenntniß durch die Wahrnehmung desjenigen, was die Ord= nung der Natur unterbricht und diejenige Macht unmittelbar bezeichnet, welcher die Natur unterworfen ist, diese Überzeugung wird durch Wun= der veranlaßt; oder die zufällige Ordnung der Natur, von der man deut= lich einsieht, daß sie auf vielerlei andere Art möglich war, in der gleich= wohl große Kunst, Macht und Güte hervorleuchtet, führt auf den gött= lichen Urheber, oder drittens die nothwendige Einheit, die in der Na= tur wahrgenommen wird, und die wesentliche Ordnung der Dinge, welche großen Regeln der Vollkommenheit gemäß ist, kurz das, was in der Regel= mäßigkeit der Natur Nothwendiges ist, leitet auf ein oberstes Principium nicht allein dieses Daseins, sondern selbst aller Möglichkeit.

Wenn Menschen völlig verwildert sind, oder eine halsstarrige Bos= heit ihre Augen verschließt, alsdann scheint das erstere Mittel einzig und allein einige Gewalt an sich zu haben, sie vom Dasein des höchsten Wesens zu überführen. Dagegen findet die richtige Betrachtung einer wohlgear= teten Seele an so viel zufälliger Schönheit und zweckmäßiger Verbindung, wie die Ordnung der Natur darbietet, Beweisthümer genug, einen mit großer Weisheit und Macht begleiteten Willen daraus abzunehmen, und es sind zu dieser Überzeugung, so fern sie zum tugendhaften Verhalten hinlänglich, das ist, moralisch gewiß sein soll, die gemeine Begriffe des Verstandes hinreichend. Zu der dritten Art zu schließen wird nothwen= diger Weise Weltweisheit erfordert, und es ist auch einzig und allein ein höherer Grad derselben fähig, mit einer Klarheit und Überzeugung, die der Größe der Wahrheit gemäß ist, zu dem nämlichen Gegenstande zu ge= langen.

OBSERVATION FIVE
In Which the Insufficiency of the Usual
Method of Physico-Theology is Indicated

1.
Physico-Theology in General

All the ways of recognizing God's existence from his effects may be brought under the three following. Either: (i) This knowledge may be achieved through perception of whatever interrupts the order of nature and immediately shows the power to which nature is subject. This conviction is occasioned by a *miracle*. (ii) Or the contingent order of *nature* in which great art, power, and goodness shine forth—though it is clearly seen that the order was possible in many other ways—leads to the divine creator. (iii) Or the *necessary* unity perceived in *nature* and the essential order of things consistent with the great rule of perfection, in short, whatever is necessary in the regularity of nature, leads to the supreme principle not only of this existence but rather of all possibility itself.

If men are entirely savage or where their eyes are closed by obstinate evil the first way appears to be the one and the only one having the force to convince them of the existence of the supreme being. On the other hand, the correct observation of a well-cultivated soul finds, in so much contingent excellence and purposeful conjunction as the order of nature provides, sufficient evidence to assume a will accompanied by great wisdom and might. And the common concepts of understanding are sufficient for this conviction so long as they are adequate to virtuous behavior, that is, so long as they are morally certain. Philosophy is necessarily required in order to reason in the third way, and it and it alone is capable of a higher degree of wisdom which reaches the aforementioned object with a clarity and conviction consistent with the magnitude of the truth.

Die beide letztere Arten kann man physikotheologische Methoden nennen; denn sie zeigen beide den Weg, aus den Betrachtungen über die Natur zur Erkenntniß Gottes hinauf zu steigen.

2.
Die Vortheile und auch die Fehler der gewöhnlichen Physikotheologie.

Das Hauptmerkmal der bis dahin gebräuchlichen physischtheolo= gischen Methode besteht darin: daß die Vollkommenheit und Regelmäßig= keit erstlich ihrer Zufälligkeit nach gehörig begriffen, und alsdann die künstliche Ordnung nach allen zweckmäßigen Beziehungen darin gewiesen wird, um daraus auf einen weisen und gütigen Willen zu schließen, nach= her aber zugleich durch die hinzugefügte Betrachtung der Größe des Werks der Begriff der unermeßlichen Macht des Urhebers damit ver= einigt wird.

Diese Methode ist vortrefflich: erstlich weil die Überzeugung über= aus sinnlich und daher sehr lebhaft und einnehmend und demnach auch dem gemeinsten Verstande leicht und faßlich ist; zweitens weil sie natür= licher ist als irgend eine andere, indem ohne Zweifel ein jeder von ihr zu= erst anfängt; drittens weil sie einen sehr anschauenden Begriff von der hohen Weisheit, Vorsorge oder auch der Macht des anbetungswürdigen Wesens verschafft, welcher die Seele füllt und die größte Gewalt hat auf Erstaunen, Demuth und Ehrfurcht zu wirken.*) Diese Beweisart ist viel praktischer als irgend eine andere selbst in Ansehung des Philosophen. Denn ob er gleich für seinen forschenden oder grüblenden Verstand hier nicht die bestimmte abgezogene Idee der Gottheit antrifft und die Gewiß=

---

*) Wenn ich unter andern die mikroskopische Beobachtungen des Doctor Hill, die man im Hamb. Magaz. antrifft, erwäge und sehe zahlreiche Thiergeschlechter in einem einzigen Wassertropfen, räuberische Arten, mit Werkzeugen des Verderbens ausgerüstet, die von noch mächtigern Tyrannen dieser Wasserwelt zerstört werden, indem sie geflissen sind andre zu verfolgen; wenn ich die Ränke, die Gewalt und die Scene des Aufruhrs in einem Tropfen Materie ansehe und erhebe von da meine Augen in die Höhe, um den unermeßlichen Raum von Welten wie von Stäubchen wimmeln zu sehen, so kann keine menschliche Sprache das Gefühl ausdrücken, was ein solcher Gedanke erregt, und alle subtile metaphysische Zergliederung weicht sehr weit der Erhabenheit und Würde, die einer solchen Anschauung eigen ist.

The latter two ways may be termed physico-theological methods, for they both show the way of ascending from observations of nature to the knowledge of God.

2.
The advantages and also the errors of ordinary physico-theology

The chief distinguishing characteristic of the physico-theological method which has hitherto been employed is this: perfection and regularity are first grasped appropriately to their contingency; then the ingenious order in all purposive relations is indicated so as to reason from that to a wise and a good will; and subsequently through the additional observation of the work's magnitude the concept of the immeasurable power of the creator is joined to it.

The method is excellent: first because the conclusion is thoroughly empirical and thus lively and engaging, and accordingly is easy and intelligible to the most common intellect. Second, because it is more natural than any other proof and without a doubt every other proof begins with it. Third, because it supplies a very radily apparent concept [anschauender Begriff] of great wisdom, providence, and even the might of a being worthy of prayer which fills the soul and has the greatest power to effect admiration, humility, and awe.* This mode of proof is far more practical than another even in the eyes of the philosopher. Although he encounters no determinate abstract idea of divinity for his inquiring or meditative understanding here, and the certainty is not mathematical but

*If I consider, amongst others, the microscopic observations of Dr. Hill[28] to be found in the *Hamburg Magazine,* and see that numerous animal species are in a single drop of water—predatory species outfitted with the tools of destruction, which are themselves destroyed by yet other more powerful tyrants of this watery world while they are busy pursuing others—when I see the intrigue, power and a scene of turmoil in a bit of matter and then turn my attention from that to boundless space, swarming with worlds like bits of dust, no human language can express the feeling such reflection excites and all subtle metaphysical analyses fall far indeed from the grandeur and value that are part and parcel of such a vision.

heit selbst nicht mathematisch, sondern moralisch ist, so bemächtigen sich
doch so viel Beweisthümer, jeder von so großem Eindruck, seiner Seele,
und die Speculation folgt ruhig mit einem gewissen Zutrauen einer Über=
zeugung, die schon Platz genommen hat. Schwerlich würde wohl jemand
seine ganze Glückseligkeit auf die angemaßte Richtigkeit eines metaphysi=
schen Beweises wagen, vornehmlich wenn ihm lebhafte sinnliche Über=
redungen entgegen ständen. Allein die Gewalt der Überzeugung, die hier=
aus erwächst, darum eben weil sie so sinnlich ist, ist auch so gesetzt und
unerschütterlich, daß sie keine Gefahr von Schlußreden und Unterscheidun=
gen besorgt und sich weit über die Macht spitzfündiger Einwürfe wegsetzt.
Gleichwohl hat diese Methode ihre Fehler, die beträchtlich genug sind, ob
sie zwar eigentlich nur dem Verfahren derjenigen zuzurechnen sind, die
sich ihrer bedient haben.

1. Sie betrachtet alle Vollkommenheit, Harmonie und Schönheit der
Natur als zufällig und als eine Anordnung durch Weisheit, da doch viele
derselben mit nothwendiger Einheit aus den wesentlichsten Regeln der
Natur abfließen. Das, was der Absicht der Physikotheologie hiebei am
schädlichsten ist, besteht darin, daß sie diese Zufälligkeit der Naturvoll=
kommenheit als höchstnöthig zum Beweise eines weisen Urhebers ansieht,
daher alle nothwendige Wohlgereimtheiten der Dinge der Welt bei dieser
Voraussetzung gefährliche Einwürfe werden.

Um sich von diesem Fehler zu überzeugen, merke man auf nachstehen=
des. Man sieht, wie die Verfasser nach dieser Methode gefließen sind, die
an unzähligen Endabsichten reiche Producte des Pflanzen= und Thierreichs
nicht allein der Macht des Ungefährs, sondern auch der mechanischen Noth=
wendigkeit nach allgemeinen Gesetzen der materialen Natur zu entreißen.
Und hierin kann es ihnen auch nicht im mindesten schwer werden. Das
Übergewicht der Gründe auf ihrer Seite ist gar zu sehr entschieden. Allein
wenn sie sich von der organischen Natur zur unorganischen wenden, so be=
harren sie noch immer auf eben derselben Methode, allein sie finden sich
daselbst fast jederzeit durch die veränderte Natur der Sachen in Schwie=
rigkeiten befangen, denen sie nicht ausweichen können. Sie reden noch
immer von der durch große Weisheit getroffenen Vereinbarung so vieler
nützlichen Eigenschaften des Luftkreises, den Wolken, dem Regen, den
Winden, der Dämmerung ꝛc. ꝛc., als wenn die Eigenschaft, wodurch die
Luft zu Erzeugung der Winde auferlegt ist, mit derjenigen, wodurch sie
Dünste aufzieht, oder wodurch sie in großen Höhen dünner wird, eben so

moral, such proofs so take possession of his soul, and each makes such a profound impression, that speculation proceeds quietly with certain confidence in the conviction which has already taken place. Of course it would be difficult to entrust one's entire blessedness to the putative certainty of a metaphysical proof, particularly if viable sensible persuasions stood in opposition to it. Still the power of the conviction that comes from this [physico-theological method] is so firm and unshakable, precisely because it is so sensible, that it need fear no danger from epilogues and distinctions and is far superior to the power of captious objections. Nevertheless this method does have its weaknesses, which are apparent enough, though they are only due to precisely the procedure which has served it:

1. It views all perfections, harmony, and excellence of nature as contingent and as an arrangement of wisdom, although many of them follow with necessary unity from the most essential rules of nature. What is most pernicious to the intent of physico-theology is that it considers the contingency of natural perfection as highly essential to the proof of a wise creator. Accordingly, with this assumption all necessary harmonious adaptations of things in the world become dangerous objections.

In order to be convinced of this defect, one may note the following: in this method authors can be seen to be studious in rescuing the products of the plant and animal kingdom, which are vastly rich in final intent, not only from the power of chance but also from the mechanical necessity of universal laws of material nature. This cannot be in the slightest way difficult for them. The preponderance of reasons on their side is far too decisive. In turning from organic to inorganic nature, however, they retain the identical method, but here they almost always find themselves enmeshed in difficulties which they cannot. escape owing to the changed nature of the things. They are forever speaking of the unification, effected by great wisdom, of so many useful properties of the atmosphere (clouds, rain, wind, twilight, and so on) as though the property by which air produces wind were joined by means of a wise choice to those

vermittelst einer weisen Wahl wäre vereinigt worden, wie etwa bei einer Spinne die verschiedene Augen, womit sie ihrem Raube auflauert, mit den Warzen, woraus die Spinnenseide als durch Ziehlöcher gezogen wird, mit den feinen Klauen oder auch den Ballen ihrer Füße, dadurch sie sie zusammenklebt oder sich daran erhält, in einem Thiere verknüpft sind. In diesem letzteren Fall ist die Einheit bei allen verbundenen Nutzbarkeiten (als in welcher die Vollkommenheit besteht) offenbar zufällig und einer weisen Willkür beizumessen, da sie im Gegentheil im ersteren Fall noth= wendig ist und, wenn nur eine Tauglichkeit von den erwähnten der Luft beigemessen wird, die andere unmöglich davon zu trennen ist. Eben da= durch daß man keine andere Art die Vollkommenheit der Natur zu be= urtheilen einräumt, als durch die Anstalt der Weisheit, so wird eine jede ausgebreitete Einheit, in so fern sie offenbar als nothwendig erkannt wird, einen gefährlichen Einwurf ausmachen. Wir werden bald sehen, daß nach unserer Methode aus einer solchen Einheit gleichwohl auch auf die göttliche Weisheit geschlossen wird, aber nicht so, daß sie von der weisen Wahl als ihrer Ursache, sondern von einem solchen Grunde in einem obersten Wesen hergeleitet wird, welcher zugleich ein Grund einer großen Weisheit in ihm sein muß, mithin wohl von einem weisen Wesen, aber nicht durch seine Weisheit.

2. Diese Methode ist nicht genugsam philosophisch und hat auch öfters die Ausbreitung der philosophischen Erkenntniß sehr gehindert. So bald eine Naturanstalt |nützlich ist, so wird sie gemeiniglich unmittel= bar aus der Absicht des göttlichen Willens, oder doch durch eine besonders durch Kunst veranstaltete Ordnung der Natur erklärt; entweder weil man einmal sich in den Kopf gesetzt hat, die Wirkungen der Natur gemäß ihren allgemeinsten Gesetzen könnten auf solche Wohlgereimtheit nicht auslaufen, oder wenn man einräumte, sie hätten auch solche Folgen, so würde dieses heißen die Vollkommenheit der Welt einem blinden Ungefähr zutrauen, wodurch der göttliche Urheber sehr würde verkannt werden. Daher werden in einem solchen Falle der Naturforschung Grenzen gesetzt. Die erniedrigte Vernunft steht gerne von einer weiteren Untersuchung ab, weil sie solche hier als Vorwitz ansieht, und das Vorurtheil ist desto gefährlicher, weil es den Faulen einen Vorzug vor dem unermüdeten Forscher giebt durch den Vorwand der Andacht und der billigen Unterwerfung unter den großen Urheber, in dessen Erkenntniß sich alle Weisheit vereinbaren muß. Man erzählt z. E. die Nutzen der Gebirge, deren es unzählige giebt, und

through which vapors rise or become more rare at greater altitudes; as perhaps the many eyes with which a spider lies in wait for its prey, the nodules from which the net is spun as by a loom, the delicate claws or even the balls of its feet by which it glues its prey together or on which it holds it, are joined in a single animal. In this latter case, the unity of all the combined ends (in which perfection consists) is obviously contingent and attributed to wise discretion, whereas in the former case, on the contrary, it is necessary. If one advantage of those mentioned be attributed to the air it is impossible to separate the other from it. Precisely because no mode of judging the perfection of nature is admitted save as a provision of wisdom, every extensive unity insofar as it is manifestly recognized as necessary will constitute a dangerous objection. We will soon see that according to our method it is nevertheless quite possible to reach a conclusion of divine intelligence from such unity. It is not deduced from wise choice as its cause, but rather is derived from such a ground in a supreme being as must simultaneously be a basis for great wisdom in him; that is, from a wise being, but not through its wisdom.

2. This method is not sufficiently philosophical, and often has much restricted the expansion of philosophical knowledge. As soon as a natural structure is useful it is commonly explained immediately by the intention of divine will or by a specially arranged order of nature elaborately prepared. This is either because it was once thought that the effects of nature according to their most general laws could not issue in such harmonious adaptation, or else because if it be admitted they might have such consequences this would mean that the perfection of the world was entrusted to blind chance. In this way the divine creator would be largely misunderstood.

In such a case, accordingly, the investigation of nature is set limits. Humiliated reason gladly stands off from further inquiry, for it sees this as impertinence and the prejudice is that much more dangerous since it grants preference to the indolent over the tireless researcher through the pretext of reverence and reasonable submission to a great creator in whose knowledge all wisdom must be united. For example, the uses of mountains, of which there are uncountably many, are recited. As soon as a

fo bald man deren recht viel und unter diefen folche, die das menfchliche
Gefchlecht nicht entbehren kann, zufammen gebracht hat, fo glaubt man
Urfache zu haben fie als eine unmittelbare göttliche Anftalt anzufehen.
Denn fie als eine Folge aus allgemeinen Bewegungsgefeßen zu betrachten
(weil man von diefen gar nicht vermuthet, daß fie auf fchöne und nüßliche
Folgen follten eine Beziehung haben, es müßte denn etwa von ungefähr
fein), das würde ihrer Meinung nach heißen, einen wefentlichen Vortheil
des Menfchengefchlechts auf den blinden Zufall ankommen laffen. Eben
fo ift es mit der Betrachtung der Flüffe der Erde bewandt. Wenn man
die phyfifchtheologifchen Verfaffer hört, fo wird man dahin gebracht fich
vorzuftellen, ihre Laufrinnen wären alle von Gott ausgehöhlt. Es heißt
auch nicht philofophiren: wenn man, indem man einen jeden einzelnen
Berg oder jeden einzelnen Strom als eine befondere Abficht Gottes betrachtet, die nach allgemeinen Gefeßen nicht würde erreicht worden fein,
wenn man, fage ich, alsdann fich diejenige Mittel erfinnt, deren befonde-
ren Vorkehrung fich etwa Gott möchte bedient haben, um diefe Individual-
Wirkungen heraus zu bringen. Denn nach demjenigen, was in der dritten
Betrachtung diefer Abtheilung gezeigt worden, ift dergleichen Product
dennoch in fo fern immer übernatürlich; ja, weil es nicht nach einer Ordnung der Natur (indem es nur als eine einzelne Begebenheit durch eigene
Anftalten entftand) erklärt werden kann, fo gründet fich ein folches Verfahren zu urtheilen auf eine verkehrte Vorftellung vom Vorzuge der Natur an fich felber, wenn fie auch durch Zwang auf einen einzelnen Fall
follte gelenkt werden müffen, welches nach aller unferer Einficht als ein
Mittel des Umfchweifs und nicht als ein Verfahren der Weisheit kann
angefehen werden.*) Als Newton durch untrügliche Beweife fich überzeugt
hatte, daß der Erdkörper diejenige Figur habe, auf der alle durch den
Drehungsfchwung veränderte Richtungen der Schwere fenkrecht ftänden,
fo fchloß er: die Erde fei im Anfange flüffig gewefen und habe nach den

---

*) Es wäre zu wünfchen, daß in dergleichen Fällen, wo die Offenbarung Nach-
richt giebt, daß eine Weltbegebenheit ein außerordentliches, göttliches Verhängniß fei,
der Vorwiß der Philofophen möchte gemäßigt werden ihre phyfifche Einfichten aus-
zukramen; denn fie thun der Religion gar keinen Dienft und machen es nur zweifelhaft, ob die Begebenheit nicht gar ein natürlicher Zufall fei; wie in demjenigen
Fall, da man die Vertilgung des Heeres unter Sanherib dem Winde Samyel beimißt. Die Philofophie kommt hiebei gemeiniglich ins Gedränge, wie in der Whifton-
fchen Theorie, die aftronomifche Kometenkenntniß zur Bibelerklärung zu gebrauchen.

fair number have been collected, and amongst them those that the human race cannot do without, that is thought sufficient reason for seeing them as an immediate divine provision. To consider them as a consequence of the universal laws of motion would, in their view, leave an essential advantage of the human race to blind chance (since they would never suppose that the laws of motion have a relation to excellent and useful consequences it would have to be from chance). The same thing is applied to observation of the earth's rivers. If one listens to the physico-theological authors he will be brought to imagine that their channels were all excavated by God.

It cannot be called philosophizing if, while one is regarding every particular mountain or every particular current as a special design of God which could not be achieved according to universal law, if as I say, one then invents that means whose special provision may perhaps have served God to produce this individual effect. For according to what has been shown in the Third Observation of this section, such a product is then in that degree supernatural. Indeed because it cannot be explained according to a natural order (since it arose as a particular event through its own design) such a procedure of judging is founded upon a preposterous notion of the excellence of nature itself when it must be directed towards a single case even if by constraint. According to our best judgment this is seen as a means of confusion and not as the procedure of wisdom.* When Newton had convinced himself by irrefutable proofs that the earth has the figure upon which all the vectors of gravity which are altered by rotary motion remain perpendicular, he concluded that in the beginning the earth was fluid and immediately obtained its shape through the laws of statics by

*It might be wished that the importunity of philosophers in showing off their insights in physics could be moderated in cases where revelation gives information that an event in the world has an extraordinary, divine relation. For they do no service to religion at all, and indeed make it questionable whether the event may not be an entirely natural coincidence, as in the case where the destruction of the army under Sennacherib is attributed to the wind of Samuel. Philosophy is usually in difficult straits when, as in Whiston's theory, astronomical knowledge of the comets is used for Biblical exposition.

Gesetzen der Statik vermittelst der Umdrehung gerade diese Gestalt ange=
nommen. Er kannte so gut wie sonst jemand die Vortheile, die in der
Kugelrundung eines Weltkörpers liegen, und auch die höchst nöthige Ab=
plattung, um den nachtheiligen Folgen der Achsendrehung vorzubeugen.
Dieses sind insgesammt Anordnungen, die eines weisen Urhebers würdig
sind. Gleichwohl trug er kein Bedenken sie den nothwendigsten mecha=
nischen Gesetzen als eine Wirkung beizumessen, und besorgte nicht, dabei
den großen Regierer aller Dinge aus den Augen zu verlieren.

Es ist also auch sicher zu vermuthen, daß er nimmermehr in An=
sehung des Baues der Planeten, ihrer Umläufe und der Stellung ihrer
Kreise unmittelbar zu einer göttlichen Anstalt seine Zuflucht würde ge=
nommen haben, wenn er nicht geurtheilt hätte: daß hier ein mechanischer
Ursprung unmöglich sei, nicht wegen der Unzulänglichkeit derselben zur
Regelmäßigkeit und Ordnung überhaupt (denn warum besorgte er nicht
diese Untauglichkeit in dem vorher erwähnten Falle?), sondern weil die
Himmelsräume leer sind, und keine Gemeinschaft der Wirkungen der Pla=
neten ineinander, ihre Kreise zu stellen, in diesem Zustande möglich ist.
Wenn es ihm indessen beigefallen wäre zu fragen, ob sie denn auch jeder=
zeit leer gewesen, und ob nicht wenigstens im allerersten Zustande, da
diese Räume vielleicht im Zusammenhange erfüllt waren, diejenige Wir=
kung möglich gewesen, deren Folgen sich seitdem erhalten haben, wenn er
von dieser alterältesten Beschaffenheit eine gegründete Vermuthung ge=
habt hätte, so kann man versichert sein, daß er auf eine der Philosophie
geziemende Art in den allgemeinen mechanischen Gesetzen die Gründe von
der Beschaffenheit des Weltbaues gesucht haben würde, ohne desfalls in
Sorgen zu sein, daß diese Erklärung den Ursprung der Welt aus den
Händen des Schöpfers der Macht des Ungefährs überlieferte. Das be=
rühmte Beispiel des Newton darf demnach nicht dem faulen Vertrauen
zum Vorwande dienen, eine übereilte Berufung auf eine unmittelbare
göttliche Anstalt für eine Erklärung in philosophischem Geschmacke aus=
zugeben.

Überhaupt haben freilich unzählbare Anordnungen der Natur, da sie
nach den allgemeinsten Gesetzen immer noch zufällig sind, keinen andern
Grund als die weise Absicht desjenigen, der gewollt hat, daß sie so und
nicht anders verknüpft werden sollten. Aber man kann nicht umgekehrt
schließen: wo eine natürliche Verknüpfung mit demjenigen übereinstimmt,
was einer weisen Wahl gemäß ist, da ist sie auch nach den allgemeinen

means of its revolution. He knew as well as anyone else the advantages accruing to the roundness of a heavenly body and also the flattening which is highly necessary to prevent untoward consequences of rotation about an axis. These are arrangements altogether worthy of a wise creator. Nevertheless he had no scruple about ascribing them to effects of the most necessary mechanical laws and was not concerned therewith to lose sight of the great ruler of all things.

Thus it is safe to suppose that he would never have taken refuge in divine origination in respect to the construction of the planets, their revolutions, and the position of their orbits, had he not judged that mechanical origination was impossible. This was not due to the insufficiency of mechanical laws in producing regularity and order in general (for then why did he not cite this insufficiency in the case just noted above?) but rather because heavenly spaces are empty, and there is no community of effects of the planets in this situation for them to establish each other in their orbits. But, however, it had occurred to him to ask whether it had always been empty and whether since, in the most primal state at least, these spaces were perhaps filled and connected, that efficacy was possible whose consequences have been continued since then; if he had had a reasonable conjecture about this most primitive state, one may be quite certain that he would have sought the reasons for the constitution of the universe in general mechanical laws in a way suitable for philosophy without being concerned in that case that this explanation of the world's origin was taking things out of the hands of the creator and giving them over to the power of chance. The famous example of Newton may not then serve as an excuse for indolent trust in giving out a rash invocation of immediate divine intention as an explanation in philosophic guise.

Certainly innumerable structures of nature, since they are still contingent according to the most general laws, can have no other ground in general than the intention of the one who has willed that they be conjoined as they are and not otherwise. But it cannot be concluded conversely that when a natural conjunction agrees with whatever is consistent with a wise will it

Wirkungsgesetzen der Natur zufällig und durch künstliche Fügung außer=
ordentlich fest gesetzt worden. Es kann bei dieser Art zu denken sich öfters
zutragen, daß die Zwecke der Gesetze, die man sich einbildet, unrichtig sind,
und dann hat man außer diesem Irrthume noch den Schaden, daß man
die wirkende Ursachen vorbeigegangen ist und sich unmittelbar an eine Ab=
sicht, die nur erdichtet ist, gehalten hat. Süßmilch hatte ehedem vermeint,
den Grund, warum mehr Knäbchen als Mägdchen geboren werden, in
dieser Absicht der Vorsehung zu finden, damit durch die größere Zahl
derer vom Mannsgeschlechte der Verlust ergänzt werde, den dieses Ge=
schlecht durch Krieg und gefährlichere Arten des Gewerbes vor dem andern
erleidet. Allein durch spätere Beobachtungen wurde eben dieser sorgfältige
und vernünftige Mann belehrt: daß dieser Überschuß der Knäbchen in den
Jahren der Kindheit durch den Tod so weggenommen werde, daß noch
eine geringere Zahl männlichen als die des weiblichen Geschlechts in die
Jahre gelangen, wo die vorher erwähnte Ursachen allererst Gründe des
Verlusts enthalten können. Man hat Ursache zu glauben, daß diese Merk=
würdigkeit ein Fall sei, der unter einer viel allgemeinern Regel stehen
mag, nämlich daß der stärkere Theil der Menschenarten auch einen größe=
ren Antheil an der Zeugungsthätigkeit habe, um in den beiderseitigen
Producten seine eigene Art überwiegend zu machen, daß aber dagegen,
weil mehr dazu gehört, daß etwas, welches die Grundlage zu größerer
Vollkommenheit hat, auch in der Ausbildung alle zu Erreichung derselben
gehörige Umstände antreffe, eine größere Zahl derer von minder voll=
kommener Art den Grad der Vollständigkeit erreichen werde, als der=
jenigen, zu deren Vollständigkeit mehr Zusammentreffung von Gründen
erfordert wird. Es mag aber mit dieser Regel eine Beschaffenheit haben,
welche es wolle, so kann man hiebei wenigstens die Anmerkung machen:
daß es die Erweiterung der philosophischen Einsicht hindere, sich an die
moralische Gründe, das ist, an die Erläuterung aus Zwecken, zu wenden,
da wo es noch zu vermuthen ist, daß physische Gründe durch eine Ver=
knüpfung mit nothwendigen allgemeineren Gesetzen die Folge bestimmen.

   3. Diese Methode kann nur dazu dienen, einen Urheber der Ver=
knüpfungen und künstlichen Zusammenfügungen der Welt, aber nicht der
Materie selbst und den Ursprung der Bestandtheile des Universum zu be=
weisen. Dieser beträchtliche Fehler muß alle diejenige, die sich ihrer allein
bedienen, in Gefahr desjenigen Irrthums lassen, den man den feineren
Atheismus nennt, und nach welchem Gott im eigentlichen Verstande als

is also contingent according to the universal efficient laws of nature and is established by extraordinary, artificial dispensation. It can often happen in this mode of thinking that the purposes which are imagined for the laws are incorrect, and thus there is in addition to this error also the damage of missing the efficient causes and of immediately fastening onto a merely fictional intention. Sussmilch[29] had earlier attempted to find the reason why more little boys than little girls are born in the intention of Providence to make up the greater loss that the male sex suffers from war and the more dangerous nature of their undertakings. Yet through later consideration even this careful and rational man was convinced that the excess of boys disappears in the childhood years, and that a smaller number of the male than of the female sex survives into the years in which the previously mentioned causes could contain the ultimate reasons for the loss. There is reason to believe that this notable fact is a case which may stand under a much more general law. That is, the more robust part of the human species also has a greater share in the reproductive activity in order to make the joint products preponderantly of its own kind. But, on the other hand, since more is requisite for something with a basis for greater perfection to encounter the circumstances pertaining to achievement of that development, a greater number of those of a less perfect type will reach a degree of completion than those to whose perfection more concurrence of grounds is required. This rule may have whatever construction it will but at least this observation can be made: it greatly impedes the extensions of philosophical insight to turn to moral reasons, that is, explanations according to purpose, where it may still be conjectured that physical grounds may determine the consequence through a conjunction with more general necessary laws.

3. This method can only serve to prove a creator of the conjunction and artificial coordination of the world, but not of the material itself and the origin of parts of the universe. This notable failing must keep those who use only it in danger of that error which is called the better atheism. According to this, in the necessary or contingent, order and manifold advantageous coordination in general designate a rational creator. In

ein Werkmeifter und nicht als ein Schöpfer der Welt, der zwar die Ma=
terie geordnet und geformt, nicht aber hervorgebracht und erschaffen hat,
angesehen werde. Da ich diese Unzulänglichkeit in der nächsten Betrach=
tung erwägen werde, so begnüge ich mich sie hier nur angemerkt zu haben.

Übrigens bleibt die gedachte Methode jederzeit eine derjenigen, die
sowohl der Würde als auch der Schwäche des menschlichen Verftandes am
meisten gemäß sind. Es sind in der That unzählbare Anordnungen in der
Natur, deren nächster Grund eine Endabsicht ihres Urhebers sein muß,
und es ist der leichtefte Weg, der auf ihn führt, wenn man diejenige An=
ftalten erwägt, die seiner Weisheit unmittelbar untergeordnet sind. Da=
her ist es billig seine Bemühungen vielmehr darauf zu wenden sie zu er=
gänzen als anzufechten, ihre Fehler zu verbessern als sie um deswillen ge=
ringschätig zu halten. Die folgende Betrachtung soll sich mit dieser Ab=
sicht beschäftigen.

Sechfte Betrachtung.
Verbefferte Methode der Phyfikotheologie.

1.
Ordnung und Anftändigkeit, wenn sie gleich nothwendig ist, bezeichnet einen verftändigen Urheber.

Es kann nichts dem Gedanken von einem göttlichen Urheber des
Univerfum nachtheiliger und zugleich unvernünftiger sein, als wenn man
bereit ist eine große und fruchtbare Regel der Anftändigkeit, Nutzbarkeit
und Übereinstimmung dem ungefähren Zufall beizumessen; dergleichen
das Clinamen der Atomen in dem Lehrgebäude des Demokritus und
Epikurs war. Ohne daß ich mich bei der Ungereimtheit und vorsetzlichen
Verblendung dieser Art zu urtheilen verweile, da sie genugsam von an=
dern ist augenscheinlich gemacht worden, so bemerke ich dagegen: daß die
wahrgenommene Nothwendigkeit in Beziehung der Dinge auf regelmäßige
Verknüpfungen und der Zusammenhang nützlicher Gesetze mit einer noth=
wendigen Einheit eben sowohl als die zufälligste und willkürlichfte Anftalt
einen Beweisthum von einem weisen Urheber abgebe; obgleich die Ab=
hängigkeit von ihm in diesem Gesichtspunkte auf andere Art muß vorge=
ftellt werden. Um dieses gehörig einzusehen, so merke ich an: daß die
Ordnung und vielfältige vortheilhafte Zusammenstimmung überhaupt

proper sense, God is regarded as the master craftsman but not the creator of the world, one who has ordered and formed matter to be sure, but has not produced and created it. Since I shall be considering this insufficiency in the next Observation I am content here simply to have noted it.

Still, the aforementioned method always remains one of those which are most consistent with both the dignity and the weaknesses of human understanding. There are in fact innumerable structures in nature whose immediate ground must be the final intention of their creator and the easiest way leading to this is to consider those provisions immediately ordered by his wisdom. Thus it is reasonable to apply one's efforts more to completing than to attacking it in order to improve its defects, rather than despising it because of them. In the following Observation I shall be concerned with this intention.

OBSERVATION SIX
Improved Method of Physico-Theology

1.
Order and suitability whenever it is necessary indicates an intelligent creator.

There can be nothing more prejudicial to the concept of a divine creator of the universe, and at the same time more irrational, than when one is prepared to attribute an extensive and fertile rule of suitability, utility, and agreement of things in nature to approximate chance. The swerve [clinamen] of atoms in the system of Democritus and Epicurus was such a thing. Without pausing to examine incoherence and deliberate delusion of this sort—for it has been made sufficiently obvious by others—I will simply note that, on the contrary, the perceived necessity in the relation of things to regular conjunction and the integration of useful laws with a necessary unity gives evidence of a wise creator as well as the most contingent and arbitrary arangement [does], although the dependence upon him must be presented in some other way in this point of view. To show this sufficiently I note that even before it be considered whether the relation to things is

einen verständigen Urheber bezeichnet, noch ehe man daran denkt, ob diese
Beziehung den Dingen nothwendig oder zufällig sei. Nach den Urtheilen
der gemeinen gesunden Vernunft hat die Abfolge der Weltveränderungen,
oder diejenige Verknüpfung, an deren Stelle eine andere möglich war, ob
sie gleich einen klaren Beweisgrund der Zufälligkeit an die Hand giebt,
wenig Wirkung, dem Verstande die Vermuthung eines Urhebers zu veranlassen. Es wird dazu Philosophie erfordert, und selbst deren Gebrauch
ist in diesem Falle verwickelt und schlüpferig. Dagegen macht große Regelmäßigkeit und Wohlgereimtheit in einem vielstimmichten Harmonischen
stutzig, und die gemeine Vernunft selbst kann sie ohne einen verständigen
Urheber nimmer möglich finden. Die eine Regel der Anständigkeit mag
in der andern schon wesentlich liegen, oder willkürlich damit verbunden
sein, so findet man es gerade zu unmöglich, daß Ordnung und Regelmäßigkeit entweder von Ungefähr, oder auch unter viel Dingen, die ihr
verschiedenes Dasein haben, so von selbst sollte statt finden, denn nimmermehr ist ausgebreitete Harmonie ohne einen verständigen Grund ihrer
Möglichkeit nach zureichend gegeben. Und hier äußert sich alsbald ein
großer Unterschied zwischen der Art, wie man die Vollkommenheit ihrem
Ursprunge nach zu beurtheilen habe.

2.

Nothwendige Ordnung der Natur bezeichnet selbst einen Urheber der Materie, die so geordnet ist.

Die Ordnung in der Natur, in so fern sie als zufällig und aus der
Willkür eines verständigen Wesens entspringend angesehen wird, ist gar
kein Beweis davon, daß auch die Dinge der Natur, die in solcher Ordnung nach Weisheit verknüpft sind, selbst von diesem Urheber ihr Dasein
haben. Denn lediglich diese Verbindung ist so bewandt, daß sie einen verständigen Plan voraussetzt, daher auch Aristoteles und viele andere Philosophen des Alterthums nicht die Materie oder den Stoff der Natur, sondern nur die Form von der Gottheit herleiteten. Vielleicht nur seit der
Zeit, als uns die Offenbarung eine vollkommene Abhängigkeit der Welt
von Gott gelehrt hat, hat auch allererst die Weltweisheit die gehörige Bemühung daran gewandt, den Ursprung der Dinge selbst, die den rohen
Zeug der Natur ausmachen, als so etwas zu betrachten, was ohne einen
Urheber nicht möglich sei. Ich zweifle, daß es jemanden hiemit gelungen

necessary or contingent, order and manifold advantageous coordination in general designate a rational creator. In they give clear evidence [*der Beweigrund*] of contingency, have little effect in providing understanding with the assumption of a creator. Philosophy is necessary for this and yet its use is complex and slippery in this case. On the other hand, great regularity and harmonious adaptation in a many-voiced harmony is surprising, and common sense can never find it possible without an intelligent creator. The one rule of suitability may already lie essentially in another or be connected with it arbitrarily, still it is found to be utterly impossible that order and regularity obtain by themselves either through chance or among a plurality of things with their divergent existence. For extensive harmony is never sufficiently given without an intelligent ground of its possibility. And this immediately expresses an important difference between the ways of evaluating perfection according to its origin.

2.
Necessary Order of Nature Itself Indicates a Creator of the Matter That Is So Ordered.

The order of nature, insofar as it is regarded as contingent and as originating from the choice of a rational being, is no proof at all that natural things which are united in such an order with wisdom have their existence from this creator. For this connection is only such as to presuppose a rational plan, and for for this reason Aristotle and other philosophers of antiquity derived only the form and not the matter or the substance of nature from divinity. Perhaps it is only since revelation has taught us the complete dependence of the world upon God that philosophy has applied the necessary effort in studying the origin of things which constitute the raw material of nature as something that would not be possible without a creator. I doubt that anyone has succeeded with this, and I shall give the reasons for my judgement in the last section. At least insofar as the contingent order of the parts of nature is regarded as originating from free choice, it can contribute nothing to the

161

sei, und ich werde in der letzten Abtheilung Gründe meines Urtheils an=
führen. Zum mindesten kann die zufällige Ordnung der Theile der Welt,
in so fern sie einen Ursprung aus Willkür anzeigt, gar nichts zum Be=
weise davon beitragen. Z. E. An dem Bau eines Thiers sind Gliedmaßen
der sinnlichen Empfindung mit denen der willkürlichen Bewegung und
der Lebenstheile so künstlich verbunden, daß man boshaft sein muß (denn
so unvernünftig kann ein Mensch nicht sein), so bald man darauf geführt
wird einen weisen Urheber zu verkennen, der die Materie, daraus ein
thierischer Körper zusammen gesetzt ist, in so vortreffliche Ordnung ge=
bracht hat. Mehr folgt hieraus gar nicht. Ob diese Materie für sich ewig
und unabhängig, oder auch von eben demselben Urheber hervorgebracht
sei, das ist darin gar nicht entschieden. Ganz anders aber fällt das Ur=
theil aus, wenn man wahrnimmt, daß nicht alle Naturvollkommenheit
künstlich, sondern Regeln von großer Nutzbarkeit auch mit nothwendiger
Einheit verbunden sind, und diese Vereinbarung in den Möglichkeiten der
Dinge selbst liegt. Was soll man bei dieser Wahrnehmung urtheilen? Ist
diese Einheit, diese fruchtbare Wohlgereimtheit ohne Abhängigkeit von
einem weisen Urheber möglich? Das Formale so großer und vielfältiger
Regelmäßigkeit verbietet dieses. Weil indessen diese Einheit gleichwohl
selbst in den Möglichkeiten der Dinge gegründet ist, so muß ein weises
Wesen sein, ohne welches alle diese Naturdinge selbst nicht möglich sind,
und in welchem als einem großen Grunde sich die Wesen so mancher Na=
turdinge zu so regelmäßigen Beziehungen vereinbaren. Alsdann aber ist
klar, daß nicht allein die Art der Verbindung, sondern die Dinge selbst
nur durch dieses Wesen möglich sind, das ist, nur als Wirkungen von ihm
existiren können, welches die völlige Abhängigkeit der Natur von Gott
allererst hinreichend zu erkennen giebt. Frägt man nun: wie hängen diese
Naturen von solchem Wesen ab, damit ich daraus die Übereinstimmung
mit den Regeln der Weisheit verstehen könne? Ich anworte: sie hängen
von demjenigen in diesem Wesen ab, was, indem es den Grund der Mög=
lichkeit der Dinge enthält, auch der Grund seiner eigenen Weisheit ist;
denn diese setzt überhaupt jene voraus.*) Bei dieser Einheit aber des

*) Die Weisheit setzt voraus: daß Übereinstimmung und Einheit in den Be=
ziehungen möglich sei. Dasjenige Wesen, welches von völlig unabhängiger Natur ist,
kann nur weise sein, in so fern in ihm Gründe, selbst solcher möglichen Harmonie
und Vollkommenheiten, die seiner Ausführung sich darbieten, enthalten sind. Wäre
in den Möglichkeiten der Dinge keine solche Beziehung auf Ordnung und Vollkommen=

proof of this. For example, in the structure of an animal, the organs of sensible perception are so ingeniously conjoined with those of voluntary motion and vitality that one must be depraved (since no human being can be so unreasonable), as soon as he is shown it, to fail to recognize that wise creator has brought the material from which an animal body is composed into such an excellent order. But nothing more than this follows. Whether the material is itself eternal and independent or produced by the same creator is by no means decided. But the judgment would be quite different were it seen that not all natural perfections are artificial but rather that rules of great utility are combined with necessary unity and that this connection lies in the possibility of the things themselves. How is one to judge this perception? Is this unity, this fecund harmonious adaptation possible without dependence upon a wise creator? The formal element of such a great and manifold regularity forbids that. However, because this unity is nevertheless itself grounded in the very possibilities of things, there must be a wise being without whom, as an eminent cause, all these natural things would not even be possible and in which the beings of so many natural things unite in such regular relations. But then it is clear that not only the mode of conjunction, but the things themselves, are possible only through this being. That is, they can exist only as effects of him, which alone gives sufficient evidence of the total dependence of nature upon God. If it be asked, "How do these beings depend upon such a being so that from it I can understand the agreement with the rules of wisdom?" I would answer, "They are dependent upon that in the being in which, while it contains the basis of the possibility of the things, is also the ground of his own wisdom; for the latter presupposes the former."* But in this unity of the ground as well as the essence of all things it is

*Wisdom presupposes that agreement and unity are possible in the relations. That being which is totally independent by nature can only be wise insofar as in him are contained the grounds even of such *possible* harmonies and perfections as his realization provides. Were no such relation to order and

Grundes sowohl des Wesens aller Dinge, als der Weisheit, Güte und Macht ist es nothwendig: daß alle Möglichkeit mit diesen Eigenschaften harmonire.

3.
Regeln der verbesserten Methode der Physikotheologie.

Ich fasse sie in folgendem kurz zusammen: Durch das Zutrauen auf die Fruchtbarkeit der allgemeinen Naturgesetze wegen ihrer Abhängigkeit vom göttlichen Wesen geleitet, suche man

1. Die Ursache selbst der vortheilhaftesten Verfassungen in solchen allgemeinen Gesetzen, die mit einer nothwendigen Einheit außer andern anständigen Folgen auch auf die Hervorbringung dieser Wirkungen in Beziehung stehen.

2. Man bemerke das Nothwendige in dieser Verknüpfung verschiedener Tauglichkeiten in einem Grunde, weil sowohl die Art, um daraus auf die Abhängigkeit von Gott zu schließen, von derjenigen verschieden ist, welche eigentlich die künstliche und gewählte Einheit zum Augenmerk hat, als auch um den Erfolg nach beständigen und nothwendigen Gesetzen vom ungefähren Zufall zu unterscheiden.

3. Man vermuthe nicht allein in der unorganischen, sondern auch der organisirten Natur eine größere nothwendige Einheit, als so gerade zu in die Augen fällt. Denn selbst im Baue eines Thieres ist zu vermuthen: daß eine einzige Anlage eine fruchtbare Tauglichkeit zu viel vortheilhaften Folgen haben werde, wozu wir anfänglich vielerlei besondere Anstalten nöthig finden möchten. Diese Aufmerksamkeit ist sowohl der Philosophie sehr gemäß, als auch der physisch-theologischen Folgerung vortheilhaft.

4. Man bediene sich der offenbar künstlichen Ordnung, um daraus auf die Weisheit eines Urhebers als einen Grund, der wesentlichen und nothwendigen Einheit aber in den Naturgesetzen, um daraus auf ein weises Wesen als einen Grund, aber nicht vermittelst seiner Weisheit, sondern vermöge desjenigen in ihm, was mit dieser harmoniren muß, zu schließen.

5. Man schließe aus den zufälligen Verbindungen der Welt auf den Urheber der Art, wie das Universum znsammengefügt ist, von der

---

heit befindlich, so wäre Weisheit eine Chimäre. Wäre aber diese Möglichkeit in dem weisen Wesen nicht selbst gegründet, so könnte diese Weisheit nimmermehr in aller Absicht unabhängig sein.

necessary that all possibility harmonize with the properties of wisdom, goodness, and power.

3.
Rules for improved physico-theology

I briefly summarize them in what follows. Directed by confidence in the productivity of universal natural laws because of their dependence on the divine being, one:

1. Seeks the cause even of the most advantageous constitution in such universal laws as stand in relation to the production of these effects with necessary unity—apart from other suitable consequences.

2. Notes the necessity in this conjunction of different excellences in one ground; for not only is this way of concluding the dependence upon God different from the one which attends to artificial and elected unity, but also the results of the constant and necessary laws are distinguished from those of approximate chance.

3. Assumes a necessary unity greater than immediately appears, not only in inorganic, but also in organic nature. For even in the structure of an animal it may be supposed that a single design will be fit to produce a good many excellent consequences, whereas at the outset we would have found a number of special provisions necessary. Attention to this is as consistent with philosophy as it is advantageous to the physico-theological inference.

4. Makes use of the obviously artificial order so as to conclude the wisdom of a creator as a ground of essential and necessary unity; but in natural laws from this to a wise being as ground; not by his wisdom, but rather because of that in him which must harmonize with this [wisdom].

5. Concludes from the *contingent* connections of the world that there is a creator of the way in which the universe is put together, but concludes from *necessary* unity that the very same

perfection to be found in the possibilities of things, wisdom would be only a chimera. But were this possibility not grounded in the wise being itself, this wisdom could never be totally independent in every respect.

nothwendigen Einheit aber auf eben daſſelbe Weſen als einen Urheber
ſogar der Materie und des Grundſtoffes aller Naturdinge.

6. Man erweitere dieſe Methode durch allgemeine Regeln, welche
die Gründe der Wohlgereimtheit desjenigen, was mechaniſch oder auch
geometriſch nothwendig iſt, mit dem Beſten des Ganzen können verſtänd=
lich machen, und verabſäume nicht, ſelbſt die Eigenſchaften des Raumes
in dieſem Geſichtspunkte zu erwägen und aus der Einheit in dem großen
Mannigfaltigen deſſelben den nämlichen Hauptbegriff zu erläutern.

4.

Erläuterung dieſer Regeln.

Ich will einige Beiſpiele anführen, um die gedachte Methode ver=
ſtändlicher zu machen. Die Gebirge der Erde ſind eine der nützlichſten
Verfaſſungen auf derſelben, und Burnet, der ſie für nichts Beſſers, als
eine wilde Verwüſtung zur Strafe unſerer Sünde anſieht, hat ohne Zweifel
Unrecht. Nach der gewöhnlichen Methode der Phyſikotheologie werden die
ausgebreitete Vortheile dieſer Bergſtrecken erzählt, und darauf werden
ſie als eine göttliche Anſtalt durch große Weisheit um ſo vielfältig abge=
zielter Nutzen willen angeſehen. Nach einer ſolchen Art zu urtheilen wird
man auf die Gedanken gebracht: daß allgemeine Geſetze ohne eine eigene
künſtliche Anordnung auf dieſen Fall eine ſolche Geſtalt der Erdfläche
nicht zuwege gebracht hätten, und die Berufung auf den allmächtigen
Willen gebietet der forſchenden Vernunft ein ehrerbietiges Schweigen. Da=
gegen iſt nach einer beſſer unterwieſenen Denkungsart der Nutze und die
Schönheit dieſer Naturanſtalt gar kein Grund, die allgemeine und ein=
fältige Wirkungsgeſetze der Materie vorbei zu gehen, um dieſe Verfaſſung
nicht als eine Nebenfolge derſelben anzuſehen. Es möchte vielleicht ſchwer
auszumachen ſein: ob die Kugelfigur der Erde überhaupt nicht von noch
beträchtlicherem Vortheile und wichtigern Folgen ſei, als diejenigen Un=
ebenheiten, die ihre Oberfläche von dieſer abgemeſſenen Rundung etwas
abweichen machen. Gleichwohl findet kein Philoſoph einiges Bedenken ſie
als eine Wirkung der allgemeinſten ſtatiſchen Geſetze in der alleräteſten
Epoche der Welt anzuſehen. Warum ſollten die Ungleichheiten und Her=
vorragungen nicht auch zu ſolchen natürlichen und ungekünſtelten Wir=
kungen gehören? Es ſcheint: daß bei einem jeden großen Weltkörper der
Zuſtand, da er aus der Flüſſigkeit in die Feſtigkeit allmählig übergeht,

being is creator of the matter and the basic substance of all natural things.

6. May expand this method through universal rules, which would make understandable the reasons for the harmony between what is mechanically or geometrically necessary and what is the best for the whole. Even the properties of space are not omitted from consideration in this view, and illustrate the aforementioned main notion by their unity in the great manifold of space.

4.
Illustration of these rules

I want to cite a few examples in order to make the method in question more intelligible.

Mountains are one of the most useful creations on earth, and Burnet, who regards them as nothing better than fierce devastations to punish our sins, is without a doubt wrong. [30] According to the usual method of physico-theology the great advantages of the mountain ranges are recounted, and they are thus regarded as a divine provision of great wisdom for the sake of such manifold intentional utility. Such a way of judging gives the idea that in this case universal laws would never have been sufficient in themselves to accomplish such a configuration of the earth's surface without a unique artificial arrangement; and invocation of almighty will demands respectful silence from inquiring reason. On the other hand, according to a better-instructed method of thought, the utility and excellence of this natural arrangement is absolutely no reason for passing over the general and simple efficient laws of matter and for not regarding this construction as a secondary consequence of them. It may be perhaps difficult to determine whether the roundness of the earth is not of greater advantage and more important consequence than those unevenesses which make its outer surfaces deviate somewhat from this exact roundness. Nevertheless there is no philosopher who has the slightest hesitation in regarding the spherical form as the effect of the most universal laws of statics in the most ancient epoch of the world. But why should the unevennesses and the projections not also belong to such natural and uncontrived effects? It seems

sehr nothwendig mit der Erzeugung weitläuftiger Höhlen verbunden sei, die sich unter seiner schon gehärteten Rinde finden müssen, wenn die leich= testen Materien seines inwendigen, noch flüssigen Klumpens, darunter auch die Luft ist, mit allmähliger Absonderung unter diesen empor steigen, und daß, da die Weitläuftigkeit dieser Höhlen ein Verhältniß zu der Größe des Weltkörpers haben muß, die Einsinkungen der festen Gewölbe eben so weit ausgebreitet sein werden. Selbst eine Art von Regelmäßigkeit, wenigstens die Kettenreihe dieser Unebenheiten, darf bei einer solchen Er= zeugungsart nicht fremd und unerwartet scheinen. Denn man weiß, daß das Aufsteigen der leichten Arten in einem großen Gemische an einem Orte einen Einfluß auf die nämliche Bewegung in dem benachbarten Theile des Gemengsels habe. Ich halte mich bei dieser Erklärungsart nicht lange auf, wie ich denn allhier keine Absicht habe, einige Ergebenheit in Ansehung derselben zu bezeigen, sondern nur eine kleine Erläuterung der Methode zu urtheilen durch dieselbe darzulegen.

Das ganze feste Land der Erde ist mit den Laufrinnen der Ströme als mit Furchen auf eine sehr vortheilhafte Art durchzogen. Es sind aber auch so viel Unebenheiten, Thäler und flache Gegenden auf allem festen Lande: daß es beim ersten Anblick scheint nothwendig zu sein, daß die Ka= näle, darin die Wasser derselben rinnen, besonders gebauet und geordnet sein müssen, widrigenfalls nach der Unregelmäßigkeit alles übrigen Bodens die von den Höhen laufende Wasser weit und breit ausschweifen, viele Flächen überschwemmen, in Thälern Seen machen und das Land eher wild und unbrauchbar als schön und wohlgeordnet machen müßten. Wer wird nicht hier einen großen Anschein zu einer nöthigen außerordentlichen Ver= anstaltung gewahr? Indessen würde aller Naturforschung über die Ur= sache der Ströme durch eine angenommene übernatürliche Anordnung ein Ende gemacht werden. Weil ich mich hingegen diese Art der Regelmäßig= keit nicht irre machen lasse und nicht sogleich ihre Ursache außer dem Be= zirk allgemeiner mechanischer Gesetze erwarte, so folge ich der Beobachtung, um daraus etwas auf die Erzeugungsart dieser Ströme abzunehmen. Ich werde gewahr: daß viele Fluthbetten der Ströme sich noch bis jetzt aus= bilden, und daß sie ihre eigene Ufer erhöhen, bis sie das umliegende Land nicht mehr so sehr wie ehedem überschwemmen. Ich werde gewiß, daß alle Ströme vor Alters wirklich so ausgeschweift haben, als wir be= sorgten, daß sie es ohne eine außerordentliche Anstalt thun müßten, und ich nehme daraus ab, daß keine solche außerordentliche Einrichtung jemals

that the condition of any large cosmic body in the process of gradually changing from fluidity to solidity is necessarily connected to the generation of extensive depressions which must be found under its already hardened crust when the lightest materials of its internal and still-fluid clumps, including air, gradually separate and rise from the crust. Since the extent of these depressions must have a relation to the size of the cosmic body, the sinking of deep caverns must be just as extensive. Indeed a sort of regularity, at least the linkage of these unevennesses into a chain, does not seem strange and unexpected with such a mode of generation. It is known that the ascent of light parts of a mixture in one place has an influence on the like motion in neighboring parts of the compound. I shall not stay long with this mode of explanation, for I have no intention of displaying any devotion to it, rather only of providing a slight illustration of judging by means of it.

All the continents of the earth are crisscrossed with the channels of streams as with furrows of an extremely advantageous sort. But there are also so many uneven places, valleys, and flat regions over all the continents that at first glance it seems necessary that the channels in which the waters of the streams run must be specially built and arranged. Otherwise, because of the irregularity of all the remaining ground, waters flowing from heights would have to cut far and wide and overflow many surfaces, making lakes in the valleys and the land savage and useless rather than fair and well ordered. Who would not see here the apparent necessity [*einen grossen Anschein*] of extraordinary management? However, assumption of supernatural arrangement would put an end to all scientific investigation into the causes of the currents. Because I, on the contrary, do not allow this sort of regularity to mislead me and do not immediately expect the cause outside the range of universal mechanical laws, I will pursue the study so as to learn something about the mode of generation of these streams from it. I see that the river beds of many streams are even now forming themselves and that they raise their own banks until they no longer overflow the surrounding land as much as before. I see that all the streams really have dug out [earth] with time, just as we have shown that they must do it, without any extraordinary provision; and from this I conclude

vorgegangen sei. Der Amazonenstrom zeigt in einer Strecke von einigen
hundert Meilen deutliche Spuren, daß er ehedem kein eingeschränktes
Fluthbette gehabt, sondern weit und breit das Land überschwemmt haben
müsse; denn das Erdreich zu beiden Seiten ist bis in große Weiten flach
wie ein See und besteht aus Flußschlamm, wo ein Kiesel eben so selten
ist wie ein Demant. Eben dasselbe findet man beim Mississippi. Und über=
haupt zeigen der Nil und andere Ströme, daß diese Kanäle mit der Zeit
viel weiter verlängert worden, und da wo der Strom seinen Ausfluß zu
haben schien, weil er sich nahe zur See über den flachen Boden ausbreitete,
bauet er allmählich seine Laufrinne aus und fließt weiter in einem ver=
längerten Fluthbette. Alsdann aber, nachdem ich durch Erfahrungen auf
die Spur gebracht worden, glaube ich die ganze Mechanik von der Bildung
der Fluthrinnen aller Ströme auf folgende einfältige Gründe bringen zu
können. Das von den Höhen laufende Quell= oder Regenwasser ergoß sich
anfänglich nach dem Abhang des Bodens unregelmäßig, füllte manche
Thäler an und breitete sich über manche flache Gegenden aus. Allein in
demjenigen Striche, wo irgend der Zug des Wassers am schnellsten war,
konnte es der Geschwindigkeit wegen seinen Schlamm nicht so wohl ab=
setzen, den es hergegen zu beiden Seiten viel häufiger fallen ließ. Dadurch
wurden die Ufer erhöht, indessen daß der stärkste Zug des Wassers seine
Rinne erhielt. Mit der Zeit, als der Zufluß des Wassers selber geringer
wurde (welches in der Folge der Zeit endlich geschehen mußte aus Ur=
sachen, die den Kennern der Geschichte der Erde bekannt sind), so über=
schritt der Strom diejenige Ufer nicht mehr, die er sich selbst aufgeführt
hatte, und aus der wilden Unordnung entsprang Regelmäßigkeit und
Ordnung. Man sieht offenbar, daß dieses noch bis auf diese Zeit, vor=
nehmlich bei den Mündungen der Ströme, die ihre jüngsten Theile sind,
vorgeht, und gleichwie nach diesem Plane das Absetzen des Schlammes
nahe bei den Stellen, wo der Strom anfangs seine neue Ufer überschritt,
häufiger als weiter davon geschehen mußte, so wird man auch noch gewahr,
daß wirklich an viel Orten, wo ein Strom durch flache Gegenden läuft,
sein Rinnsal höher liegt als die umliegende Ebenen.

Es giebt gewisse allgemeine Regeln, nach denen die Wirkungen der
Natur geschehen, und die einiges Licht in der Beziehung der mechanischen
Gesetze auf Ordnung und Wohlgereimtheit geben können, deren eine ist:
die Kräfte der Bewegung und des Widerstandes wirken so lange auf ein=
ander, bis sie sich die mindeste Hinderniß leisten. Die Gründe dieses Ge=

that there has never been any such extraordinary arrangement. The Amazon, in a stretch of several hundred miles, shows clear evidence that earlier it had no restricted bed, but rather must have flowed far and wide over the land, for the land on either side of the river is flat like a lake for great distances and consists of river mud where gravel is as rare as a diamond. Exactly the same thing is found with the Mississippi. And in general the Nile and other streams show that these channels have been much extended with the passage of time. Where the stream seems to have its estuary, because it extends over flat ground near the sea, it gradually constructs its channel and so flows further in a lengthened river bed.

But then, after I have been put on to the evidence through experience, I believe I can bring the entire mechanism for the construction of river channels onto the following simple grounds. Spring water or rain water which flows from a height initially spilled out irregularly according to the profile of the ground, filling many a valley and spreading out over many a flat region. But in that stretch where the flow of the water was the swiftest, because of its speed, it could not deposit so much of its mud and on the contrary often let it pile up much more frequently on either side. In this way banks were raised while the strongest flow of the water obtained its channel. When the flow of the water itself became slighter (which must happen in the course of time for reasons that are known to experts in the history of the earth), the stream no longer overflowed those banks which it itself had constructed. Regularity and order thus developed from wild disorder. It can manifestly be seen that this proceeds even now, principally at the estuaries of streams, which are the streams' most recent parts. Similarly, in this plan, the deposit of mud must take place closer to the places where the stream initially overflowed its new banks [rather] than farther from it. It will be seen that in many places where a stream runs through flat regions its channel lies higher than the surrounding plains.

There are certain universal rules according to which the effects of nature obtain, and which can shed the only light on the relation of mechanical laws to order and harmonious adaptation. One of them is: the forces of motion and of resistance have an effect on each other until they produce the

seßes lassen sich sehr leicht einsehen; allein die Beziehung, die dessen Folge auf Regelmäßigkeit und Vortheil hat, ist bis zur Bewunderung weit= läuftig und groß. Die Epicykloide, eine algebraische Krümmung, ist von dieser Natur: daß Zähne und Getriebe, nach ihr abgerundet, die mindest mögliche Reibung an einander erleiden. Der berühmte Herr Prof. Käst= ner erwähnt an einem Orte: daß ihm von einem erfahrnen Bergwerks= verständigen an den Maschinen, die lange im Gebrauche gewesen, gezeigt worden, daß sich wirklich diese Figur endlich durch lange Bewegung ab= schleife; eine Figur, die eine ziemlich verwickelte Construction zum Grunde hat, und die mit aller ihrer Regelmäßigkeit eine Folge von einem gemeinen Gesetze der Natur ist.

Um etwas aus den schlechten Naturwirkungen anzuführen, was, in= dem es unter dem eben erwähnten Gesetze steht, um deswillen einen Aus= schlag auf Regelmäßigkeit an sich zeigt, führe ich eine von den Wirkungen der Flüsse an. Es ist wegen der großen Verschiedenheiten des Abschusses aller Gegenden des festen Landes sehr zu erwarten, daß die Ströme, die auf diesem Abhange laufen, hin und wieder steile Stürze und Wasserfälle haben würden, deren auch wirklich einige, obzwar selten, vorkommen und eine große Unregelmäßigkeit und Unbequemlichkeit enthalten. Allein es fällt leicht in die Augen: daß, wenn gleich (wie zu vermuthen) in dem ersten verwilderten Zustande dergleichen Wasserfälle häufig waren, dennoch die Gewalt des Absturzes das lockere Erdreich, ja selbst einige noch nicht genugsam gehärtete Felsarten werde eingegraben und weggewaschen haben, bis der Strom seinen Rinnsal zu einem ziemlich gleichförmichten Abhang gesenkt hatte, daher, wo auch noch Wasserfälle sind, der Boden felsicht ist und in sehr viel Gegenden der Strom zwischen zwei steil abgeschnittenen Ufern läuft, wozwischen er sein tiefliegendes Bette vermuthlich selbst ein= geschnitten hat. Man findet es sehr nützlich, daß fast alle Ströme in dem größten Theile ihres Laufes einen gewissen Grad Geschwindigkeit nicht überschreiten, der ziemlich mäßig ist und wodurch sie schiffbar sind. Ob= gleich nun dieses im Anfange von der so sehr verschiedenen Abschießigkeit des Bodens, worüber sie laufen, kaum allein ohne besondere Kunst zu er= warten stände, so läßt sich doch leichtlich erachten, daß mit der Zeit ein gewisser Grad der Schnelligkeit sich von selbst habe finden müssen, den sie nicht leichtlich übertreffen können, der Boden des Landes mag abschießig sein, wie er will, wenn er nur locker ist. Denn sie werden ihn so lange abspühlen, sich hineinarbeiten und ihr Bette an einigen Orten senken, an

slightest resistance. The reasons for this law are readily apparent. Yet the relation that its consequences have to regularity and advantage are great and extensive, even to the point of admiration. The epicycloid, an algebraic curve, is of such a nature that teeth and gears rounded off according to it suffer the least possible friction from one another. The celebrated Professor Kastner[31] mentions in one place that he was shown by a mining expert of long experience that machines which had been in use for a long time really did themselves take on this figure. This is a figure which has a fairly sophisticated construction as its foundation, and yet with all its regularity is a consequence of a general law of nature.

In order to cite something among the bad effects of nature which, however, stand under the law just mentioned and for this reason display an outcome of regularity, I cite one of the effects of rivers. Because of the great differences of the profiles of all the regions of the continent, it is certainly to be expected that the streams which flow on these slopes now and again will have steep drops and waterfalls. Some of these actually do obtain—though seldom—and entail great irregularity and inconvenience. Yet it is clear that whenever (as may be assumed) in the first primitive state such waterfalls were frequent, the power of the plunge would have undermined and washed away the spongy earth and even the rocky ground which was not yet sufficiently hardened until the stream had sunk its channel into a rather uniform slope. For that reason, where there are still waterfalls, the earth is rocky; and in very many regions the stream flows between two steeply cut-out banks between which the river itself has probably cut its own deep-lying bed. It is very useful that nearly all streams, in the greater part of their courses, do not exceed a certain relatively moderate speed and that thereby they are navigable. Now although at the outset this would hardly be expected without some special arrangement, just because of the different profiles of the ground through which they flow, it can be clearly seen that with time they have found a certain speed by themselves which they cannot easily exceed no matter how slanted the ground is in the country so long as it is spongy. They will so long wash over the ground and work themselves into it, sinking their beds in some places and

andern erhöhen, bis dasjenige, was sie vom Grunde fortreißen, wenn sie angeschwollen sind, demjenigen, was sie in den Zeiten der trägeren Bewegung fallen lassen, ziemlich gleich ist. Die Gewalt wirkt hier so lange, bis sie sich selbst zum gemäßigtern Grade gebracht hat, und bis die Wechselwirkung des Anstoßes und des Widerstandes zur Gleichheit ausgeschlagen ist.

Die Natur bietet unzählige Beispiele von einer ausgebreiteten Nutzbarkeit einer und eben derselben Sache zu einem vielfältigen Gebrauche dar. Es ist sehr verkehrt diese Vortheile sogleich als Zwecke und als diejenigen Erfolge anzusehen, welche die Bewegungsgründe enthielten, weswegen die Ursachen derselben durch göttliche Willkür in der Welt angeordnet würden. Der Mond schafft unter andern Vortheilen auch diesen, daß Ebbe und Fluth Schiffe auch wider oder ohne Winde vermittelst der Ströme in den Straßen und nahe beim festen Lande in Bewegung setzen. Vermittelst seiner und der Jupiters-Trabanten findet man die Länge des Meers. Die Producte aus allen Naturreichen haben ein jedes eine große Nutzbarkeit, wovon man einige auch zum Gebrauche macht. Es ist eine widersinnige Art zu urtheilen, wenn man, wie es gemeiniglich geschieht, diese alle zu den Bewegungsgründen der göttlichen Wahl zählt und sich wegen des Vortheils der Jupitersmonde auf die weise Anstalt des Urhebers beruft, die den Menschen dadurch ein Mittel die Länge der Örter zu bestimmen hat an die Hand geben wollen. Man hüte sich, daß man die Spötterei eines Voltaire nicht mit Recht auf sich ziehe, der in einem ähnlichen Tone sagt: sehet da, warum wir Nasen haben; ohne Zweifel damit wir Brillen darauf stecken könnten. Durch die göttliche Willkür wird noch nicht genugsamer Grund angegeben, weswegen eben dieselbe Mittel, die einen Zweck zu erreichen allein nöthig wären, noch in so viel anderer Beziehung vortheilhaft seien. Diejenige bewundernswürdige Gemeinschaft, die unter den Wesen alles Erschaffenen herrscht, daß ihre Naturen einander nicht fremd sind, sondern, in vielfacher Harmonie verknüpft, sich zu einander von selbst schicken und eine ausgebreitete nothwendige Vereinbarung zur gesammten Vollkommenheit in ihren Wesen enthalten, das ist der Grund so mannigfaltiger Nutzbarkeiten, die man nach unserer Methode als Beweisthümer eines höchst weisen Urhebers, aber nicht in allen Fällen als Anstalten, die durch besondere Weisheit mit den übrigen um der besondern Nebenvortheile willen verbunden worden, ansehen kann. Ohne Zweifel sind die Bewegungsgründe, weswegen Jupiter Monde

9*

raising them at others, until what they sweep away from the ground when they are swollen will be pretty much equal to what they deposit in times of a more sluggish motion. Force is effective here until it has moderated itself and until the reciprocal effect of the flow and resistance has been extinguished in equilibrium.

Nature offers innumerable examples of the extensive use one and the same thing has for many applications. It is most preposterous immediately to regard these advantages as being the goals and the results that contained the motivating reasons why the grounds for them were arranged in the world by divine choice. Among the other advantages of the moon is that it creates the ebb and flow by which ships can be put into motion by means of the current in straits near land, even against or without wind. By means of the moon and Jupiter's satellites the longitude of the oceans may be determined. The products from all realms of nature each have great utility, some of which can be employed. It is a senseless way of judging if—as usually is done—these are all counted as motivating reasons of the divine choice, so that on account of the advantage of Jupiter's moons, one invokes the wise preparation of the creator who wanted thereby to give men a handy means of determining the longitude of places. One must take care not justifiably to call upon himself the satire of a Voltaire, who said in a similar tone: "See, the reason why we have noses is without a doubt to have a place to put our spectacles."[32] Divine choice does not give a sufficient reason why the same means which would be necessary to achieve one purpose should still be advantageous in so many other connections. That remarkable community which dominates in the essence of every created being, so that their natures are not foreign one to the other but rather are joined in manifold harmony and of themselves blend with each other and contain an extensive necessary union of collective perfection in their essences, is the ground of such manifold utilities. According to our method these [utilities] may be regarded as evidence of a supremely wise creator, but not in all cases as arrangements which are joined with the rest by special wisdom for the sake of subsidiary advantages. Without a doubt the

haben sollte, vollständig, wenn gleich niemals durch die Erfindung der Sehrohre dieselbe zu Messung der Länge genutzt würden. Diese Nutzen, die als Nebenfolgen anzusehen sind, kommen gleichwohl mit in Anschlag, um die unermeßliche Größe des Urhebers aller Dinge daraus abzunehmen. Denn sie sind nebst Millionen anderer ähnlicher Art Beweisthümer von der großen Kette, die selbst in den Möglichkeiten der Dinge die Theile der Schöpfung vereinbart, die einander nichts anzugehen scheinen; denn sonst kann man auch nicht allemal die Nutzen, die der Erfolg einer freiwilligen Anstalt nach sich zieht und die der Urheber kennt und in seinem Rathschlusse mit befaßt, um deswillen zu den Bewegungsgründen solcher Wahl zählen, wenn diese nämlich auch unangesehen solcher Nebenfolgen schon vollständig waren. Ohne Zweifel hat das Wasser darum nicht die Natur sich wagrecht zu stellen, damit man sich darin spiegeln könne. Dergleichen beobachtete Nutzbarkeiten können, wenn man mit Vernunft urtheilen will, nach der eingeschränkten physischtheologischen Methode, die im Gebrauche ist, gar nicht zu der Absicht, die man hier vor Augen hat, genutzt werden. Nur einzig und allein der Zusatz, den wir ihr zu geben gesucht haben, kann solche gesammelte Beobachtungen zu Gründen der wichtigen Folgerung auf die allgemeine Unterordnung aller Dinge unter ein höchst weises Wesen tüchtig machen. Erweitert eure Absichten, so viel ihr könnt, über die unermeßliche Nutzen, die ein Geschöpf in tausendfacher Beziehung wenigstens der Möglichkeit nach darbietet (der einzige Kokosbaum schafft dem Indianer unzählige), verknüpfet in dergleichen Beziehungen die entlegensten Glieder der Schöpfung mit einander. Wenn ihr die Producte der unmittelbar künstlichen Anstalten geziemend bewundert habt, so unterlasset nicht, auch in dem ergötzenden Anblick der fruchtbaren Beziehung, die die Möglichkeiten der erschaffenen Dinge auf durchgängige Harmonie haben, und der ungekünstelten Abfolge so mannigfaltiger Schönheit, die sich von selbst darbietet, diejenige Macht zu bewundern und anzubeten, in deren ewigen Grundquelle die Wesen der Dinge zu einem vortrefflichen Plane gleichsam bereit darliegen.

Ich merke im Vorübergehen an, daß das große Gegenverhältniß, das unter den Dingen der Welt in Ansehung des häufigen Anlasses, den sie zu Ähnlichkeiten, Analogien, Parallelen und, wie man sie sonst nennen will, geben, nicht so ganz flüchtig verdient übersehen zu werden. Ohne mich bei dem Gebrauch, den dieses auf Spiele des Witzes hat und der mehrentheils nur eingebildet ist, aufzuhalten, liegt hierin noch für den

motivating reasons why Jupiter must have moons would be complete even if they had never been used to measure longitude owing to the discovery of the telescope. These uses which are to be regarded as subsidiary consequences nevertheless enter into the estimate of the immeasurable magnitude of the creator of all things. For they are, among millions of other things of a similar sort, evidence of the great chain uniting, even in the possibilities of things, parts of the creation which seem to have nothing to do with each other. Otherwise of course one cannot for this reason count the utilities, which the result of a freely willed choice entails and which the creator knows and is concerned with in his decree, among the motives of such a choice, that is when they are complete irrespective of such secondary consequences. Without a doubt the nature of water to hold itself level is not so that people can be mirrored in it. Such like utilities cannot be used for the purpose in view here to judge rationally in terms of the limited physico-theological method being applied. Only the supplement we have attempted to give it can make such collected observations adequate to serve as the bases for the important consequence of the universal subordination of all things under a supremely wise being. Extend your intentions as much as you can over the immeasurable uses that a creature has, in a thousand ways, at least the possibility of providing (the single coconut tree provides the Indian with innumerable ones); join the most remote members of the creation with one another in these relations; when you have suitably admired the products of immediately artificial provisions do not neglect, in the delightful spectacle of the fruitful relation between the possibilities of created things and a thoroughgoing harmony and the natural succession of such manifold beauty it holds out, also to admire and to pray to that power in whose eternal fundamental principle the essences of things lie prepared, as it were, to accord with an excellent plan.

I note in passing that the great reciprocal relation among things in the world does not merit being passed over so fleetingly in respect to the frequent reason which it gives for similarities, analogies, parallels, and whatever else one calls them. Without stopping with the use of these in a game of wits, which for the

Philosophen ein, wie mir dünkt, wichtiger Gegenstand des Nachdenkens
verborgen, wie solche Übereinkunft sehr verschiedener Dinge in einem ge=
wissen gemeinschaftlichen Grunde der Gleichförmigkeit so groß und weit=
läuftig und doch zugleich so genau sein könne. Diese Analogien sind auch
sehr nöthige Hülfsmittel unserer Erkenntniß, die Mathematik selber liefert
deren einige. Ich enthalte mich Beispiele anzuführen, denn es ist zu be=
sorgen, daß nach der verschiedenen Art, wie dergleichen Ähnlichkeiten
empfunden werden, sie nicht dieselbe Wirkung über jeden andern Verstand
haben möchten, und der Gedanke, den ich hier einstreue, ist ohnedem un=
vollendet und noch nicht genugsam verständlich.

Wenn man fragen sollte, welches denn der Gebrauch sei, den man
von der großen Einheit in den mancherlei Verhältnissen des Raumes,
welche der Meßkünstler erforscht, machen könnte, so vermuthe ich, daß all=
gemeine Begriffe von der Einheit der mathematischen Objecte auch die
Gründe der Einheit und Vollkommenheit in der Natur könnten zu er=
kennen geben. Z. E. Es ist unter allen Figuren die Cirkelfigur diejenige,
darin eben der Umkreis den größt möglichen Raum beschließt, den ein
solcher Umfang nur befassen kann, darum nämlich, weil eine genaue
Gleichheit in dem Abstande dieser Umgränzung von einem Mittelpunkte
darin durchgängig herrscht. Wenn eine Figur durch gerade Linien soll
eingeschlossen werden, so kann die größt mögliche Gleichheit in Ansehung
des Abstandes derselben vom Mittelpunkte nur statt finden, wenn nicht
allein die Entfernungen der Winkelpunkte von diesem Mittelpunkte unter=
einander, sondern auch die Perpendikel aus diesem auf die Seiten ein=
ander völlig gleich sind. Daraus wird nun ein regelmäßiges Polygon,
und es zeigt sich durch die Geometrie, daß mit eben demselben Umkreise
ein anderes Polygon von eben der Zahl Seiten jederzeit einen kleinern
Raum einschließen würde als das reguläre. Noch ist eine und zwar die
einfachste Art der Gleichheit in dem Abstande von einem Mittelpunkte
möglich, nämlich wenn blos die Entfernung der Winkelpunkte des Vielecks
von demselben Mittelpunkte durchgängig gleich ist, und da zeigt sich, daß
ein jedes irreguläre Polygon, welches im Cirkel stehen kann, den größten
Raum einschließt unter allen, der von eben denselben Seiten nur immer
kann beschlossen werden. Außer diesem ist zuletzt dasjenige Polygon, in
welchem noch überdem die Größe der Seite dem Abstande des Winkel=
punkts vom Mittelpunkte gleich ist, das ist, das regelmäßige Sechseck,
unter allen Figuren überhaupt diejenige, die mit dem kleinsten Umfange

most part is only imagined, I think there is an important object of reflection for the philosopher concealed here: namely, how can such agreement of very different things in a certain single ground of uniformity be at once so extensive and far-reaching and yet also so precise? These analogies are such necessary aids to our knowledge that mathematics itself provides some of them. I hesitate to cite examples, fearing that because of the different way in which they are felt they would not exercise the same effect on every understanding. Yet the idea which I am throwing out here is otherwise not complete or sufficiently comprehensible without them.

If it should be asked what use may be made of the great unity in the diverse relations of space which the geometer investigates, I would conjecture that universal concepts of the unity of mathematical objects can also give grounds for recognition of unity and perfection in nature. For example, among all figures it is the circle whose planar circumference encloses the greatest possible space, because in a circle there is an exact equality of distance of the circumference from a middle point. If a figure is to be enclosed by straight lines, the greatest possible equality with respect to their distance from a center can only obtain when not only the distances of the angles from the center are themselves exactly equal but also when the perpendiculars from this center to the sides are exactly equal. Now this [construction] gives a regular polygon and geometry demonstrates that with the same circumference another polygon with an equal number of sides would always enclose a smaller space than a regular one. But one, and certainly the simplest, sort of equality of the distance from a center is possible when merely the distance of the angles of the polygon are equidistant from the same center, and this shows that every regular polygon [33] which may be inscribed in a circle encloses a greater space than can ever be enclosed by the same [number of] sides. Moreover, that polygon in which the size of the side is equal to the distance from the midpoint (that is, a regular hexagon) is in general the figure among all of them which encloses the greatest space with the smallest circumference such that it leaves

den größten Raum so einschließt, daß sie zugleich, äußerlich mit anderen gleichen Figuren zusammengesetzt, keine Zwischenräume übrig läßt. Es bietet sich hier sehr bald diese Bemerkung dar, daß das Gegenverhältniß des Größten und Kleinsten im Raume auf die Gleichheit ankomme. Und da die Natur sonst viel Fälle einer nothwendigen Gleichheit an die Hand giebt, so können die Regeln, die man aus den gedachten Fällen der Geometrie in Ansehung des allgemeinen Grundes solches Gegenverhältnisses des Größten und Kleinsten zieht, auch auf die nothwendige Beobachtung des Gesetzes der Sparsamkeit in der Natur angewandt werden. In den Gesetzen des Stoßes ist in so fern jederzeit eine gewisse Gleichheit nothwendig: daß nach dem Stoße, wenn sie unelastisch sind, beider Körper Geschwindigkeit jederzeit gleich sei, daß, wenn sie elastisch sind, beide durch die Federkraft immer gleich gestoßen werden und zwar mit einer Kraft, womit der Stoß geschah, daß der Mittelpunkt der Schwere beider Körper durch den Stoß in seiner Ruhe oder Bewegung gar nicht verändert wird 2c. 2c. Die Verhältnisse des Raums sind so unendlich mannigfaltig und verstatten gleichwohl eine so gewisse Erkenntniß und klare Anschauung, daß, gleichwie sie schon öfters zu Symbolen der Erkenntnisse von ganz anderer Art vortrefflich gedient haben (z. E. die Erwartungen in den Glücksfällen auszudrücken), also auch Mittel an die Hand geben können, die Regeln der Vollkommenheit in natürlich nothwendigen Wirkungsgesetzen, in so fern sie auf Verhältnisse ankommen, aus den einfachsten und allgemeinsten Gründen zu erkennen.

Ehe ich diese Betrachtung beschließe, will ich alle verschiedene Grade der philosophischen Erklärungsart der in der Welt vorkommenden Erscheinungen der Vollkommenheit, in so fern man sie insgesammt unter Gott betrachtet, anführen, indem ich von derjenigen Art zu urtheilen anfange, wo die Philosophie sich noch verbirgt, und bei derjenigen endige, wo sie ihre größte Bestrebung zeigt. Ich rede von der Ordnung, Schönheit und Anständigkeit, in so fern sie der Grund ist, die Dinge der Welt auf eine der Weltweisheit anständige Art einem göttlichen Urheber unter zu ordnen.

Erstlich, man kann eine einzelne Begebenheit in dem Verlaufe der Natur als etwas unmittelbar von einer göttlichen Handlung Herrührendes ansehen, und die Philosophie hat hier kein ander Geschäfte als nur einen Beweisgrund dieser außerordentlichen Abhängigkeit anzuzeigen.

Zweitens, man betrachtet eine Begebenheit der Welt als eine, worauf als auf einen einzelnen Fall die Mechanik der Welt von der

no interstices if it is adjoined externally to other equivalent figures. It emerges very soon from this study that the reciprocal relations of the maximums and the minimum in space depend upon equality. And since nature has so many cases handy of a necessary equality, the rule that is derived in the cases of geometry just mentioned in regard to the universal ground for such a correlation of the maximum and minimum can also be applied to the necessary law of parsimony in nature.

In the laws of collision, a certain equality is always necessary in that if both bodies are inelastic after the impact the speed of both is always equal. If they are elastic, both are moved proportionately by the driving force, and the force with which they are struck is such that the center of gravity of neither body is altered in its motion or rest by the impetus and so on. The relations of space are so endlessly diverse and nevertheless allow such certain knowledge and such a clear view that they have often served admirably as symbols of knowledge of a completely different sort (for example, to express expectation in matters of luck); thus they also can provide a handy means of recognizing the rules of perfection in naturally necessary laws of efficacy insofar as they come to be known from relations of simple and universal causes.

Before closing this Observation, I want to cite all the different degrees of the philosophic mode of explanation of appearances of perfection occurring in the world as they are seen together under God, beginning with that mode of judging where philosophy is still concealed, and finishing where she shows her greatest effort. I am speaking of order, excellence, and regularity [die Anständigkeit], insofar as it is the reason for ordering things under a divine creator in a philosophically appropriate way.

First, a single event in the course of nature may be regarded as following immediately from divine activity. Here philosophy has no other business than to indicate a proof [der Beweisgrund] of this extraordinary dependence.

Second, an event in the world may be regarded as one single case toward which the mechanism of the world was

Schöpfung her besonders abgerichtet war, wie z. E. die Sündfluth nach
dem Lehrgebäude verschiedener Neuern. Alsdann ist aber die Begebenheit
nicht weniger übernatürlich. Die Naturwissenschaft, wovon die gedachte
Weltweise hiebei Gebrauch machen, dient nur dazu ihre eigene Geschick-
lichkeit zu zeigen und etwas zu ersinnen, was sich etwa nach allgemeinen
Naturgesetzen eräugnen könnte, und dessen Erfolg auf die vorgegebene
außerordentliche Begebenheit hinausliefe. Denn sonst ist ein solches Verfahren der göttlichen Weisheit nicht gemäß, die niemals darauf abzielt
mit unnützer Kunst zu prahlen, welche man selbst an einem Menschen
tadeln würde, der, wenn ihn z. E. nichts abhielte eine Kanone unmittelbar abzufeuren, ein Feuerschloß mit einem Uhrwerk anbringen wollte,
wodurch sie in dem gesetzten Augenblick durch mechanische sinnreiche Mittel
losbrennen sollte.

Drittens, wenn gewisse Stücke der Natur als eine von der Schöpfung her daurende Anstalt, die unmittelbar von der Hand des großen
Werkmeisters herrührt, angesehen werden; und zwar wie eine Anstalt, die
als ein einzelnes Ding und nicht wie eine Anordnung nach einem beständigen Gesetze eingeführt worden; z. E. wenn man behauptet, Gott habe
die Gebirge, die Flüsse, die Planeten und ihre Bewegung mit dem Anfange aller Dinge zugleich unmittelbar geordnet. Da ohne Zweifel ein
Zustand der Natur der erste sein muß, in welchem die Form der Dinge
eben so wohl wie die Materie unmittelbar von Gott abhängt, so hat diese
Art zu urtheilen in so fern einen philosophischen Grund. Indessen weil
es übereilt ist, ehe und bevor man die Tauglichkeit, die den Naturdingen
nach allgemeinen Gesetzen eigen ist, geprüft hat, eine Anstalt unmittelbar
der Schöpfungshandlung beizumessen, darum weil sie vortheilhaft und
ordentlich ist, so ist sie in so weit nur in sehr kleinem Grade philosophisch.

Viertens, wenn man einer künstlichen Ordnung der Natur etwas
beimißt, bevor die Unzulänglichkeit, die sie hiezu nach gemeinen Gesetzen
hat, gehörig erkannt worden, z. E. wenn man etwas aus der Ordnung
des Pflanzen- und Thierreichs erklärt, was vielleicht in gemeinen mechanischen Kräften liegt, blos deswegen weil Ordnung und Schönheit darin
groß sind. Das Philosophische dieser Art zu urtheilen ist alsdann noch
geringer, wenn ein jedes einzelne Thier oder Pflanze unmittelbar der
Schöpfung untergeordnet wird, als wenn außer einigem unmittelbar Erschaffenen die andere Producte demselben nach einem Gesetze der Zeu-
gungsfähigkeit (nicht blos des Auswickelungsvermögens) untergeordnet

particularly directed at creation—for example, the flood in the systems of diverse moderns.[34] But then the event is not less supernatural. Natural science, which the aforementioned philosophers make use of, here serves only to show their own skill and to devise something which could happen according to universal natural laws and whose result issues in the previously given extraordinary event. Otherwise such a procedure is not consistent with divine wisdom, which never intends to show off with needless art something that would be censured in a human being. For instance, [such a person might] want to add a firing pin with a clockwork mechanism to a cannon which nothing prevented him from firing off directly so that it would be discharged at the given moment by mechanically sensible means.

Third, when a certain aspect of nature is seen as a provision that follows directly from the hand of the great craftsman enduring from creation until now and indeed is a provision introduced as a particular thing and not as a structure according to constant laws; as, for example, when it is maintained that God has immediately ordered the mountains, the rivers, the planets, and their motions at the beginning of things. Since without a doubt there must be an initial condition in which the form as well as the matter of things depends directly on God, this mode of thought has to that extent a philosophical basis. However, because it is overquick to attribute advantageous and orderly structure immediately to the creative act before probing the fitness attaching to natural things according to universal laws, it is philosophical only to a slight extent.

Fourth, when something is attributed to an artificial order of nature before the insufficiency of common laws for it is adequately known; as, for example, when something is explained in the plant or animal kingdoms which might perhaps lie within the powers of common mechanics simply because its order and excellence are great. The philosophic nature of this mode of judging is less if each particular plant or animal is immediately subordinated to creation than when—apart from a few immediately created things—other products of the plant or the animal kingdoms are subordinated to the law of generation

werden, weil im letztern Fall mehr nach der Ordnung der Natur erklärt
wird; es müßte denn ſein, daß dieſer ihre Unzulänglichkeit in Anſehung
deſſen klar erwieſen werden könnte. Es gehört aber auch zu dieſem Grade
der philoſophiſchen Erklärungsart eine jede Ableitung einer Anſtalt in
der Welt aus künſtlichen und um einer Abſicht willen errichteten Geſetzen
überhaupt und nicht blos im Thier= und Pflanzenreiche;*) z. E. wenn
man vom Schnee und den Nordſcheinen ſo redet, als ob die Ordnung der
Natur, die beide hervorbringt, um des Nutzens des Grönländers oder
Lappen willen (damit er in den langen Nächten nicht ganz im Finſtern
ſei) eingeführt wäre, obgleich es noch immer zu vermuthen iſt, daß dieſes
eine wohlpaſſende Nebenfolge mit nothwendiger Einheit aus andern Ge=
ſetzen ſei. Man iſt faſt jederzeit in Gefahr dieſes Fehlers, wenn man
einige Nutzen der Menſchen zum Grunde einer beſondern göttlichen Ver=
anſtaltung angiebt, z. E. daß Wald und Feld mehrentheils mit grüner
Farbe bedeckt iſt, weil dieſe unter allen Farben die mittlere Stärke hat,
um das Auge in mäßiger Übung zu erhalten. Hiegegen kann man ein=
wenden, daß der Bewohner der Davisſtraße vom Schnee faſt blind wird
und ſeine Zuflucht zu den Schneebrillen nehmen muß. Es iſt nicht tadel=
haft, daß man die nützliche Folgen aufſucht und ſie einem gütigen Ur=
heber beimißt, ſondern daß die Ordnung der Natur, darnach ſie geſchehen,
als künſtlich und willkürlich mit andern verbunden vorgeſtellt wird, da ſie
doch vielleicht mit andern in nothwendiger Einheit ſteht.

　　Fünftens. Am mehrſten enthält die Methode über die vollkommene
Anſtalten der Natur zu urtheilen den Geiſt wahrer Weltweisheit, wenn
ſie, jederzeit bereit, auch übernatürliche Begebenheiten zuzulaſſen, im=
gleichen die wahrhaftig künſtliche Anordnungen der Natur nicht zu ver=
kennen, hauptſächlich die Abzielung auf Vortheile und alle Wohlgereimt=
heit ſich nicht hindern läßt, die Gründe davon in nothwendigen allgemeinen
Geſetzen aufzuſuchen, mit großer Achtſamkeit auf die Erhaltung der Ein=
heit und mit einer vernünftigen Abneigung, die Zahl der Natururſachen
um derentwillen zu vervielfältigen. Wenn hiezu noch die Aufmerkſamkeit

---

　　*) Ich habe in der zweiten Nummer der dritten Betrachtung dieſes Abſchnittes
unter den Beiſpielen der künſtlichen Naturordnung blos die aus dem Pflanzen= und
Thierreiche angeführt. Es iſt aber zu merken, daß eine jede Anordnung eines Ge=
ſetzes um eines beſondern Nutzens willen, darum weil ſie hiedurch von der noth=
wendigen Einheit mit andern Naturgeſetzen ausgenommen wird, künſtlich ſei, wie
aus einigen hier erwähnten Beiſpielen zu erſehen.

(not merely of evolution),[35] because in the latter case more is explained by the order of nature; [to justify this mode of philosophical explanation] it would have to be possible clearly to indicate the insufficiency of the order of nature in respect to plants and animals. But it pertains to this degree of philosophic explanation that every derivation of a structure in the world in general, and not just in the plant and animal kingdoms, be from artificial laws, ones established for the sake of a purpose.* This happens, for example, when the snow and the northern lights are spoken of as though the order of nature which produces them were introduced for the sake of the advantage of Greenlanders and Lapps (so that in the long nights they are not entirely in the dark), though it may still be conjectured that this is a well-harmonized secondary consequence of other laws [which it follows] with a necessary unity. One is almost always in danger of this error when he gives a few human advantages as the basis for special divine arrangements; for instance that forests and fields are for the most part covered with green because, of all the colors, these are such as to keep the eye in moderate practice. Against this it may be objected that an inhabitant of the Davis Strait must be almost blinded by the snow and required to take refuge in snowglasses. It is not a matter of censure that useful consequences are sought and attributed to a good creator, but [it is a matter of censure] rather that the order of nature according to which they obtain is conceived as artificial and arbitrarily connected to others, since perhaps they stand in a necessary unity with these others.

Fifth, the method of judging the perfect provisions of nature most contains the spirit of true philosophy if, though prepared at any time to admit supernatural events and not to mistake true artificial structures of nature, especially the aim at advantage and harmonious adaptation, it does not refrain from seeking the grounds of these in universal laws, giving great

---

*In the second paragraph of the third Observation of this Part, I have cited as examples only those drawn from the plant and animal kingdoms among the instances of artificial natural order. It should be noted, however, that every ordering of laws for the sake of a particular advantage is artificial since it is an exception to the necessary unity with other natural laws, as may be seen from the examples mentioned here.

auf die allgemeine Regeln gefügt wird, welche den Grund der nothwendi=
gen Verbindung desjenigen, was natürlicher Weise ohne besondere Anstalt
vorgeht, mit den Regeln des Vortheils oder der Annehmlichkeit vernünf=
tiger Wesen können begreiflich machen, und man alsdann zu dem gött=
lichen Urheber hinauf steigt, so erfüllt diese physischtheologische Art zu ur=
theilen ihre Pflichten gehörig.*)

Siebente Betrachtung.

Kosmogonie.

Eine Hypothese mechanischer Erklärungsart des Ursprungs
der Weltkörper und der Ursachen ihrer Bewegungen gemäß
den vorher erwiesenen Regeln.

Die Figur der Himmelskörper, die Mechanik, nach der sie sich bewegen
und ein Weltsystem ausmachen, imgleichen die mancherlei Veränderun=
gen, denen die Stellung ihrer Kreise in der Folge der Zeit unterworfen ist,
alles dieses ist ein Theil der Naturwissenschaft geworden, der mit so gro=
ßer Deutlichkeit und Gewißheit begriffen wird, daß man auch nicht eine
einzige andere Einsicht sollte aufzeigen können, welche einen natürlichen
Gegenstand (der nur einigermaßen dieses seiner Mannigfaltigkeit bei=
käme) auf eine so ungezweifelt richtige Art und mit solcher Augenschein=
lichkeit erklärte. Wenn man dieses in Erwägung zieht, sollte man da nicht
auch auf die Vermuthung gerathen, daß der Zustand der Natur, in wel=
chem dieser Bau seinen Anfang nahm, und ihm die Bewegungen, die jetzt
nach so einfältigen und begreiflichen Gesetzen fortdauern, zuerst einge=
drückt worden, ebenfalls leichter einzusehen und faßlicher sein werde, als
vielleicht das mehrste, wovon wir sonst in der Natur den Ursprung suchen.
Die Gründe, die dieser Vermuthung günstig sind, liegen am Tage. Alle
diese Himmelskörper sind runde Massen, so viel man weiß, ohne Organi=
sation und geheime Kunstzubereitung. Die Kraft, dadurch sie gezogen

---

*) Ich will hiemit nur sagen, daß dieses der Weg für die menschliche Vernunft
sein müsse. Denn wer wird es gleichwohl jemals verhüten können hiebei vielfältig
zu irren, nach dem Pope:

Geh, schreibe Gottes weiser Ordnung des Regimentes Regeln vor,
Dann kehre wieder in dich selber zuletzt zurück und sei ein Thor.

attention to the maintenance of unity and keeping a reasonable aversion to multiplying the number of natural causes for their sakes. If to this be added attention to the universal laws which are able to make understandable the ground of the necessary connection between that which proceeds naturally without special cause and the rules of advantage or convenience of rational creatures, and if after that one ascends to the divine creator, this physico-theological mode of judging satisfactorily performs its duties.*

OBSERVATION SEVEN
Cosmogony
An Hypothetical and Mechanical Explanation of
the Origin of Heavenly Bodies and the Causes of
their Motions According to the Rules Previously
Demonstrated

The shape of heavenly bodies, the mechanics according to which they move and constitute a universe, as well as the many alterations that the position of their orbits are subjected to in the course of time—all of this has become a portion of natural science. And it is understood so distinctly and certainly that it is impossible to point to a single other insight (that even comes close to the complexity of this one) in which a natural object is explained in such an indubitably true fashion and so evidently. If this be taken into consideration, should not one conjecture that the condition of nature in which this structure originated, on which were initially impressed motions which even now continue according to simple and comprehensible laws, will likewise be more comprehensible and easier to understand than perhaps most things whose origin we normally seek in nature? The reasons favorable to this assumption are obvious. All these heavenly bodies are round masses, and so far as is known,

*I want to say only that this must be the way of human reason. Yet nevertheless who will never be able to avoid frequent error, as Pope has it:

Go teach eternal Wisdom how to rule—
Then drop into thyself and be a fool [36]

werden, ist allem Ansehen nach eine der Materie eigene Grundkraft, darf also und kann nicht erklärt werden. Die Wurfsbewegung, mit welcher sie ihren Flug verrichten, und die Richtung, nach der dieser Schwung ihnen ertheilt worden, ist zusammt der Bildung ihrer Massen das Hauptsäch=lichste, ja fast das einzige, wovon man die erste natürliche Ursachen zu suchen hat: einfältige und bei weitem nicht so verwickelte Wirkungen, wie die meisten andere der Natur sind, bei welchen gemeiniglich die Gesetze gar nicht mit mathematischer Richtigkeit bekannt sind, nach denen sie ge=schehen, da sie im Gegentheil hier in dem begreiflichsten Plane vor Augen liegen. Es ist auch bei einem so großen Anschein eines glücklichen Erfolgs sonst nichts im Wege, als der Eindruck von der rührenden Größe eines solchen Naturstücks, als ein Sonnensystem ist, wo die natürlichen Ursachen alle verdächtig sind, weil ihre Zulänglichkeit viel zu nichtig und dem Schöpfungsrechte des obersten Urhebers entgegen zu sein scheint. Allein könnte man eben dieses nicht auch von der Mechanik sagen, wodurch ein großer Weltbau, nachdem er einmal da ist, seine Bewegungen forthin er=hält? Die ganze Erhaltung derselben kommt auf eben dasselbe Gesetz an, wornach ein Stein, der in der Luft geworfen ist, seine Bahn beschreibt; ein einfältiges Gesetz, fruchtbar an den regelmäßigsten Folgen und würdig, daß ihm die Aufrechthaltung eines ganzen Weltbaues anvertraut werde.

Von der andern Seite, wird man sagen, ist man nicht vermögend die Naturursachen deutlich zu machen, wodurch das verächtlichste Kraut nach völlig begreiflichen mechanischen Gesetzen erzeugt werde, und man wagt sich an die Erklärung von dem Ursprunge eines Weltsystems im Großen. Allein ist jemals ein Philosoph auch im Stande gewesen, nur die Gesetze, wornach der Wachsthum oder die innere Bewegung in einer schon vorhandenen Pflanze geschieht, dermaßen deutlich und mathematisch sicher zu machen, wie diejenige gemacht sind, welchen alle Bewegungen der Weltkörper gemäß sind. Die Natur der Gegenstände ist hier ganz ver=ändert. Das Große, das Erstaunliche ist hier unendlich begreiflicher als das Kleine und Bewundernswürdige, und die Erzeugung eines Planeten zusammt der Ursache der Wurfsbewegung, wodurch er geschleudert wird, um im Kreise zu laufen, wird allem Anscheine nach leichter und deutlicher einzusehen sein, als die Erzeugung einer einzigen Schneeflocke, in der die abgemessene Richtigkeit eines sechseckichten Sternes dem Ansehen nach ge=nauer ist als die Rundung der Kreise, worin Planeten laufen, und an welcher die Strahlen viel richtiger sich auf eine Fläche beziehen, als die

without organization and esoteric preparation. The power by which they are moved is, according to all opinion, one of the basic forces of matter itself and thus may not and cannot be further explained. The initiation of the motion with which they accomplish their flight and the direction communicated to them by this impulse together with the constitution of the masses is the chief, indeed almost the only, thing whose first, original natural causes have to be sought. [These are] simple effects and by no means as complicated as the majority of those in nature whose laws are not commonly understood with mathematical rigor. On the contrary, here they are obvious in a most comprehensible plan. Nothing stands in the way of the appearance of such a happy consequence except the impression of the stirring magnitude of a work of nature such as a solar system is, where natural causes all are suspect because their sufficiency is much too nugatory and seems to be adverse to the power of the original creator. And yet cannot the same thing be said of the mechanics through which a large cosmic system continually retains its motion once it exists? Retention of such motion turns upon the very same law by which a stone thrown into the air describes its trajectory, a simple law rich in the most regular consequences and worthy of having entrusted to it maintenance of an entire universe.

On the other hand it will be said that it is not possible to discover the natural causes through which the most lowly cabbage is generated according to completely mechanical laws, and yet one dares an explanation of the origin of the universe at large. But still no philosopher has ever been in a position to render any of the laws of the growth or inner movement of an already existing plant as distinct and mathematically certain as those to which all motions of the heavenly bodies conform. The nature of the objects is completely altered here. The large, the astonishing, is infinitely more comprehensible than the small and marvelous. The generation of a planet, together with the cause of the impulse with which it is slung into motion so as to revolve in orbit, is to all appearances more easily and more distinctly comprehended than the generation of a single snowflake, where the precise proportion of the six-sided star seems more exact than the roundness of the orbits in which the planets revolve, and

Bahnen dieser Himmelskörper es gegen den gemeinschaftlichen Plan ihrer Kreisbewegungen thun.

Ich werde den Versuch einer Erklärung von dem Ursprunge des Weltbaues nach allgemeinen mechanischen Gesetzen darlegen, nicht von der gesammten Naturordnung, sondern nur von den großen Massen und ihren Kreisen, welche die roheste Grundlage der Natur ausmachen. Ich hoffe einiges zu sagen, was andern zu wichtigen Betrachtungen Anlaß geben kann, obgleich mein Entwurf grob und unausgearbeitet ist. Einiges davon hat in meiner Meinung einen Grad der Wahrscheinlichkeit, der bei einem kleinern Gegenstande wenig Zweifel übrig lassen würde, und der nur das Vorurtheil einer größern erforderlichen Kunst, als man den allgemeinen Naturgesetzen zutraut, entgegen stehen kann. Es geschieht oft: daß man dasjenige zwar nicht findet, was man eigentlich sucht, aber doch auf diesem Wege andere Vortheile, die man nicht vermuthet, antrifft. Auch ein solcher Nutze würde ein genugsamer Gewinn sein, wenn er sich dem Nachdenken anderer darböte, gesetzt auch daß die Hauptzwecke der Hypothese dabei verschwinden sollten. Ich werde die allgemeine Gravitation der Materie nach dem Newton oder seinen Nachfolgern hiebei voraussetzen. Diejenige, welche etwa durch eine Definition der Metaphysik nach ihrem Geschmacke glauben die Folgerung scharfsinniger Männer aus Beobachtung und mathematischer Schlußart zu vernichten, werden die folgende Sätze als etwas, das überdem mit der Hauptabsicht dieser Schrift nur eine entfernte Verwandtschaft hat, überschlagen können.

1.

Erweiterte Aussicht in den Inbegriff des Universum.

Die sechs Planeten mit ihren Begleitern bewegen sich in Kreisen, die nicht weit von einem gemeinschaftlichen Plane, nämlich der verlängerten Äquatorsfläche der Sonne, abweichen. Die Kometen dagegen laufen in Bahnen, die sehr weit davon abstehen, und schweifen nach allen Seiten weit von dieser Beziehungsfläche aus. Wenn nun anstatt so weniger Planeten oder Kometen einige tausend derselben zu unserer Sonnenwelt gehörten, so würde der Thierkreis als eine von unzähligen Sternen erleuchtete Zone, oder wie ein Streif, der sich in einem blassen Schimmer verliert, erscheinen, in welchem einige nähere Planeten in ziemlichem Glanze, die entfernten aber durch ihre Menge und Mattigkeit des Lichts nur eine

where the rays relate to each other on a surface far more accurately than the paths of these heavenly bodies do in the direction of the common plane of their orbital motions.

I shall attempt to set down an explanation of the origin of the universe according to general mechanical laws, not of the entire natural order but only of the large masses and their orbits which constitute the most primitive basis of nature. I hope to say a few things that will give others a start toward important considerations, though my draft is crude and not worked out. In my view, some of these things have a degree of probability which would leave little doubt with less significant objects of inquiry, and which can be opposed only by the prejudice of demanding more art than is accorded to universal laws. It often happens that one does not find exactly what he is searching for, but in this way comes upon other advantages that he had not imagined. Indeed, such an advantage would be sufficient profit if it only provided for the reflection of others, even if in this way the chief intentions of the hypothesis should disappear. I shall be presupposing the universal gravitation of matter according to Newton or his followers. Those who simply by defining metaphysics according to their own tastes think to destroy the conclusions which these perspicuous men reach both from observation and from mathematical deduction will take the following propositions as something which can be passed over as having only a remote relation to the chief intention of this work.

1.
Expanded view of the content of the universe

The six planets with their satellites move in orbits that do not deviate much from a common plane which is the extended equatorial plane of the sun. Comets, on the other hand, circulate in orbits that are very far from this and stray far on all sides from this connecting surface. Now if instead of so few planets or comets several thousand of them belonged to our solar system, the zodiac would appear as one zone illuminated by countless stars or as a streak which dies away in a weak glimmer, in which a few nearer planets would still appear in

neblichte Erscheinung darstellen würden. Denn es würden bei der Kreisbewegung, darin alle diese insgesammt um die Sonne ständen, jederzeit
in allen Theilen dieses Thierkreises einige sein, wenn gleich andre ihren
Platz verändert hätten. Dagegen würden die Kometen die Gegenden zu
beiden Seiten dieser lichten Zone in aller möglichen Zerstreuung bedecken.
Wenn wir, durch diese Erdichtung vorbereitet (in welcher wir nichts weiter
als die Menge der Körper unserer Planetenwelt in Gedanken vermehrt
haben), unsere Augen auf den weiteren Umfang des Universum richten,
so sehen wir wirklich eine lichte Zone, in welcher Sterne, ob sie zwar allem
Ansehen nach sehr ungleiche Weiten von uns haben, dennoch zu einer und
eben derselben Fläche dichter wie anderwärts gehäuft sind, dagegn die
Himmelsgegenden zu beiden Seiten mit Sternen nach aller Art der Zerstreuung bedeckt sind. Die Milchstraße, die ich meine, hat sehr genau die
Richtung eines größten Zirkels, eine Bestimmung, die aller Aufmerksamkeit werth ist, und daraus sich verstehen läßt, daß unsere Sonne und wir
mit ihr uns in demjenigen Heere der Sterne mit befinden, welches sich zu
einer gewissen gemeinschaftlichen Beziehungsfläche am meisten drängt,
und die Analogie ist hier ein sehr großer Grund zu vermuthen: daß diese
Sonnen, zu deren Zahl auch die unsrige gehört, ein Weltsystem ausmachen,
das im Großen nach ähnlichen Gesetzen geordnet ist, als unsre Planetenwelt im Kleinen; daß alle diese Sonnen sammt ihren Begleitern irgend
einen Mittelpunkt ihrer gemeinschaftlichen Kreise haben mögen, und daß
sie nur um der unermeßlichen Entfernung willen und wegen der langen
Zeit ihrer Kreisläufe, ihre Örter gar nicht zu verändern scheinen, ob zwar
dennoch bei etlichen wirklich einige Verrückung ihrer Stellen ist beobachtet
worden; daß die Bahnen dieser großen Weltkörper sich eben so auf eine
gemeinschaftliche Fläche beziehen, von der sie nicht weit abweichen, und
daß diejenige, welche mit weit geringerer Häufung die übrige Gegenden
des Himmels einnehmen, den Kometen unserer Planetenwelt darin ähn-
lich sind.

Aus diesem Begriffe, der, wie mich dünkt, die größte Wahrscheinlichkeit hat, läßt sich vermuthen, daß, wenn es mehr solche höhere Weltord-
nungen giebt, als diejenige, dazu unsre Sonne gehört, und die dem, der
in ihr seinen Stand hat, die Erscheinung der Milchstraße verschafft, in
der Tiefe des Weltraums einige derselben wie blasse, schimmernde Plätze
werden zu sehen sein und, wenn der Beziehungsplan einer solchen andern
Zusammenordnung der Firsterne schief gegen uns gestellt ist, wie elliptische

some brilliance but the more distant ones—owing to their crowding and to the weakness of their light—would present only a dim appearance. For, given the orbital motion with which all of these together are situated about the sun, there will always be some in all parts of the zodiac even if others should change their plac' ˠn the other hand, the comets would cover the regions on boι sides of this radiant zone in all possible dispersion. If we are prepared through this fiction (in which we have done no more than multiply, in thought, the number of heavenly bodies in our solar system) to pay attention to the great expanse of the universe we will see a radiant zone in which stars are more thickly clustered in one part of the same plane, though certainly to all appearances they are at highly unequal distances from us. By contrast, the heavenly regions on either side are covered with stars in every sort of dispersion. The Milky Way, which I have in mind, has precisely the track of a great circle, a characteristic worth great attention. It follows as a matter of course from this that our sun and with it we ourselves are found in that hoard of stars which for the most part crowd into a certain common connecting surface. The analogy is a very good reason here to conjecture that these suns, to whose number our own belongs, constitute a universe which in the large is regulated according to laws analogous to those of our solar system as a miniature. All these suns together with their satellites may have a center of their common orbits, and it is only because of their immeasurable distance and the long period of their orbital motions that they seem not to change their positions, although for a few to be sure, real deviation of position is noted. The orbits of these large masses are related within a common plane from which they do not greatly deviate. Those which occupy the remaining regions of the heavens, with much less frequency, are analogous in that respect to the comets of our solar system.

From this conception, which seems to me to be highly probable, it may be assumed that if there be other higher world orders, such as that to which our suns belongs [wherein] whatever is positioned in it causes the appearance of the Milky Way, some of these would be visible as dimly shimmering spots in the depths of space; and if the plane of such another

Figuren erscheinen werden, die in einem kleinen Raum aus großer Weite ein Sonnensystem, wie das von unsrer Milchstraße ist, darstellen. Und dergleichen Plätzchen hat wirklich die Astronomie schon vorlängst entdeckt, obgleich die Meinung, die man sich davon gemacht hat, sehr verschieden ist, wie man in des Herrn von Maupertuis Buche von der Figur der Sterne sehen kann.

Ich wünsche, daß diese Betrachtung mit einiger Aufmerksamkeit möchte erwogen werden; nicht allein weil der Begriff, der dadurch von der Schöpfung erwächst, erstaunlich viel rührender ist, als er sonst sein kann (indem ein unzählbares Heer Sonnen wie die unsrige ein System ausmacht, dessen Glieder durch Kreisbewegungen verbunden sind, diese Systeme selbst aber, deren vermuthlich wieder unzählige sind, wovon wir einige wahrnehmen können, selbst Glieder einer noch höhern Ordnung sein mögen), sondern auch weil selbst die Beobachtung der uns nahen Fixsterne oder vielmehr langsam wandelnden Sonnen, durch einen solchen Begriff geleitet, vielleicht manches entdecken kann, was der Aufmerksamkeit entwischt, in so fern nicht ein gewisser Plan zu untersuchen ist.

2.
Gründe für einen mechanischen Ursprung unserer Planetenwelt überhaupt.

Die Planeten bewegen sich um unsere Sonne insgesammt nach einerlei Richtung und nur mit geringer Abweichung von einem gemeinschaftlichen Beziehungsplane, welcher die Ekliptik ist, gerade so, als Körper, die durch eine Materie fortgerissen werden, die, indem sie den ganzen Raum anfüllt, ihre Bewegung wirbelnd um eine Achse verrichtet. Die Planeten sind insgesammt schwer zur Sonne hin, und die Größe des Seitenschwungs müßte eine genau abgemessene Richtigkeit haben, wenn sie dadurch in Cirkelkreisen zu laufen sollen gebracht werden; und wie bei dergleichen mechanischer Wirkung eine geometrische Genauigkeit nicht zu erwarten steht, so weichen auch alle Kreise, obzwar nicht viel, von der Cirkelrundung ab. Sie bestehen aus Materien, die nach Newtons Berechnungen, je entfernter sie von der Sonne sind, von desto minderer Dichtigkeit sind, so wie auch ein jeder es natürlich finden würde, wenn sie sich in dem Raume, darin sie schweben, von einem daselbst zerstreuten Weltstoff gebildet hätten. Denn bei der Bestrebung, womit alles zur Sonne sinkt,

aggregation of fixed stars is set obliquely to us it will appear as an elliptical figure, which represents a system of stars such as our Milky Way in a small space because of the vast distance. These very spots were in fact discovered long ago by astronomy, though the opinion held of them is very different, as can be seen from Maupertuis's book [37] on the figuration of the stars.

I wish that this observation might be considered with some attention, because the notion of the creation which grows from it is astonishingly more moving than otherwise it would be, for it makes a system out of an innumerably great throng of suns like ours, a system whose members are united by their circular motion. These systems are presumably innumerable, though we can perceive only a few of them; and they may themselves be members of a still higher order. It should also be considered because observation of the fixed stars near us or of the more slowly moving suns, if directed by such a concept, can perhaps discover much which would escape attention were there not a certain plan to be investigated.

2.
Reasons for a mechanical origin of our solar system in general

The planets move around our sun together in a single direction and with only a slight deviation from a common plane, the elliptic, exactly as bodies which speed through matter filling the entire space assume a whirling motion around an axis. All the planets gravitate towards the sun, and the magnitude of their lateral momentum must be in exact proportion if they are to be caused to rotate in circular orbits by it. As geometric precision is not to be expected with such mechanical effects all orbits deviate from circularity, though not by much. The planets consist of materials which, according to Newton's computations, are less dense the further removed they are from the sun, so that everyone would find it natural that they had formed themselves from cosmic matter scattered in the space in which they move. For with the tendency of everything to sink towards the sun, more matter of the denser

müssen die Materien dichterer Art sich mehr zur Sonne drängen und sich in der Naheit zu ihr mehr häufen, als die von leichterer Art, deren Fall wegen ihrer mindern Dichtigkeit mehr verzögert wird. Die Materie der Sonne aber ist nach des v. Buffon Bemerkung an Dichtigkeit derjenigen, die die summirte Masse aller Planeten zusammen haben würde, ziemlich gleich, welches auch mit einer mechanischen Bildung wohl zusammen stimmt, nach welcher in verschiedenen Höhen aus verschiedenen Gattungen der Elemente die Planeten sich gebildet haben mögen, sonst alle übrige aber, die diesen Raum erfüllten, vermengt auf ihren gemeinschaftlichen Mittelpunkt, die Sonne, mögen niedergestürzt sein.

Derjenige, welcher diesem ungeachtet dergleichen Bau unmittelbar in die Hand Gottes will übergeben wissen, ohne desfalls den mechanischen Gesetzen etwas zuzutrauen, ist genöthigt etwas anzuführen, weswegen er hier dasjenige nothwendig findet, was er sonst in der Naturlehre nicht leichtlich zuläßt. Er kann gar keine Zwecke nennen, warum es besser wäre, daß die Planeten vielmehr nach einer Richtung als nach verschiedenen, nahe zu einem Beziehungsplane als nach allerlei Gegenden in Kreisen liefen. Der Himmelsraum ist anjetzt leer, und bei aller dieser Bewegung würden sie einander keine Hindernisse leisten. Ich bescheide mich gerne, daß es verborgene Zwecke geben könne, die nach der gemeinen Mechanik nicht wären erreicht worden und die kein Mensch einsieht; allein es ist keinem erlaubt sie voraus zu setzen, wenn er eine Meinung darauf gründen will, ohne daß er sie anzuzeigen vermag. Wenn denn endlich Gott unmittelbar den Planeten die Wurfskraft ertheilt und ihre Kreise gestellt hätte, so ist zu vermuthen, daß sie nicht das Merkmal der Unvollkommenheit und Abweichung, welches bei jedem Product der Natur anzutreffen, an sich zeigen würden. War es gut, daß sie sich auf eine Fläche beziehen sollten, so ist zu vermuthen, er würde ihre Kreise genau darauf gestellt haben, war es gut, daß sie der Cirkelbewegung nahe kämen, so kann man glauben, ihre Bahn würde genau ein Cirkelkreis geworden sein, und es ist nicht abzusehen, weswegen Ausnahmen von der genauesten Richtigkeit selbst bei demjenigen, was eine unmittelbare göttliche Kunsthandlung sein sollte, übrig bleiben mußten.

Die Glieder der Sonnenwelt aus den entferntesten Gegenden, die Kometen, laufen sehr eccentrisch. Sie könnten, wenn es auf eine unmittelbare göttliche Handlung ankäme, eben so wohl in Cirkelkreisen bewegt sein, wenn gleich ihre Bahnen von der Ekliptik noch so sehr abweichen.

kind must press toward the sun and accumulate in its vicinity than of the lighter sort, whose fall is retarded by its more modest density. But the density of the sun's matter is, according to Buffon's study,[38] about equal to the cumulative mass the planets would have together. This is quite consistent with a mechanical formation according to which the planets may have formed themselves from different species of elements in different altitudes while all the rest of whatever filled this space crowded around the common center, the sun, and may have been thrust down.

He who, not withstanding this, wants to ascribe this same structure immediately to the hand of God and does not trust anything to mechanical laws, would have to show why in this case he finds it necessary to do something which he would not otherwise easily admit in natural science. He can cite no reason why it should be better that the planets revolve in one direction rather than in several and circulate closer to a common plane rather than in all sorts of different regions. The expanse of space is now empty and would present no barrier for any of these motions. I am readily resigned to the fact that there may be hidden purposes which could not be reached by general mechanics and which no human being can discern. But nobody is allowed to assume these for the purpose of grounding an opinion without being able to indicate them. Had God ultimately communicated the planets' initial impulse to them and immediately set them in their orbits, it may be supposed that they would not bear the marks of imperfection and deviation which are to be encountered with any natural products. Were it good that they should lie in one plane, then it may be supposed that he would have established their orbits in precisely that way; were it good that they came close to circular motion, it may be believed that their paths would have been precise circles. It is not easy to conceive why exceptions from the most precise regularity should have to remain in things that are immediately produced by a divine act.

The members of the solar system from the most distant regions, the comets, circulate very eccentrically. Were it a matter of immediate divine production, they could just as well be moved in circular orbits even if their paths deviated greatly

Die Nutzen der so großen Eccentricität werden in diesem Fall mit großer Kühnheit ersonnen, denn es ist eher begreiflich, daß ein Weltkörper, in einer Himmelsregion, welche es auch sei, in gleichem Abstande immer bewegt, die dieser Weite gemäße Einrichtung habe, als daß er auf die große Verschiedenheit der Weiten gleich vortheilhaft eingerichtet sei; und was die Vortheile, die Newton anführt, anlangt, so ist sichtbar, daß sie sonst nicht die mindeste Wahrscheinlichkeit haben, außer daß bei der einmal voraus gesetzten unmittelbaren göttlichen Anordnung sie doch zum mindesten zu einigem Vorwande eines Zweckes dienen können.

Am deutlichsten fällt dieser Fehler, den Bau der Planetenwelt göttlichen Absichten unmittelbar unter zu ordnen, in die Augen, da wo man von der mit der Zunahme der Entfernungen umgekehrt abnehmenden Dichtigkeit der Planeten Bewegungsgründe erdichten will. Der Sonnen Wirkung, heißt es, nimmt in diesem Maße ab, und es war anständig, daß die Dichtigkeit der Körper, die durch sie sollten erwärmt werden, auch dieser proportionirlich eingerichtet würde. Nun ist bekannt, daß die Sonne nur eine geringe Tiefe unter die Oberfläche eines Weltkörpers wirkt, und aus ihrem Einflusse denselben zu erwärmen kann also nicht auf die Dichtigkeit des ganzen Klumpens geschlossen werden. Hier ist die Folgerung aus dem Zwecke viel zu groß. Das Mittel, nämlich die verminderte Dichtigkeit des ganzen Klumpens, begreift eine Weitläuftigkeit der Anstalt, welche für die Größe des Zwecks überflüssig und unnöthig ist.

In allen natürlichen Hervorbringungen, in so fern sie auf Wohlgereimtheit, Ordnung und Nutzen hinauslaufen, zeigen sich zwar Übereinstimmungen mit göttlichen Absichten, aber auch Merkmale des Ursprungs aus allgemeinen Gesetzen, deren Folgen sich noch viel weiter als auf solchen einzelnen Fall erstrecken und demnach in jeder einzelnen Wirkung Spuren von einer Vermengung solcher Gesetze an sich zeigen, die nicht lediglich auf dieses einzige Product gerichtet waren. Um deswillen finden auch Abweichungen von der größt möglichen Genauigkeit in Ansehung eines besondern Zwecks statt. Dagegen wird eine unmittelbar übernatürliche Anstalt, darum weil ihre Ausführung gar nicht die Folgen aus allgemeinern Wirkungsgesetzen der Materie voraus setzt, auch nicht durch besondere sich einmengende Nebenfolgen derselben entstellt werden, sondern den Plan der äußerst möglichen Richtigkeit genau zu Stande bringen. In den näheren Theilen der Planetenwelt zum gemeinschaftlichen Mittelpunkte ist eine größere Annäherung zur völligen Ordnung und abgemesse-

from the elliptic. The utilities of such a great eccentricity will be invented with great boldness in this case. For that a heavenly body, in whatever region of space it may be, will always move conformably to its distance is more understandable than that it be arranged with equal advantage for the great difference of distance. So far as the advantages that Newton cites are concerned, it is obvious that they do not have the slightest probability except that at least they can serve as the pretext of a goal for the immediate divine arrangement already assumed.

The defect of immediately ordering the construction of the universe under divine intention becomes most apparent where motives must be invented for the decrease in the density of the planets with an increase in the distance. The efficacy of the sun, it is said, is decreased to this extent, and it would be appropriate were the density of those bodies to be warmed by it adjusted proportionately. Now, it is known that the sun is effective to only a slight depth under the surface of a planet, and so nothing may be concluded about the density of the entire mass from the sun's influence in warming these surfaces. The consequence is much too extensive here for the purpose. The means, namely the diminished density of the entire mass, comprehends a widely ramified cause which is superfluous and unnecessary for the extent of the purpose.

All natural productions show agreement with divine intentions insofar as they tend towards harmonious adaptation, order, and utility, to be sure; but they also show marks of universal laws whose consequences extend much farther than such merely particular cases and accordingly in every particular effect show traces of a collection of such laws that were not simply directed toward this single product alone. For that reason deviations from the greatest possible exactitude in respect to a particular purpose obtain. On the other hand, an immediately supernatural provision would achieve exactly the plan of greatest possible precision, for its operation in no way presupposes the consequence of more general laws of the action of matter and is not marred by the interference of secondary consequences of the law. In parts of the solar system near the common center, there is a greater approach to full order and

nen Genauigkeit, die nach den Grenzen des Systems hinaus, oder weit von dem Beziehungsplane zu den Seiten in Regellofigkeit und Abweichun= gen ausartet, gerade so wie es von einer Verfassung zu erwarten ist, die mechanischen Ursprungs ist. Bei einer unmittelbar göttlichen Anordnung können niemals unvollständig erreichte Zwecke angetroffen werden, sondern allenthalben zeigt sich die größte Richtigkeit und Abgemessenheit, wie man unter andern am Bau der Thiere gewahr wird.

3.

Kurzer Abriß der wahrscheinlichsten Art, wie ein Planeten= system mechanisch hat gebildet werden können.

Die eben jetzt angeführte Beweisgründe für einen mechanischen Ur= sprung sind so wichtig, daß selbst nur einige derselben vorlängst alle Natur= forscher bewogen haben, die Ursache der Planetenkreise in natürlichen Bewegkräften zu suchen, vornehmlich weil die Planeten in eben derselben Richtung, worin die Sonne sich um ihre Achse schwingt, um sie in Kreisen laufen, und ihre Bahnen so sehr nahe mit dieser ihrer Äquatorsfläche zu= sammen treffen. Newton war der große Zerstörer aller dieser Wirbel, an denen man gleichwohl noch lange nach seinen Demonstrationen hing, wie an dem Beispiel des berühmten Herrn von Mairan zu sehen ist. Die sichere und überzeugende Beweisthümer der Newtonischen Weltweisheit zeigten augenscheinlich, daß so etwas, wie die Wirbel sein sollten, welche die Planeten herum führten, gar nicht am Himmel angetroffen werde und daß so ganz und gar kein Strom solcher Flüssigkeit in diesen Räumen sei, daß selbst die Kometenschweife quer durch alle diese Kreise ihre unver= rückte Bewegung fortsetzen. Es war sicher hieraus zu schließen: daß, so wie der Himmelsraum jetzt leer oder unendlich dünne ist, keine mechanische Ursache statt finden könne, die den Planeten ihre Kreisbewegung ein= drückte. Allein sofort alle mechanische Gesetze vorbei gehen und durch eine kühne Hypothese Gott unmittelbar die Planeten werfen zu lassen, damit sie in Verbindung mit ihrer Schwere sich in Kreisen bewegen sollten, war ein zu weiter Schritt, als daß er innerhalb dem Bezirke der Weltweisheit hätte bleiben können. Es fällt alsbald in die Augen, daß noch ein Fall übrig bleibe, wo mechanische Ursachen dieser Verfassung möglich seien: wenn nämlich der Raum des Planetenbaues, der anjetzt leer ist, vorher erfüllt war, um eine Gemeinschaft der Bewegkräfte durch alle Gegenden

exact precision, which degenerates into irregularity and deviations towards the limits of the system or on the sides far from the plane, precisely what would be expected where the composition is mechanical in origin. In an arrangement immediately from God incompletely achieved purposes would never be encountered; rather, maximum proportion and exactitude would be evidenced everywhere as is seen, among other places in the structure of animals.

3.
Brief abstract of the most probable way in which the planetary system could have been mechanically formed

The arguments cited for a mechanical origin are so important that long ago only some of them induced all natural scientists to seek the causes of planetary orbits in natural impetus to motion, principally because the planets revolve through their orbits in the very same direction as the sun swings around on its axis and their courses so very nearly coincide with those of the sun's equatorial surface. Newton was the great destroyer of all those vortices to which people nevertheless still cling long after his demonstrations—as the example of the famous Mairan [39] shows. The certain and convincing arguments of the Newtonian philosophy showed clearly that something which leads the planets about, such as the vortices are supposed to do, is simply not to be found in the heavens, and that there is absolutely no current of such fluidity in these spaces, for even the comet's tails continue their undisturbed motion straight through all of these orbits. It was safe to conclude this much: that since space is now empty or infinitely thin, no mechanical cause can impress their orbital motion upon the planets. But immediately to pass over all mechanical laws and by bold hypothesis to allow God to set the planets in motion so that they move in proportion to their weight was too great a step to allow him to remain within the domain of philosophy. It is apparent that there remains one situation where mechanical causes of this composition might yet be possible—that is if the space of planetary structure which now is empty previously was filled in order to provide a community of moving forces through all the

dieses Bezirks, worin die Anziehung unserer Sonne herrscht, zu veran=
lassen.

Und hier kann ich diejenige Beschaffenheit anzeigen, welche die einzige
mögliche ist, unter der eine mechanische Ursache der Himmelsbewegungen
statt findet, welches zur Rechtfertigung einer Hypothese ein beträchtlicher
Umstand ist, dessen man sich nur selten wird rühmen können. Da die Räume
anjetzt leer sind, so müssen sie ehedem erfüllt gewesen sein, sonst hat niemals
eine ausgebreitete Wirkung der in Kreisen treibenden Bewegkräfte statt
finden können. Und es muß demnach diese verbreitete Materie sich hernach
auf die Himmelskörper versammelt haben, das ist, wenn ich es näher be=
trachte, diese Himmelskörper selbst werden sich aus dem verbreiteten Grund=
stoffe in den Räumen des Sonnenbaues gebildet haben, und die Bewegung,
die die Theilchen ihres Zusammensatzes im Zustande der Zerstreuung
hatten, ist bei ihnen nach der Vereinbarung in abgesonderte Massen übrig
geblieben. Seitdem sind diese Räume leer. Sie enthalten keine Materie,
die unter diesen Körpern zur Mittheilung des Kreisschwunges dienen
könnte. Aber sie sind es nicht immer gewesen, und wir werden Bewegun=
gen gewahr, wovon jetzt keine natürliche Ursachen statt finden können, die
aber Überbleibsel des allerältesten rohen Zustandes der Natur sind.

Von dieser Bemerkung will ich nur noch einen Schritt thun, um
mich einem wahrscheinlichen Begriff von der Entstehungsart dieser großen
Massen und der Ursache ihrer Bewegungen zu nähern, indem ich die
gründlichere Vollführung eines geringen Schattenrisses dem forschenden
Leser selbst überlasse. Wenn demnach der Stoff zu Bildung der Sonne
und aller Himmelskörper, die ihrer mächtigen Anziehung zu Gebote stehen,
durch den ganzen Raum der Planetenwelt zerstreuet war, und es war ir=
gend in dem Orte, den jetzt der Klumpe der Sonne einnimmt, Materie
von stärkeren Anziehungskräften, so entstand eine allgemeine Senkung
hiezu, und die Anziehung des Sonnenkörpers wuchs mit ihrer Masse. Es
ist leicht zu vermuthen, daß in dem allgemeinen Fall der Partikeln selbst
von den entlegensten Gegenden des Weltbaues die Materien dichterer Art
in den tiefern Gegenden, wo sich alles zum gemeinschaftlichen Mittelpunkte
hindrängte, sich nach dem Maße werden gehäuft haben, als sie dem Mittel=
punkte näher waren, obzwar in allen Regionen Materien von allerlei Art
der Dichtigkeit waren. Denn nur die Theilchen von der schwersten Gattung
konnten das größte Vermögen haben in diesem Chaos durch das Gemenge
der leichteren zu bringen, um in größere Naheit zum Gravitationspunkte

regions of this domain in which the attraction of sun dominates.

And I can indicate here that condition which is the only one possible in which a mechanical cause of motion of the heavens occurs. This is a significant circumstance for the substantiation of an hypothesis of which one can seldom boast. Where spaces are now empty they must have once been full, for otherwise there could never have obtained an extensive efficacy of moving forces in setting the planets in orbits. And accordingly the widely dispersed matter subsequently must have collected on heavenly bodies; or examined a bit more fully, the heavenly bodies must have formed themselves out of the widely dispersed basic matter in the region of the sun, and the motion that the particles had in their dispersed condition has remained in the separated masses after their coalescence. Since that time these spaces have been empty. They contain no matter which could serve to communicate orbital motion of these bodies. But they have not always been this way, and we note motions of which no natural cause could now take place, but which are a carry-over from the most primitive, virgin state of nature.

I will go just a step further from these observations in order to come closer to a notion of the probable way in which these great masses originated and the causes of their motions, whilst leaving the more thorough execution of a sketchy outline to the inquiring reader himself. Accordingly, when the matter of the formation of the sun and of all the heavenly bodies that are at the disposal of its powerful attraction was scattered through the entire planetary space, there was matter with stronger powers of attraction somewhere in the area now occupied by the bulk of the sun. So a general inclination towards [such matter] developed, and the power of attraction of the sun's body grew with its mass. It is easy to conjecture that in the general case of particles, even from the most remote regions of the universe where everything pressed toward a common center, matter of a denser kind will have accumulated in the innermost regions according to the distance from the center, though matter of every kind of density was in all regions. Only the heaviest sorts of particles could have the greatest capacity of pressing through the aggregation of lighter ones in this chaos to arrive at the maximum proximity to the center of gravity. In the motion,

zu gelangen. In den Bewegungen, die von verschiedentlich hohem Fall in der Sphäre umher entsprangen, konnte niemals der Widerstand der einander hindernden Partikeln so vollkommen gleich sein, daß nicht nach irgend einer Seite die erworbene Geschwindigkeiten in eine Abbeugung ausschlagen sollten. Und in diesem Umstande zeigt sich eine sehr gemeine Regel der Gegenwirkung der Materien, daß sie einander so lange treiben oder lenken und einschränken, bis sie sich die mindeste Hinderniß leisten; welchem gemäß die Seitenbewegungen sich endlich in eine gemeinschaft= liche Umdrehung nach einer und eben derselben Richtung vereinigen mußten. Die Partikeln demnach, woraus die Sonne gebildet wurde, kamen auf ihr schon mit dieser Seitenbewegung an, und die Sonne, aus diesem Stoffe gebildet, mußte eine Umdrehung in eben derselben Richtung haben.

Es ist aber aus den Gesetzen der Gravitation klar: daß in diesem herumgeschwungenen Weltstoffe alle Theile müssen bestrebt gewesen sein, den Plan, der in der Richtung ihres gemeinschaftlichen Umschwunges durch den Mittelpunkt der Sonne geht, und der nach unseren Schlüssen mit der Äquatorsfläche dieses Himmelskörpers zusammentrifft, zu durch= schneiden, wofern sie nicht schon sich in demselben befanden. Demnach werden alle diese Theile vornehmlich nahe zur Sonne ihre größte Häufung in dem Raume haben, der der verlängerten Äquatorsfläche derselben nahe ist. Endlich ist es auch sehr natürlich, daß, da die Partikeln einander so lange hindern oder beschleunigen, mit einem Worte, einander stoßen oder treiben müssen, bis eines des andern Bewegung gar nicht mehr stören kann, zuletzt alles auf den Zustand ausschlage, daß nur diejenige Theil= chen schweben bleiben, die gerade den Grad des Seitenschwunges haben, der erfordert wird in dem Abstande, darin sie von der Sonne sind, der Gravitation das Gleichgewicht zu leisten, damit ein jegliches sich in freier Bewegung in concentrischen Cirkeln herumschwinge. Diese Schnelligkeit ist eine Wirkung des Falles und die Bewegung zur Seiten eine Folge des so lange dauernden Gegenstoßes, bis alles in die Verfassung der mindesten Hindernisse sich von selbst geschickt hat. Die übrigen Theilchen, die eine solche abgemessene Genauigkeit nicht erreichen konnten, müssen bei all= mählig abnehmender Bewegung zum Mittelpunkte der allgemeinen Gra= vitation gesunken sein, um den Klumpen der Sonne zu vermehren, der demnach eine Dichtigkeit haben wird, welche der von den übrigen Mate= rien in dem um sie befindlichen Raume im Durchschnitte genommen ziem= lich gleich ist; so doch, daß nach den angeführten Umständen ihre Masse

which developed from tumbling from different heights through the sphere, the resistance of the particles hindering each other could never be so completely equal that the speed achieved might not be extinguished in deflection toward some one side. And in this event a very common rule of the reciprocal effect of matter is demonstrated: that they [the particles] strike against, bend, and restrict each other until they afford the least resistance which must finally unite them in a common revolution in one and the same direction in accordance with lateral motion. Accordingly, the particles out of which the sun was constituted came to it with their lateral motion, and the sun formed from this matter must have a revolution in that very same direction.

Now, it is clear from the laws of gravity that all the parts of this swirling cosmic matter must attempt to cut through the plane that runs in the direction of their common rotation through the midpoint of the sun and, according to our conclusions, intersect the equatorial surface of this heavenly body in so far as they are not already in it. Thus all these particles, especially those near the sun, will have their greatest accumulation in the space near the extended equatorial plane itself. Finally, it is also quite natural that, since the particles must so long hinder or accelerate each other—in a word, push or jostle—until one can no longer interrupt the motion of the other, everything finally ends in the state where only those particles remain floating which have the exact degree of lateral motion required to achieve equilibrium with gravitation at the distance they are from the sun. Thus each will swing round in concentric circles in free motion. This velocity is an effect of the fall, and the motion away from the plane is a consequence of the opposition which has long endured until everything in the structure spontaneously has achieved the least resistance. The remaining particles, which could not achieve such a precise exactitude, must have sunk with gradually decreased motion to the center of universal gravitation, there to increase the mass of the sun, which thus will have a density that is on the average nearly equal to that of the rest of the matter in the space about it. Yet its mass will, according to the conditions just indicated, necessarily far exceed that of the collection of matter which

nothwendig die Menge der Materie, die in dem Bezirke um sie schweben geblieben, weit übertreffen wird.

In diesem Zustande, der mir natürlich zu sein scheint, da ein ver=
breiteter Stoff zu Bildung verschiedener Himmelskörper in einem engen
Raum zunächst der verlängerten Fläche des Sonnenäquators von desto
mehrer Dichtigkeit, je näher dem Mittelpunkte, und allenthalben mit einem
Schwunge, der in diesem Abstande zur freien Cirkelbewegung hinlänglich
war, nach den Centralgesetzen bis in große Weiten um die Sonne sich
herumschwang, wenn man da setzt, daß sich aus diesen Theilchen Planeten
bildeten, so kann es nicht fehlen, daß sie nicht Schwungskräfte haben soll=
ten, dadurch sie in Kreisen, die den Cirkeln sehr nahe kommen, sich be=
wegen sollten, ob sie gleich etwas davon abweichen, weil sie sich aus Theil=
chen von unterschiedlicher Höhe sammleten. Es ist eben so wohl sehr natür=
lich, daß diejenige Planeten, die sich in großen Höhen bilden, (wo der
Raum um sie viel größer ist, der da veranlaßt, daß der Unterschied der
Geschwindigkeit der Partikeln die Kraft, womit sie zum Mittelpunkte des
Planeten gezogen werden, übertreffe) daselbst auch größere Klumpen als
nahe zur Sonne gewinnen. Die Übereinstimmung mit vielen andern
Merkwürdigkeiten der Planetenwelt übergehe ich, weil sie sich von selbst
darbietet.*) In den entlegensten Theilen des Systems und vornehmlich
in großen Weiten vom Beziehungsplane werden die sich bildende Körper,
die Kometen, diese Regelmäßigkeit nicht haben können. Und so wird der
Raum der Planetenwelt leer werden, nachdem sich alles in abgesonderte
Massen vereinbart hat. Doch können noch in späterer Epoche Partikeln
aus den äußersten Grenzen dieser Anziehungssphäre herabgesunken sein,
die forthin jederzeit frei im Himmelsraume in Kreisen sich um die Sonne
bewegen mögen: Materien von der äußersten Dünnigkeit und vielleicht
der Stoff, woraus das Zodiakallicht besteht.

4.
Anmerkung.

Die Absicht dieser Betrachtung ist vornehmlich, um ein Beispiel von
dem Verfahren zu geben, zu welchem uns unsere vorige Beweise berechtigt

---

*) Die Bildung eines kleineren Systems, das als ein Theil zu der Planeten=
welt gehört, wie des Jupiters und Saturns, imgleichen die Achsendrehungen dieser
Himmelskörper werden wegen der Analogie unter dieser Erklärung mit begriffen.

10*

remains circulating in regions around it.

Since the dispersed material for the constitution of the different heavenly bodies was initially in the narrow space of the extended plane of the sun's equatorial surface, and of. greater density the nearer it was to the midpoint, and everywhere with a momentum that was adequate for free circular motion at this distance, it whirled about the sun at great distances according to the laws of central force.[40] In this situation it seems natural to me that if it be assumed that the planets formed themselves from these particles, they cannot fail to have motive forces which move them in very nearly circular orbits, though they deviate somewhat from circularity because they are composed from particles at different altitudes. It is likewise very natural that those planets which form themselves in great altitudes (where the space about them is much greater, causing the difference in the speed of the particles to exceed the force with which they are attracted to the midpoint of the planet) win to themselves even greater masses than those near the sun. I will pass over here the agreement with many other noteworthy features of the solar system since they emerge themselves.*

In the most remote parts of the system, and principally at great remove from elliptic, the self-forming bodies, the comets, cannot have this regularity. And so the space of the solar system is emptied after everything has collected in separated masses. Yet in still later epochs particles from the most distant borders of this sphere of attraction may sink and move freely in the heavenly space in orbits about the sun: matter of the thinnest sort and perhaps that of which the zodiacal light consists.

4.

Note.

The intention of this observation is principally to give an

*The formation of a smaller system that belongs as a part of the solar system, such as that of Jupiter or Saturn, as well as the rotation of these heavenly bodies about their axis, may be understood on analogy with this explanation.

haben, da man nämlich die ungegründete Besorgniß wegschafft, als wenn eine jede Erklärung einer großen Anstalt der Welt aus allgemeinen Naturgesetzen den boshaften Feinden der Religion eine Lücke öffne, in ihre Bollwerke zu dringen. Meiner Meinung nach hat die angeführte Hypothese zum mindesten Gründe genug für sich, um Männer von ausgebreiteter Einsicht zu einer nähern Prüfung des darin vorgestellten Plans, der nur ein grober Umriß ist, einzuladen. Mein Zweck, in so fern er diese Schrift betrifft, ist erfüllt, wenn man, durch das Zutrauen zu der Regelmäßigkeit und Ordnung, die aus allgemeinen Naturgesetzen fließen kann, vorbereitet, nur der natürlichen Weltweisheit ein freieres Feld öffnet und eine Erklärungsart, wie diese oder eine andere als möglich und mit der Erkenntniß eines weisen Gottes wohl zusammenstimmend anzusehen kann bewogen werden.

Es wäre übrigens der philosophischen Bestrebung wohl würdig, nachdem die Wirbel, das beliebte Werkzeug so vieler Systeme, außerhalb der Sphäre der Natur auf des Miltons Limbus der Eitelkeit verwiesen worden, daß man gleichwohl gehörig forschte, ob nicht die Natur ohne Erdichtung besonderer Kräfte selber etwas darböte, was die durchgehends nach einerlei Gegend gerichtete Schwungsbewegung der Planeten erklären könnte, da die andere von den Centralkräften in der Gravitation als einem dauerhaften Verbande der Natur gegeben ist. Zum wenigsten entfernt sich der von uns entworfene Plan nicht von der Regel der Einheit, denn selbst diese Schwungskraft wird als eine Folge aus der Gravitation abgeleitet, wie es zufälligen Bewegungen anständig ist, denn diese sollen als Erfolge aus den der Materie auch in Ruhe beiwohnenden Kräften hergeleitet werden.

Überdies merke ich an, daß das atomistische System des Demokritus und Epikurs unerachtet des ersten Anscheins von Ähnlichkeit doch eine ganz verschiedene Beziehung zu der Folgerung auf einen Urheber der Welt habe, als der Entwurf des unsrigen. In jenem war die Bewegung ewig und ohne Urheber und der Zusammenstoß, der reiche Quell so vieler Ordnung, ein Ungefähr und ein Zufall, wozu sich nirgend ein Grund fand. Hier führt ein erkanntes und wahres Gesetz der Natur nach einer sehr begreiflichen Voraussetzung mit Nothwendigkeit auf Ordnung, und da hier ein bestimmender Grund eines Ausschlags auf Regelmäßigkeit angetroffen wird und etwas, was die Natur im Gleise der Wohlgereimtheit und Schönheit erhält, so wird man auf die Vermuthung eines Grundes geführt, aus

example of the procedure to which our previous proofs have entitled us for disposing of the baseless fear that every explanation of a great constitution of the world from universal natural laws would open a breach for the evil enemies of religion to pierce its bulwarks. In my view the hypothesis cited has at least sufficient evidence to invite men of extensive insight to a further examination of the plan suggested by it, which is only a crude outline. My intention so far as this treatise is concerned is achieved if, disposed to faith in the regularity and order that can follow from natural laws, one can just be induced to see a wider field opened to natural philosophy and to regard an explanation such as this one or some other as possible and consistent with the knowledge of a wise God.

For the rest it would be quite worthy of philosophical effort if, after the vortex which is the favorite tool of so many systems has been exiled from the sphere of nature to Milton's limbo of conceit,[41] one were to examine sufficiently whether nature itself does not provide something that can explain the [orbital] motion of the planets in the same direction without the invention of special forces, since the other of the fundamental forces in gravitation is given as an enduring bond of nature. At least the plan such as the one we have drafted does not deviate from the rule of unity, for even this [orbital] power [*die Schwungskraft*][42] is deduced as a consequence of gravitation, as is appropriate for contingent motions, since these are to be derived as results of forces inherent in matter even at rest.

Additionally I note that the atomistic system of Democritus and Epicurus has a totally different relation to the inference to the creator of the world than the outline of ours does, notwithstanding the first appearance of similarities. In the former, motion was eternal and without creator, and mutual impact, the rich source of so much order, was a coincidence and an accident for which there is nowhere a reason. Here an acknowledged and true law of nature leads of necessity to order according to a highly reasonable assumption. And since a determinate reason for a conclusion in regularity is encountered here, and something that nature contains in the way of harmonious adaptation and beauty, one is led to the

dem die Nothwendigkeit der Beziehung zur Vollkommenheit kann ver=
standen werden.

Um indessen noch durch ein ander Beispiel begreiflich zu machen, wie
die Wirkung der Gravitation in der Verbindung zerstreuter Elemente
Regelmäßigkeit und Schönheit hervor zu bringen nothwendiger Weise be=
stimmt sei, so will ich eine Erklärung von der mechanischen Erzeugungsart
des Saturnusringes beifügen, die, wie mir dünkt, so viel Wahrscheinlich=
keit hat, als man es von einer Hypothese nur erwarten kann. Man räume
mir nur ein: daß Saturn in dem ersten Weltalter mit einer Atmosphäre
umgeben gewesen, dergleichen man an verschiednen Kometen gesehen, die
sich der Sonne nicht sehr nähern und ohne Schweife erscheinen, daß die
Theilchen des Dunstkreises von diesem Planeten (dem wir eine Achsen=
drehung zugestehen wollen) aufgestiegen sind, und daß in der Folge diese
Dünste, es sei darum, weil der Planet verkühlte, oder aus andern Ur=
sachen, anfingen sich wieder zu ihm nieder zu senken, so erfolgt das übrige
mit mechanischer Richtigkeit. Denn da alle Theilchen von dem Punkte der
Oberfläche, da sie aufgestiegen, eine diesem Orte gleiche Geschwindigkeit
haben müssen, um die Achse des Planeten sich zu bewegen, so müssen alle
vermittelst dieses Seitenschwungs bestrebt gewesen sein, nach den Regeln
der Centralkräfte freie Kreise um den Saturn zu beschreiben.*) Es müssen
aber alle diejenige Theilchen, deren Geschwindigkeit nicht gerade den Grad
hat, die der Attraction der Höhe, wo sie schweben, durch Centrifugalkraft
genau das Gleichgewicht leistet, einander nothwendig stoßen und ver=
zögern, bis nur diejenige, die in freier Cirkelbewegung nach Centralgesetzen
umlaufen können, um den Saturn in Kreisen bewegt, übrig bleiben, die
übrige aber nach und nach auf dessen Oberfläche zurück fallen. Nun müssen
nothwendig alle diese Cirkelbewegungen die verlängerte Fläche des Sa=
turnusäquators durchschneiden, welches einem jeden, der die Centralgesetze
weiß, bekannt ist; also werden sich endlich um den Saturn die übrige
Theilchen seiner vormaligen Atmosphäre zu einer zirkelrunden Ebene
drängen, die den verlängerten Äquator dieses Planeten einnimmt, und
deren äußerster Rand durch eben dieselbe Ursache, die bei den Kometen
die Grenze der Atmosphäre bestimmt, auch hier abgeschnitten ist. Dieser

---

*) Saturn bewegt sich um seine Achse, nach der Voraussetzung. Ein jedes
Theilchen, das von ihm aufsteigt, muß daher eben dieselbe Seitenbewegung haben
und sie, zu welcher Höhe es auch gelangt, daselbst fortsetzen.

assumption of a ground from which the necessity of the relation to perfection may be understood.

But in order to make understandable by another example how the effects of gravity may be determined to produce regularity and beauty in a necessary fashion in the combination of dispersed elements, I want to add an explanation of the mechanical generation of Saturn's rings. This, it seems to me, has as much probability as can ever be expected from an hypothesis. One needs only to grant me that in the primal state Saturn was enveloped with an atmosphere like that seen around different comets which do not approach very close to the sun and appear without tails; and that particles of the atmosphere of this planet (for which we shall admit motion about its axis) arose; and subsequently that this dust—perhaps because the planet cooled off or for some other reason—began to settle toward the planet again. Then the rest follows with mechanical precision. For since all the particles which ascend from a point on the surface must have a speed equal to that of this place in order to move around the axis, all of them must have striven by means of this lateral motion to describe free circles around Saturn* according to the rules of the central forces. But all those particles whose speed is not of the exact degree to achieve equilibrium with the attraction of centrifugal force at the altitude in which they circulate must necessarily shove against and retard each other until only those which can circulate in free circular motion around Saturn according to the laws of the central force can remain and the rest gradually fall back to the surface. Now all the circular motions must necessarily intersect the extended plane of Saturn's equator, which is clear to everyone who knows the laws of the central force. Thus the remaining parts of Saturn's former atmosphere are forced into a circular plane that occupies the extended equator of this planet, its outermost edge being cut off by the same cause that determines the limits of the atmosphere of comets. This limbus

*Saturn moves around its axis, according to this assumption. Every particle that ascends from it must thus have the same lateral motion and continue it at whatever height it may reach.

Limbus von frei bewegtem Weltstoffe muß nothwendig ein Ring werden, oder vielmehr es können gedachte Bewegungen auf keine andre Figur als die eines Ringes ausschlagen. Denn da sie alle ihre Geschwindigkeit zur Cirkelbewegung nur von den Punkten der Oberfläche des Saturns haben können, von da sie aufgestiegen sind, so müssen diejenige, die von dessen Äquator sich erhoben haben, die größte Schnelligkeit besitzen. Da nun unter allen Weiten von dessen Mittelpunkte nur eine ist, wo diese Geschwindigkeit gerade zur Cirkelbewegung taugt, und in jeder kleinern Entfernung zu schwach ist, so wird ein Cirkelkreis in diesem Limbus aus dem Mittelpunkt des Saturns gezogen werden können, innerhalb welchem alle Partikeln zur Oberfläche dieses Planeten niederfallen müssen, alle übrige aber zwischen diesem gedachten Cirkel und dem seines äußersten Randes (folglich die in einem ringförmichten Raum enthaltene) werden forthin frei schwebend in Cirkelkreisen um ihn in Bewegung bleiben.

Nach einer solchen Auflösung gelangt man auf Folgen, durch die die Zeit der Achsendrehung des Saturns gegeben ist, und zwar mit so viel Wahrscheinlichkeit, als man diesen Gründen einräumt, wodurch sie zugleich bestimmt wird. Denn weil die Partikeln des inneren Randes eben dieselbe Geschwindigkeit haben wie diejenige, die ein Punkt des Saturnusäquators hat, und überdem diese Geschwindigkeit nach den Gesetzen der Gravitation den zur Cirkelbewegung gehörigen Grad hat, so kann man aus dem Verhältnisse des Abstandes eines der Saturnus-Trabanten zu dem Abstande des innern Randes des Ringes vom Mittelpunkte des Planeten, imgleichen aus der gegebenen Zeit des Umlaufs des Trabanten die Zeit des Umschwungs der Theilchen in dem inwendigen Rande finden, aus dieser aber und dem Verhältniß des kleinsten Durchmessers vom Ringe zu dem des Planeten dieses seine Achsendrehung. Und so findet sich durch Rechnung: daß Saturn sich in 5 Stunden und ungefähr 40 Minuten um seine Achse drehen müsse, welches, wenn man die Analogie mit den übrigen Planeten hiebei zu Rathe zieht, mit der Zeit der Umwendung derselben wohl zu harmoniren scheint.

Und so mag denn die Voraussetzung der kometischen Atmosphäre, die der Saturn im Anfange möchte gehabt haben, zugestanden werden oder nicht, so bleibt diejenige Folgerung, die ich zur Erläuterung meines Hauptsatzes daraus ziehe, wie mich dünkt, ziemlich sicher: daß, wenn ein solcher Dunstkreis um ihn gewesen, die mechanische Erzeugung eines schwebenden Ringes eine nothwendige Folge daraus hat sein müssen, und daß daher

of freely moving cosmic matter must become a ring, or rather the aforementioned motion can result in no other figure than a ring. For since they can inherit their speed for circular motion only from the points of the surface of Saturn from which they have ascended, those which have ascended from the equator must have the greatest speed. Since among all the distances there is only one where the speed serves exactly for circular motion, and is too weak in every lesser distance, a circle can be derived from the midpoint of Saturn in this limbus. Inside of all this all particles must fall to the surface; but all of the others, between the aforementioned circle and its outermost limit (and thus contained within a ringed space), will continue in motion around it in circular orbit.

According to such a solution one arrives at consequences through which the time of Saturn's rotation is given, and with as much probability as is granted the grounds through which it is determined. For since these particles of the inner border have the same velocity as that of a point on Saturn's equator, and moreover since this velocity is sufficient to achieve circular motion according to the laws of gravity, one may find the time of the revolution of the particles in the inner border from the relation of the distance of one of the satellites of Saturn to the distance of the inner border of the ring from the center of the planet; similarly, from the time taken for the revolution of the satellite one may infer the time for the revolution of particles in the inner border of the ring. And from this and from the relation of the smallest diameter from the ring to that of the planet, its revolution about its axis [may be found]. By computation it is found that Saturn must turn around its axis in five hours and approximately 40 minutes, which, considering the analogy with the rest of the planets, seems to harmonize well with the time of their rotations.

And so whether the assumption of a comet-like atmosphere that Saturn may have had at the outset be admitted or not, the consequence that I have deduced for explication of my chief proposition seem to me to remain rather safe: that if there was such an atmosphere about Saturn, the mechanical generation of a floating ring must have been a necessary consequence of it,

der Ausschlag der allgemeinen Gesetzen überlassenen Natur selbst aus dem Chaos auf Regelmäßigkeit abziele.

Achte Betrachtung.
Von der göttlichen Allgenugsamkeit.

Die Summe aller dieser Betrachtungen führt uns auf einen Begriff von dem höchsten Wesen, der alles in sich faßt, was man nur zu gedenken vermag, wenn Menschen, aus Staube gemacht, es wagen ausspähende Blicke hinter den Vorhang zu werfen, der die Geheimnisse des Unerforsch= lichen für erschaffene Augen verbirgt. Gott ist allgenugsam. Was da ist, es sei möglich oder wirklich, das ist nur etwas, in so fern es durch ihn ge= geben ist. Eine menschliche Sprache kann den Unendlichen so zu sich selbst reden lassen: Ich bin von Ewigkeit zu Ewigkeit, außer mir ist nichts, ohne in so fern es durch mich etwas ist. Dieser Gedanke, der erhabenste unter allen, ist noch sehr vernachlässigt, oder mehrentheils gar nicht berührt worden. Das, was sich in den Möglichkeiten der Dinge zu Vollkommenheit und Schönheit in vortrefflichen Planen darbietet, ist als ein für sich nothwendiger Gegenstand der göttlichen Weisheit, aber nicht selbst als eine Folge von diesem unbegreiflichen Wesen angesehen worden. Man hat die Abhängigkeit anderer Dinge blos auf ihr Dasein eingeschränkt, wodurch ein großer Antheil an dem Grunde von so viel Vollkommenheit jener obersten Natur entzogen und ich weiß nicht welchem ewigen Undinge beigemessen wird.

Fruchtbarkeit eines einzigen Grundes an viel Folgen, Zusammen= stimmung und Schicklichkeit der Naturen, nach allgemeinen Gesetzen ohne öftern Widerstreit in einem regelmäßigen Plane zusammen zu passen, müssen zuvörderst in den Möglichkeiten der Dinge angetroffen werden, und nur alsdann kann Weisheit thätig sein sie zu wählen. Welche Schran= ken, die dem Unabhängigen aus einem fremden Grunde gesetzt sein wür= den, wenn selbst diese Möglichkeiten nicht in ihm gegründet wären? Und was für ein unverständliches Ungefähr, daß sich in diesem Felde der Mög= lichkeit ohne Voraussetzung irgend eines Existirenden Einheit und frucht= bare Zusammenpassung findet, dadurch das Wesen von den höchsten Gra= den der Macht und Weisheit, wenn jene äußere Verhältnisse mit seinem innern Vermögen verglichen werden, sich im Stande sieht große Voll=

and that therefore the outcome of nature left to universal laws is aimed at the evolution of regularity from chaos.

OBSERVATION EIGHT
The Total Sufficiency of the Divine

The sum of all these observations leads us to the notion of a supreme being which comprehends within itself everything that may only be conjectured when men, fashioned from the dust, dare to cast curious glances behind the curtain which veils the mysteries of the inscrutable from the sight of creatures. God is all sufficient. Whatever is, be it possible or actual, is something only insofar as it is given through him. A human language allows the infinite to speak of himself thusly: "I am from eternity to eternity. Apart from me nothing is without being something through me." This concept, the most sublime of all, is still much neglected, or for the most part has not been touched at all. That which provides for perfection and excellence in the possibilities of things in superb plans is itself a necessary object of divine wisdom, but it has not been regarded as a consequence of this incomprehensible being. The dependence of other things has been restricted to their existence, and therewith a great portion of the reason for so much perfection is excluded from the supreme Nature and attributed to who knows what eternal non-being.

Productivity of a single ground for many consequences, harmony, and the fitness of natures to be coordinated in a regular plan according to universal laws without frequent conflict must first be encountered in the possibilities of things, and only then can wisdom be engaged in choosing them. What restrictions would be placed upon the independent being from external sources were not these very possibilities grounded in him! And what an incomprehensible coincidence that in this field of possibility, unity and a productive co-ordination obtain without the assumption of something existent through which the being of supreme degrees of power and wisdom—if those external relations be compared to his internal faculties—finds

kommenheit zuwege zu bringen? Gewiß, eine solche Vorstellung überliefert
nimmermehr den Ursprung des Guten ohne allen Abbruch in die Hand
eines einzigen Wesens. Als Hugen die Pendeluhr erfand, so konnte er,
wenn er daran dachte, sich diese Gleichförmigkeit, welche ihre Vollkommen=
heit ausmacht, nimmer gänzlich beimessen; die Natur der Cykloide, die es
möglich macht, daß kleine und große Bogen durch freien Fall in derselben
in gleicher Zeit beschrieben werden, konnte diese Ausführung lediglich in
seine Gewalt setzen. Daß aus dem einfachen Grunde der Schwere so ein
großer Umfang von schönen Folgen auch nur möglich ist, würde, wenn
es nicht von dem, der durch wirkliche Ausübung allen diesen Zusammen=
hang hervor gebracht hat, selbst abhinge, seinen Antheil an der reizenden
Einheit und dem großen Umfange so vieler, auf einem einzigen Grunde
beruhender Ordnung offenbar schmälern und theilen.

Die Bewunderung über die Abfolge einer Wirkung aus einer Ur=
sache hört auf, so bald ich die Zulänglichkeit der Ursache zu ihr deutlich
und leicht einsehe. Auf diesen Fuß kann keine Bewunderung mehr statt
finden, wenn ich den mechanischen Bau des menschlichen Körpers, oder
welcher künstlichen Anordnung ich auch will, als ein Werk des Allmäch=
tigen betrachte und blos auf die Wirklichkeit sehe, denn es ist leicht und
deutlich zu verstehen: daß der, so alles kann, auch eine solche Maschine,
wenn sie möglich ist, hervorbringen könne. Allein es bleibt gleichwohl Be=
wunderung übrig, man mag gleich dieses zur leichteren Begreifung ange=
führt haben, wie man will. Denn es ist erstaunlich, daß auch nur so etwas
wie ein thierischer Körper möglich war. Und wenn ich gleich alle Federn
und Röhren, alle Nervengefäße, Hebel und mechanische Einrichtung des=
selben völlig einsehen könnte, so bliebe doch immer Bewunderung übrig,
wie es möglich sei, daß so vielfältige Verrichtungen in einem Bau ver=
einigt worden, wie sich die Geschäfte zu einem Zwecke mit denen, wodurch
ein anderer erreicht wird, so wohl paaren lassen, wie eben dieselbe Zu=
sammenfügung außerdem noch dazu dient die Maschine zu erhalten und
die Folgen aus zufälligen Verletzungen wieder zu verbessern, und wie es
möglich war, daß ein Mensch konnte ein so feines Gewebe sein und uner=
achtet so vieler Gründe des Verderbens noch so lange dauern. Nachdem
ich auch endlich mich belehrt habe, daß so viel Einheit und Harmonie
darum möglich sei, weil ein Wesen da ist, welches nebst den Gründen der
Wirklichkeit auch die von aller Möglichkeit enthält, so hebt dieses noch
nicht den Grund der Bewunderung auf. Denn man kann sich zwar durch

himself in a position to bring about great perfection! Such a view certainly never leaves the origin of the good to the hand of a single being without the greatest disruption. When Huygens discovered the pendulum clock he could never—had he thought of it—attribute entirely to himself this uniformity which constitutes its perfection; [yet] the nature of the cycloid which makes it possible for small and large arcs of free fall through it to be described in the same time could have set this execution purely within his power. That such a great extent of excellent consequences is even possible from the simple ground of gravity, did it not itself depend upon the one who through actual execution has produced this conjunction, would obviously diminish and divide his share in the captivating unity and the great extent of so much order resting upon a single ground

Amazement at the sequence of effects from a cause ceases as soon as I see, clearly and easily, the sufficiency of the cause for this sequence. This way there can be no more amazement if I regard the mechanical structure of the human body—or whatever artificial arrangement—as a work of the omnipotent and pay attention only to the actuality; for it is clear and easy to understand that he who can do anything could also produce such a machine if it is possible. Nevertheless something astonishing remains, regardless of what one may have cited to make it more easily understood. For it is astonishing that something like an animal body was possible. And even if I could fully appreciate its springs and tubes, the nerve fibers and levers and mechanical structures, astonishment would still remain as to how it is possible for such manifold functions to be united in one structure; and how the items which serve one purpose are paired so well with those which achieve another; how in addition the very same composition also serves to conserve the machine and to restore it again after accidental damage; and that a human being can be such a fine fabric and endure so long despite so many grounds for destruction. And even when I am convinced that there is so much unity and harmony possible because there is a being which contains, in addition to all the grounds for actuality, all those of possibility, the reason for this astonishment is still not abolished. For certainly one can create

die Analogie deſſen, was Menſchen ausüben, einigen Begriff davon machen, wie ein Weſen die Urſache von etwas Wirklichem ſein könne, nimmermehr aber, wie es den Grund der innern Möglichkeit von andern Dingen ent= halte, und es ſcheint, als wenn dieſer Gedanke viel zu hoch ſteigt, als daß ihn ein erſchaffenes Weſen erreichen könnte.

Dieſer hohe Begriff der göttlichen Natur, wenn wir ſie nach ihrer Allgenugſamkeit gedenken, kann ſelbſt in dem Urtheil über die Beſchaffen= heit möglicher Dinge, wo uns unmittelbar Gründe der Entſcheidung fehlen, zu einem Hülfsmittel dienen, aus ihr als einem Grunde auf fremde Möglichkeit als eine Folge zu ſchließen. Es iſt die Frage: ob nicht unter allen möglichen Welten eine Steigerung ohne Ende in den Graden der Vollkommenheit anzutreffen ſei, da gar keine natürliche Ordnung möglich iſt, über die nicht noch eine vortrefflichere könne gedacht werden; ferner, wenn ich auch hierin eine höchſte Stufe zugäbe, ob nicht wenigſtens ſelbſt verſchiedene Welten, die von keiner übertroffen werden, einander an Voll= kommenheit gänzlich gleich wären. Bei dergleichen Fragen iſt es ſchwer und vielleicht unmöglich aus der Betrachtung möglicher Dinge allein et= was zu entſcheiden. Allein wenn ich beide Aufgaben in Verknüpfung mit dem göttlichen Weſen erwäge und erkenne, daß der Vorzug der Wahl, der einer Welt vor der andern zu Theil wird, ohne den Vorzug in dem Ur= theile eben deſſelben Weſens, welches wählt, oder gar wider dieſes Urtheil einen Mangel in der Übereinſtimmung ſeiner verſchiedenen thätigen Kräfte und eine verſchiedene Beziehung ſeiner Wirkſamkeit ohne eine proportio= nirte Verſchiedenheit in den Gründen, mithin einen Übelſtand in dem vollkommenſten Weſen abnehmen laſſe, ſo ſchließe ich mit großer Über= zeugung: daß die vorgelegten Fälle erdichtet und unmöglich ſein müſſen. Denn ich begreife nach den geſammten Vorbereitungen, die man geſehen hat: daß man viel weniger Grund habe, aus vorausgeſetzten Möglich= keiten, die man gleichwohl nicht genug bewähren kann, auf ein nothwen= diges Betragen des vollkommenſten Weſens zu ſchließen (welches ſo be= ſchaffen iſt, daß es den Begriff der größten Harmonie in ihm zu ſchmälern ſcheint), als aus der erkannten Harmonie, die die Möglichkeiten der Dinge mit der göttlichen Natur haben müſſen, von demjenigen, was dieſem We= ſen am anſtändigſten zu ſein erkannt wird, auf die Möglichkeit zu ſchließen. Ich werde alſo vermuthen, daß in den Möglichkeiten aller Welten keine ſolche Verhältniſſe ſein können, die einen Grund der Verlegenheit in der vernünftigen Wahl des höchſten Weſens enthalten müßten; denn eben

some concept of a being which is the cause of something actual through analogy with what human beings exercise, but never a concept of how that being may contain the ground of the inner possibility of other things. It seems as though this notion ascends much too far for a created being to be able to reach it.

If we reflect upon the total sufficiency of divine nature, this elevated notion can serve as an aid in judging the constitution of possible things, even where we lack immediate grounds for decision, by inferring from it as a ground to a foreign possibility as a consequence. There is the question of whether or not among all possible worlds there is not to be encountered an endless ascent in degrees of perfection, since there is no natural order possible for which a still more excellent one cannot be conceived. And further, if I were to grant a supreme level, might there not at least be different worlds, exceeded by no other, which would be entirely equivalent to each other in perfection? In such questions it is difficult and perhaps impossible to conclude anything from the study of possible things alone. Only when I consider both problems in conjunction with divine being and realize that the preference assigned the choice of one world over others, without a preference in the *judgment* of the same being which chooses—or completely in opposition to this judgment— allows assumption of a defect in the agreement of his different active powers and a different relation of his efficacy without a corresponding difference in the grounds and thus a deficiency in the most perfect being, then I conclude with uttermost conviction that the hypothesized cases must be contrived and impossible. For after all the preparations that have been seen, I well understand that one would have much less reason to infer the necessary behavior of the most perfect being (which is constituted so that the concept of maximum harmony seems to be diminished in him) from possibilities assumed but which cannot sufficiently be verified, than to infer such possibility from the known harmonies which the possibilities of things must have with divine nature, that is, from what is known to be most appropriate to this being. Thus I will assume that in the possibilities of all worlds there can be no such relations as would have to contain a ground for embarrassment in the

dieses oberste Wesen enthält den letzten Grund aller dieser Möglichkeit, in welcher also niemals etwas anders, als was mit ihrem Ursprunge harmonirt, kann anzutreffen sein.

Es ist auch dieser über alles Mögliche und Wirkliche erweiterte Begriff der göttlichen Allgenugsamkeit ein viel richtigerer Ausdruck, die größte Vollkommenheit dieses Wesens zu bezeichnen, als der des Unendlichen, dessen man sich gemeiniglich bedient. Denn ob man diesen letztern zwar auslegen kann, wie man will, so ist er seiner eigentlichen Bedeutung nach doch offenbar mathematisch. Er bezeichnet das Verhältniß einer Größe zu einer andern als dem Maße, welches Verhältniß größer ist als alle Zahl. Daher in dem eigentlichen Wortverstande die göttliche Erkenntniß unendlich heißen würde, in so fern sie vergleichungsweise gegen irgend eine angebliche andere Erkenntniß ein Verhältniß hat, welches alle mögliche Zahl übersteigt. Da nun eine solche Vergleichung göttliche Bestimmungen mit denen der erschaffenen Dinge in eine Gleichartigkeit, die man nicht wohl behaupten kann, versetzt und überdem das, was man dadurch will, nämlich den unverringerten Besitz von aller Vollkommenheit, nicht gerade zu verstehen giebt, so findet sich dagegen alles, was man hiebei zu denken vermag, in dem Ausdrucke der Allgenugsamkeit beisammen. Die Benennung der Unendlichkeit ist gleichwohl schön und eigentlich ästhetisch. Die Erweiterung über alle Zahlbegriffe rührt und setzt die Seele durch eine gewisse Verlegenheit in Erstaunen. Dagegen ist der Ausdruck, den wir empfehlen, der logischen Richtigkeit mehr angemessen.

rational choice of the supreme being. For this very being contains the ultimate ground of all this possibility in which therefore nothing other than what harmonizes with its origin can be encountered.

The notion of divine *sufficiency* extended over all possibility and actuality is thus a far more accurate expression to describe the great perfection than that of *infinity*, which commonly is used. For though one may construe this latter however he will its literal significance is still palpably mathematical. It describes the relation of one magnitude to another as the measure whose relation is greater than all number. Thus, for divine intelligence to be termed infinite in the literal sense would mean that, insofar as it can be compared to some other given intelligence, it has a relation which exceeds all possible number. Now while such comparison of divine attributes with those of created things transposes them into a homogeniety that cannot be maintained, and moreover does not provide for understanding what one wants with this, namely the unbounded possession of all perfections; on the other hand everything that one is able to conceive in this connection is contained in the expression "total sufficiency." The designation "infinite" is nevertheless excellent and properly aesthetic. Extension beyond all numerical concepts stirs the soul; and, through a certain bafflement, astonishes it. But on the other hand, the expression we recommend is more in conformity with the demands of logical rigor.

Dritte Abtheilung,

Worin dargethan wird: daß außer dem ausgeführten Beweis=
grunde kein anderer zu einer Demonstration vom Dasein
Gottes möglich sei.

1.

Eintheilung aller möglichen Beweisgründe vom Dasein Gottes.

Die Überzeugung von der großen Wahrheit: es ist ein Gott, wenn
sie den höchsten Grad mathematischer Gewißheit haben soll, hat dieses
Eigne: daß sie nur durch einen einzigen Weg kann erlangt werden, und
giebt dieser Betrachtung den Vorzug, daß die philosophische Bemühungen
sich bei einem einzigen Beweisgrunde vereinigen müssen, um die Fehler,
die in der Ausführung desselben möchten eingelaufen sein, vielmehr zu
verbessern als ihn zu verwerfen, so bald man überzeugt ist, daß keine Wahl
unter mehr dergleichen möglich sei.

Um dieses darzuthun, so erinnere ich, daß man die Forderung nicht
aus den Augen verlieren müsse, welche eigentlich zu erfüllen ist: nämlich
nicht das Dasein einer sehr großen und sehr vollkommenen ersten Ursache,
sondern des allerhöchsten Wesens, nicht die Existenz von einem oder meh=
reren derselben, sondern von einem einzigen und dieses nicht durch bloße
Gründe der Wahrscheinlichkeit, sondern mit mathematischer Evidenz zu
beweisen.

Alle Beweisgründe für das Dasein Gottes können nur entweder aus
den Verstandsbegriffen des blos **Möglichen**, oder aus dem Erfahrungs=

PART THREE
In Which It Is Shown That No Argument for a
Demonstration of the Existence of God Is Possible
Save That Which Has Been Cited

1.
Division of all possible proofs for the existence of God

Conviction of the great truth, *that there is a God,* must, if it is to be of the highest degree of mathematical certainty, have this property: that it can be achieved in only one way. This provides the study with the advantage that as soon as one is convinced there is no choice possible among several proofs, philosophic endeavors must be united in one single one in order to rectify the errors which may have entered through its execution, far more to correct than to reject it.

In order to demonstrate this I recall that one must not lose sight of the demand which particularly is to be met, namely that it is not the existence of a great and most perfect first cause but rather of the supreme being which is to be proved; and not the existence of one or more of them but of a unique entity; and this is proved not on grounds of mere probability but rather with mathematical clarity.

All arguments for the existence of God may be taken only either from rational concepts of the merely possible, or from the empirical concepts of the *existent*. In the first case either the

begriffe des **Exiſtirenden,** hergenommen werden. In dem erſteren Falle
wird entweder von dem Möglichen als einem Grunde auf das Daſein
Gottes als eine Folge, oder aus dem Möglichen als einer Folge auf die
göttliche Exiſtenz als einen Grund geſchloſſen. Im zweiten Falle wird
wiederum entweder aus demjenigen, deſſen Daſein wir erfahren, blos auf
die Exiſtenz einer erſten und unabhängigen Urſache, vermittelſt der
Zergliederung dieſes Begriffs aber auf die göttliche Eigenſchaften derſel=
ben geſchloſſen, oder es werden aus dem, was die Erfahrung lehrt, ſowohl
das Daſein als auch die Eigenſchaften deſſelben unmittelbar gefolgert.

2.
Prüfung der Beweisgründe der erſten Art.

Wenn aus dem Begriffe des blos Möglichen als einem Grunde
das Daſein als eine Folgerung ſoll geſchloſſen werden, ſo muß durch die
Zergliederung dieſes Begriffes die gedachte Exiſtenz darin können ange=
troffen werden; denn es giebt keine andere Ableitung einer Folge aus
einem Begriffe des Möglichen als durch die logiſche Auflöſung. Alsdann
müßte aber das Daſein wie ein Prädicat in dem Möglichen enthalten ſein.
Da dieſes nun nach der erſten Betrachtung der erſten Abtheilung nimmer=
mehr ſtatt findet, ſo erhellt: daß ein Beweis der Wahrheit, von der wir
reden, auf die erwähnte Art unmöglich ſei.

Indeſſen haben wir einen berühmten Beweis, der auf dieſen Grund
erbauet iſt, nämlich den ſo genannten Carteſianiſchen. Man erdenkt ſich
zuvörderſt einen Begriff von einem möglichen Dinge, in welchem man alle
wahre Vollkommenheit ſich vereinbart vorſtellt. Nun nimmt man an, das
Daſein ſei auch eine Vollkommenheit der Dinge; alſo ſchließt man aus
der Möglichkeit eines vollkommenſten Weſens auf ſeine Exiſtenz. Eben ſo
könnte man aus dem Begriffe einer jeden Sache, welche auch nur als die
vollkommenſte ihrer Art vorgeſtellt wird, z. E. daraus allein ſchon, daß
eine vollkommenſte Welt zu gedenken iſt, auf ihr Daſein ſchließen. Allein
ohne mich in eine umſtändliche Widerlegung dieſes Beweiſes einzulaſſen,
welche man ſchon bei andern antrifft, ſo beziehe ich mich nur auf das=
jenige, was im Anfange dieſes Werks iſt erklärt worden, daß nämlich
das Daſein gar kein Prädicat, mithin auch kein Prädicat der Vollkommen=
heit ſei, und daher aus einer Erklärung, welche eine willkürliche Verein=
barung verſchiedener Prädicate enthält, um den Begriff von irgend einem

existence of God as a consequence is concluded from the possible as a *ground*, or else divine existence as a ground is concluded from the possible as a *consequence*. In the second case again the existence of an ultimate and *independent cause* is inferred either from that whose existence we experience, and through analysis of this concept the divine properties of the independent cause are inferred; or else from what experience teaches, not only the existence, but also the *properties* of this ultimate cause are immediately concluded.

2.
Examination of proofs of the first kind

If existence is to be inferred as a consequence from the ground of the merely *possible,* that existence must be encountered in an analysis of the concept, for there is no other derivation of a consequence from a concept of possibility except through logical analysis. But then existence must be contained as a predicate in the possibility. Now since this can never be, according to the First Observation of the First Part, it appears that a proof of the truth in question is impossible in the way mentioned.

We have, of course, a famous proof which is based on this ground, namely the so-called Cartesian. First one conceives the notion of a possible thing in which all true perfections are represented as being combined. Now it is assumed that existence also is a perfection of things, and thus the existence of a most perfect being is concluded from its possibility. In the same way the existence of anything represented as the most perfect of its kind could be concluded from its concept; for instance, from only that a most perfect world may be conceived its existence is concluded. Without engaging in a detailed rebuttal of this proof, which may already be found in other places, I will only refer to what is explained at the beginning of this work, namely: existence is no predicate, and can be no predicate of perfection. Thus, from a definition which contains an arbitrary unification of diverse predicates in order to constitute the concept of some

möglichen Dinge aus zu machen, nimmermehr auf das Dasein dieses Dinges und folglich auch nicht auf das Dasein Gottes könne geschlossen werden.

Dagegen ist der Schluß von den Möglichkeiten der Dinge als Folgen auf das Dasein Gottes als einen Grund von ganz andrer Art. Hier wird untersucht, ob nicht dazu, daß etwas möglich sei, irgend etwas Existiren= des vorausgesetzt sein müsse, und ob dasjenige Dasein, ohne welches selbst keine innere Möglichkeit statt findet, nicht solche Eigenschaften enthalte, als wir zusammen in dem Begriffe der Gottheit verbinden. In diesem Falle ist zuvorderst klar, daß ich nicht aus der bedingten Möglichkeit auf ein Dasein schließen könne, wenn ich nicht die Existenz dessen, was nur unter gewissen Bedingungen möglich ist, voraussetze, denn die bedingte Möglichkeit giebt lediglich zu verstehen, daß etwas nur in gewissen Ver= knüpfungen existiren könne, und das Dasein der Ursache wird nur in so fern dargethan, als die Folge existirt, hier aber soll sie nicht aus dem Da= sein derselben geschlossen werden, daher ein solcher Beweis nur aus der innern Möglichkeit geführt werden kann, wofern er gar statt findet. Fer= ner wird man gewahr, daß er aus der absoluten Möglichkeit aller Dinge überhaupt entspringen müsse. Denn es ist nur die innere Möglichkeit selbst, von der erkannt werden soll, daß sie irgend ein Dasein voraus setze, und nicht die besondere Prädicate, dadurch sich ein Mögliches von dem andern unterscheidet; denn der Unterschied der Prädicate findet auch beim blos Möglichen statt und bezeichnet niemals etwas Existirendes. Dem= nach würde auf die erwähnte Art aus der innern Möglichkeit alles Denk= lichen ein göttliches Dasein müssen gefolgert werden. Daß dieses geschehen könne, ist in der ganzen ersten Abtheilung dieses Werks gewiesen worden.

3.

Prüfung der Beweisgründe der zweiten Art.

Der Beweis, da man aus den Erfahrungsbegriffen von dem, was da ist, auf die Existenz einer ersten und unabhängigen Ursache nach den Regeln der Causalschlüsse, aus dieser aber durch logische Zergliederung des Begriffes auf die Eigenschaften derselben, welche eine Gottheit be= zeichnen, kommen will, ist berühmt und vornehmlich durch die Schule der Wolffischen Philosophen sehr in Ansehen gebracht worden, allein er ist gleichwohl ganz unmöglich. Ich räume ein, daß bis zu dem Satze: wenn

possible thing, the existence of the thing—and consequently the existence of God—can never be concluded.

On the other hand, the conclusion from the possibilities of things, as consequences, to the existence of God as a ground, is of an entirely different sort. Here we investigate whether it is not true that because something is possible something else which is actual must be presupposed, and whether that existence without which there would be no internal possibility does not involve such properties as we unify in the concept of divinity. In this case it is abundantly clear that I could not infer from conditioned possibility to existence did I not presuppose the existence of what is possible only under certain conditions, for conditioned possibility means simply that something may exist only in certain combinations and the existence of the cause is demonstrated only insofar as the consequence exists. It is not deduced from the existence of the consequence, however; for such a proof, provided that it occurs at all, can only proceed from internal possibility. Further, it will be noted that this proof must be developed from the absolute possibility of all things in general. For only of the internal possibility, and not the special predicates through which one possibility is distinguished from another, is it known that it presupposes some existence; the difference of predicates occurs amongst the merely possible, and never distinguishes something existent. Accordingly, in the way mentioned, divine existence must be deduced from the internal possibility of everything conceivable. The entire first part of this work indicates that this can be done.

3.
Examination of proofs of the second kind

The proof proceeding from the empirical concepts of what exists to the existence of a first and independent cause according to the rules of causal inference and from this by means of logical analysis of the concept to properties of the independent cause which describe divinity is famous and has gained much attention through the Wolffian school of philosophy;[44] but nevertheless it is completely impossible. I agree that, until the

etwas da ist, so existirt auch etwas, was von keinem andern
Dinge abhängt, alles regelmäßig gefolgert sei, ich gebe also zu, daß
das Dasein irgend eines oder mehrer Dinge, die weiter keine Wirkungen
von einem andern sind, wohl erwiesen darliege. Nun ist der zweite Schritt
zu dem Satze, daß dieses unabhängige Ding schlechterdings noth=
wendig sei, schon viel weniger zuverlässig, da er vermittelst des Satzes
vom zureichenden Grunde, der noch immer angefochten wird, geführt wer=
den muß; allein ich trage kein Bedenken auch bis so weit alles zu unter=
schreiben. Es existirt demnach etwas schlechterdings nothwendiger Weise.
Aus diesem Begriffe des absolut nothwendigen Wesens sollen nun seine
Eigenschaften der höchsten Vollkommenheit und Einheit hergeleitet werden.
Der Begriff der absoluten Nothwendigkeit aber, der hier zum Grunde
liegt, kann auf zwiefache Art genommen werden, wie in der ersten Ab=
theilung gezeigt ist. In der ersten Art, da sie die logische Nothwendigkeit
von uns genannt worden, müßte gezeigt werden: daß das Gegentheil des=
jenigen Dinges sich selbst widerspreche, in welchem alle Vollkommenheit
oder Realität anzutreffen, und also dasjenige Wesen einzig und allein
schlechterdings nothwendig im Dasein sei, dessen Prädicate alle wahr=
haftig bejahend sind. Und da aus eben derselben durchgängigen Verein=
barung aller Realität in einem Wesen soll geschlossen werden, daß es ein
einziges sei, so ist klar, daß die Zergliederung der Begriffe des Noth=
wendigen auf solchen Gründen beruhen werde, nach denen ich auch umge=
kehrt müsse schließen können: worin alle Realität ist, das existirt noth=
wendiger Weise. Nun ist nicht allein diese Schlußart nach der vorigen
Nummer unmöglich, sondern es ist insonderheit merkwürdig, daß auf diese
Art der Beweis gar nicht auf den Erfahrungsbegriff, der ganz, ohne ihn
zu brauchen, voraus gesetzt ist, erbauet wird, sondern eben so wie der Car=
tesianische lediglich auf Begriffe, in welchen man in der Identität oder
dem Widerstreit der Prädicate das Dasein eines Wesens zu finden ver=
meint.*)

_____

*) Dieses ist das Vornehmste, worauf ich hier ausgehe. Wenn ich die Noth=
wendigkeit eines Begriffes darin setze, daß sich das Gegentheil widerspricht, und als=
dann behaupte, das Unendliche sei so beschaffen, so war es ganz unnöthig die Existenz
des nothwendigen Wesens voraus zu setzen, indem sie schon aus dem Begriffe des
Unendlichen folgt. Ja jene vorangeschickte Existenz ist in dem Beweise selbst völlig
müßig. Denn da in dem Fortgang desselben der Begriff der Nothwendigkeit und
Unendlichkeit als Wechselbegriffe angesehen werden, so wird wirklich darum aus der

proposition "If something exists, then there exists something else which depends upon no other thing" is reached, everything proceeds regularly. I admit thus that the existence of one or more things which are not the effects of another is certainly clearly demonstrated. But the second step to the claim that this independent thing is *absolutely necessary* is much less infallible, for it must be derived from the principle of sufficient reason, which is always under attack. But I have no scruple against going so far as to endorse this. Thus something exists absolutely necessarily. From this concept of the absolutely necessary being the properties of the greatest perfection and unity are supposed to be derived. But the concept of absolute necessity that is at the base of this can be taken in a two-fold way as was shown in the first part. In the first way, which we have termed "logical necessity," it must be shown that the contrary of that in which all perfection and reality is met is self-contradictory, and thus that being and only that one whose predicates are all truly affirmed is absolutely necessary in existence. Since it is to be concluded from the same thoroughgoing unification of all reality in one being that this being is *singular,* it is clear that the analysis of the concept will necessarily be based upon such grounds as make it possible to infer inversely that that in which all reality is included exists necessarily. Not only is this argument impossible according to the foregoing article, but it is also particularly noteworthy that this mode of proof is by no means built upon an empirical concept, which [concept] is assumed but not used at all. Rather, it is built, just like the Cartesian one, entirely on the concepts in which one presumes to find the existence of a being in the identity or opposition of predicates.*

*This is as far as I shall proceed here. If the necessity of a concept be assumed so that the contrary is self-contradictory and then if it be maintained that the infinite is so constituted, it would be entirely unnecessary further to assume the existence of the necessary being, for that follows from the concept of the infinite. Indeed, the premised existence is utterly useless in the proof itself. For in its procedure, the concepts of necessity and infinity are regarded as being synonymous. Really, the existence of the necessary being is inferred

Es ist meine Absicht nicht, die Beweise selber zu zergliedern, die man dieser Methode gemäß bei verschiedenen antrifft. Es ist leicht ihre Fehl= schlüsse aufzudecken, und dieses ist auch schon zum Theil von andern ge= schehen. Indessen da man gleichwohl noch immer hoffen könnte, daß ihrem Fehler durch einige Verbesserungen abzuhelfen sei, so ersieht man aus unserer Betrachtung, daß, es mag auch aus ihnen werden, was da wolle, sie doch niemals etwas anders als Schlüsse aus Begriffen möglicher Dinge, nicht aber aus Erfahrung werden können und also allenfalls den Beweisen der ersten Art beizuzählen sind.

Was nun den zweiten Beweis von derjenigen Art anlangt, da aus Erfahrungsbegriffen von existirenden Dingen auf das Dasein Gottes und zugleich seine Eigenschaften geschlossen wird, so verhält es sich hiemit ganz anders. Dieser Beweis ist nicht allein möglich, sondern auch auf alle Weise würdig durch vereinigte Bemühungen zur gehörigen Vollkommenheit ge= bracht zu werden. Die Dinge der Welt, welche sich unsern Sinnen offen= baren, zeigen sowohl deutliche Merkmale ihrer Zufälligkeit, als auch durch die Größe, die Ordnung und zweckmäßige Anstalten, die man allenthalben gewahr wird, Beweisthümer eines vernünftigen Urhebers von großer Weisheit, Macht und Güte. Die große Einheit in einem so weitläuftigen Ganzen läßt abnehmen, daß nur ein einziger Urheber aller dieser Dinge sei, und wenn gleich in allen diesen Schlüssen keine geometrische Strenge hervorblickt, so enthalten sie doch unstrittig so viel Nachdruck, daß sie einen jeden Vernünftigen nach Regeln, die der natürliche gesunde Verstand be= folgt, keinen Augenblick hierüber im Zweifel lassen.

4.

Es sind überhaupt nur zwei Beweise vom Dasein Gottes möglich.

Aus allen diesen Beurtheilungen ist zu ersehen: daß, wenn man aus Begriffen möglicher Dinge schließen will, kein ander Argument für das Dasein Gottes möglich sei, als dasjenige, wo selbst die innere Möglichkeit aller Dinge als etwas angesehen wird, was irgend ein Dasein voraus= setzt, wie es von uns in der ersten Abtheilung dieses Werks geschehen ist.

Existenz des Nothwendigen auf die Unendlichkeit geschlossen, weil das Unendliche (und zwar allein) nothwendig existirt.

It is not my intention further to analyze the proofs consistent with this method that one finds in various [philosophers]. It is easy enough to discover their fallacies, and this has been partially accomplished by others. However, because it may nevertheless still be hoped that these errors may be meliorated through a few improvements, it appears from our study that no matter what is deduced from them still they can be nothing but conclusions from the concepts of possible things, not from experience, and thus they are to be counted at most among the proofs of the first species.

As far as the second proof of that kind is concerned, where both the existence and the properties of God are deduced from empirical concepts of existent things, the matter is quite different. This proof is not only possible, but also worthy of being brought to its proper perfection through concerted efforts. Things of the world which our senses reveal to us give clear signs of their contingency as well as evidence of a rational creator of great wisdom, power and goodness through the magnitude, order, and purposive arrangement which one is aware of everywhere. The vast unity in such an extensive totality allows the conclusion that there can be only one single creator of all these things. And even if geometric rigor does not appear in all of these conclusions, still incontestably they contain such an impression that all reasoning according to rules following commonsense will remain in doubt not one moment longer.

4.

In general only two proofs of the existence of God are possible

From all this review it can be seen that if one is to conclude from the concepts of possible things, no argument is possible for the existence of God except the one which regards the internal possibility of things as something presupposing some existence, as has been done in the first part of this work. Similarly it appears that, if the inference is to ascend to the same truth from whatever the experience of existing things

from that of the infinite, for the infinite (and that alone) necessarily exists.

Imgleichen erhellt, daß, wenn von dem, was uns Erfahrung von existi=
renden Dingen lehrt, der Schluß zu eben derselben Wahrheit soll hinauf
steigen, der Beweis nur durch die in den Dingen der Welt wahrgenommene
Eigenschaften und die zufällige Anordnung des Weltganzen auf das Da=
sein sowohl als auch die Beschaffenheit der obersten Ursache kann geführt
werden. Man erlaube mir, daß ich den ersten Beweis den ontologischen,
den zweiten aber den kosmologischen nenne.

Dieser kosmologische Beweis ist, wie mich dünkt, so alt wie die
menschliche Vernunft. Er ist so natürlich, so einnehmend und erweitert
sein Nachdenken auch so sehr mit dem Fortgang unserer Einsichten, daß
er so lange dauern muß, als es irgend ein vernünftig Geschöpf geben wird,
welches an der edlen Betrachtung Theil zu nehmen wünscht, Gott aus
seinen Werken zu erkennen. Derhams, Nieuwentyts und vieler ande=
rer Bemühungen haben der menschlichen Vernunft in dieser Absicht Ehre
gemacht, obgleich bisweilen viel Eitelkeit mit untergelaufen ist, allerlei
physischen Einsichten oder auch Hirngespinsten durch die Losung des Re=
ligionseifers ein ehrwürdig Ansehen zu geben. Bei aller dieser Vortreff=
lichkeit ist diese Beweisart doch immer der mathematischen Gewißheit und
Genauigkeit unfähig. Man wird jederzeit nur auf irgend einen unbegreif=
lich großen Urheber desjenigen Ganzen, was sich unsern Sinnen darbietet,
schließen können, nicht aber auf das Dasein des vollkommensten unter
allen möglichen Wesen. Es wird die größte Wahrscheinlichkeit von der
Welt sein, daß nur ein einiger erster Urheber sei, allein dieser Überzeu=
gung wird viel an der Ausführlichkeit, die der frechsten Zweifelsucht trotzt,
ermangeln. Das macht: wir können nicht auf mehr oder größere Eigen=
schaften in der Ursache schließen, als wir gerade nöthig finden, um den
Grad und Beschaffenheit der Wirkungen daraus zu verstehen; wenn wir
nämlich von dem Dasein dieser Ursache keinen andern Anlaß zu urtheilen
haben, als den, so uns die Wirkungen geben. Nun erkennen wir viel
Vollkommenheit, Größe und Ordnung in der Welt und können daraus
nichts mehr mit logischer Schärfe schließen, als daß die Ursache derselben
viel Verstand, Macht und Güte besitzen müsse, keinesweges aber daß sie
alles wisse, vermöge 2c. 2c. Es ist ein unermeßliches Ganze, in welchem
wir Einheit und durchgängige Verknüpfung wahrnehmen, und wir können
mit großem Grunde daraus ermessen, daß ein einiger Urheber desselben
sei. Allein wir müssen uns bescheiden, daß wir nicht alles Erschaffene
kennen, und daher urtheilen, daß, was uns bekannt ist, nur einen Ur=

teaches, the proof can lead only from the properties perceived in things of the world and the contingent arrangement of the world to the existence as well as to the properties of the supreme cause. I take the liberty of terming the first proof the ontological, but the second one the cosmological.

This cosmological proof is, as I believe, as old as human reason. It is so natural, engaging, and extends its reflections so well with the growth of our understanding that it must endure for so long as there is any rational creature who wants to take part in the noble study of knowing God in his work. The efforts of Derham,[45] Nieuwentyt[46] and many others have done honor to human reason in this respect—although occasionally a good deal of vanity has crept in so as to give various physical insights, and even illusions, a worthy guise through the password of religious zeal. Yet for all this excellence, this mode of proof is incapable of mathematical precision and certainty. It will always be possible to conclude from what our senses provide to an incomprehensibly great creator of this totality; but not to the existence of the most perfect of all possible beings. It may be the most probable thing in the world that there is only one single first creator; yet this conclusion will lack much detail to baffle the most impudent skepticism. That is, we cannot infer more or greater properties in the cause than we find necessary to understand the degree and constitution of the effects from them if we have no other reason for judging the existence of this cause than what the effects give us. We recognize much perfection, greatness, and order in the world and may conclude with logical rigor from it only that the cause of this must possess much understanding, power, and goodness; but by no means that it knows everything, is capable of everything, etc. It is an immeasurable whole in which we perceive unity and thoroughgoing coordination, and with good reason we can estimate from this that there is a single creator of it. But we must resign ourselves to the fact that we do not know all created things and thus judge that what is known to us appears to have only one creator, from which we conjecture that what is not known to us is similarly constituted. To be sure this is very

heber blicken lasse, woraus wir vermuthen, was uns auch nicht bekannt
ist, werde eben so bewandt sein; welches zwar sehr vernünftig gedacht ist,
aber nicht strenge schließt.

Dagegen wofern wir uns nicht zu sehr schmeicheln, so scheint unser
entworfener ontologische Beweis derjenigen Schärfe fähig zu sein, die
man in einer Demonstration fordert. Indessen wenn die Frage wäre,
welcher denn überhaupt unter beiden der beste sei, so würde man ant=
worten: so bald es auf logische Genauigkeit und Vollständigkeit ankommt,
so ist es der ontologische, verlangt man aber Faßlichkeit für den ge=
meinen richtigen Begriff, Lebhaftigkeit des Eindrucks, Schönheit und Be=
wegkraft auf die moralische Triebfedern der menschlichen Natur, so ist
dem kosmologischen Beweise der Vorzug zuzugestehen. Und da es ohne
Zweifel von mehr Erheblichkeit ist, den Menschen mit hohen Empfindun=
gen, die fruchtbar an edler Thätigkeit sind, zu beleben, indem man zu=
gleich den gesunden Verstand überzeugt, als mit sorgfältig abgewogenen
Vernunftschlüssen zu unterweisen, dadurch daß der feinern Speculation
ein Gnüge gethan wird, so ist, wenn man aufrichtig verfahren will, dem
bekannten kosmologischen Beweise der Vorzug der allgemeinern Nutzbar=
keit nicht abzusprechen.

Es ist demnach kein schmeichlerischer Kunstgriff, der um fremden Bei=
fall buhlt, sondern Aufrichtigkeit, wenn ich einer solchen Ausführung der
wichtigen Erkenntniß von Gott und seinen Eigenschaften, als Reimarus
in seinem Buche von der natürlichen Religion liefert, den Vorzug der
Nutzbarkeit gerne einräume über einen jeden andern Beweis, in welchem
mehr auf logische Schärfe gesehen worden, und über den meinigen. Denn
ohne den Werth dieser und anderer Schriften dieses Mannes in Erwä=
gung zu ziehen, der hauptsächlich in einem ungekünstelten Gebrauche einer
gesunden und schönen Vernunft besteht, so haben dergleichen Gründe wirk=
lich eine große Beweiskraft und erregen mehr Anschauung als die logisch
abgezogene Begriffe, obgleich die letztere den Gegenstand genauer zu ver=
stehen geben.

Gleichwohl da ein forschender Verstand, wenn er einmal auf die
Spur der Untersuchung gerathen ist, nicht eher befriedigt wird, als bis
alles um ihn licht ist und bis sich, wenn ich mich so ausdrücken darf, der
Zirkel, der seine Frage umgrenzt, völlig schließt, so wird niemand eine
Bemühung, die wie die gegenwärtige auf die logische Genauigkeit in

reasonable, but it is not strictly deduced.

On the other hand, provided we are not flattering ourselves too much, our proposed ontological proof seems to be the one capable of the rigor demanded of a demonstration. However, the question of which of the two is better in general may be answered this way: insofar as logical precision and completeness are concerned, the ontological. But if comprehension of a common, true concept, the vivacity of its impression and excellence and attraction for the moral drives of human nature be required, preference is accorded the cosmological proof. And because it is without a doubt of more importance to vitalize mankind with elevated sentiments which are productive of noble activity, whilst at the same time convincing common sense, than it is to instruct it with carefully measured syllogisms through which more refined speculation is satisfied; if one proceed candidly the famous cosmological proof cannot be denied the preference of general utility.

It is not, then, a flattering maneuver seeking extraneous applause, but sincerity, when I freely grant the advantage of utility which an achievement of the important knowledge of God and his properties such as Reimarus[47] provides in his book on natural religion has over every other proof in which more attention is paid to logical rigor—and over my own. For without drawing the value of this and other writings of the man into consideration, a value which consists chiefly in the natural use of robust and excellent common sense, these grounds really have a great attraction and excite more attention than logically abstract concepts, though the latter permit more precise understanding of the object.

Nevertheless, since an inquisitive intelligence, once it stumbles upon the track of an investigation, cannot be satisfied until everything is clear to it; and, if I may express myself this way, until the circle of its questioning is completely closed, nobody will regard endeavors such as the present one, which are devoted to logical precision of such an important kind of knowledge, as being useless or superfluous—especially since there are cases where without such care the application of his

einem so sehr wichtigen Erkenntnisse verwandt ist, für unnütz und über=
flüssig halten, vornehmlich weil es viele Fälle giebt, da ohne solche Sorg=
falt die Anwendung seiner Begriffe unsicher und zweifelhaft bleiben
würde.

5.

Es ist nicht mehr als eine einzige Demonstration vom Dasein Gottes möglich, wovon der Beweisgrund oben gegeben worden.

Aus dem bisherigen erhellt: daß unter den vier erdenklichen Beweis=
gründen, die wir auf zwei Hauptarten gebracht haben, der Cartesianische
sowohl, als der, so aus dem Erfahrungsbegriffe vom Dasein vermittelst
der Auflösung des Begriffes von einem unabhängigen Dinge geführt
worden, falsch und gänzlich unmöglich seien, das ist, daß sie nicht etwa
mit keiner gehörigen Schärfe, sondern gar nicht beweisen. Es ist ferner
gezeigt worden, daß der Beweis aus den Eigenschaften der Dinge der
Welt auf das Dasein und die Eigenschaften der Gottheit zu schließen
einen tüchtigen und sehr schönen Beweisgrund enthalte, nur daß er
nimmermehr der Schärfe einer Demonstration fähig ist. Nun bleibt
nichts übrig, als daß entweder gar kein strenger Beweis hievon möglich
sei, oder daß er auf demjenigen Beweisgrunde beruhen müsse, den wir
oben angezeigt haben. Da von der Möglichkeit eines Beweises schlechthin
die Rede ist, so wird niemand das erstere behaupten, und die Folge fällt
demjenigen gemäß aus, was wir angezeigt haben. Es ist nur ein Gott
und nur ein Beweisgrund, durch welchen es möglich ist, sein Dasein mit
der Wahrnehmung derjenigen Nothwendigkeit einzusehen, die schlechter=
dings alles Gegentheil vernichtigt: ein Urtheil, darauf selbst die Be=
schaffenheit des Gegenstandes unmittelbar führen könnte. Alle andere
Dinge, welche irgend da sind, könnten auch nicht sein. Die Erfahrung
von zufälligen Dingen kann demnach keinen tüchtigen Beweisgrund ab=
geben, das Dasein desjenigen daraus zu erkennen, von dem es unmöglich
ist, daß er nicht sei. Nur lediglich darin, daß die Verneinung der gött=
lichen Existenz völlig Nichts ist, liegt der Unterschied seines Daseins von
anderer Dinge ihrem. Die innere Möglichkeit, die Wesen der Dinge sind
nun dasjenige, dessen Aufhebung alles Denkliche vertilgt. Hierin wird

concepts would remain uncertain and doubtful.

5.

There is not more than one possible demonstration of the existence of God; and the argument for it has been given above

From the foregoing it appears that: among the four conceivable arguments which we have collected into two main species, the Cartesian one as well as the one which is adduced from the empirical concept of existence by means of an analysis of the concept of an independent being, are false and completely impossible. That is, not only do they not prove something with sufficient rigor, but rather they prove nothing at all. It is further shown that the proof which infers the existence and properties of divinity from the properties of things in the world contains a good and excellent argument, but that it is never capable of the rigor of demonstration. Thus nothing remains save either that there is no strict proof possible or else that it must rest upon the argument which we have indicated above. Since the whole point of this is the possibility of a proof, nobody will maintain the former, and the result is consistent with what we have indicated. There is only one God and only one argument through which it is possible to apprehend his existence with the perception of that necessity which positively eliminates any opposition. A judgment of this sort can lead immediately to the nature of the object itself. Any other thing that may exist anywhere may also not exist. Accordingly, experience of contingent things cannot give an adequate argument by which to comprehend the existence of something of which it is impossible that it not be. It is solely in that the denial of divine existence is absolutely nothing that the difference between this [divine] existence and that of other things lies. Internal possibility, the essence of things, is precisely

also das eigene Merkmal von dem Dasein des Wesens aller Wesen bestehen. Hierin sucht den Beweisthum, und wenn ihr ihn nicht daselbst anzutreffen vermeint, so schlaget euch von diesem ungebähnten Fußsteige auf die große Heeresstraße der menschlichen Vernunft. Es ist durchaus nöthig, daß man sich vom Dasein Gottes überzeuge; es ist aber nicht eben so nöthig, daß man es demonstrire.

Ende.

11*

that whose negation cancels all thought. This is what constitutes the unique characteristic of the existence of the essence of all being. Seek the proof here. And if you are not prepared to meet it on this ground, turn from this unfamiliar path to the highway of human reason. It is thoroughly necessary that one be convinced of God's existence; but it is not nearly so necessary that it be demonstrated.

Notes

1. "... that my gifts here set forth for you with faithful solicitude, may not by you be contemptuously discarded before they have been understood" (*De rerum natura*, I, 52-53, W.H.D. Rouse translation).

2. As the text makes clear Kant is intending to enforce a strict distinction between the basis of a demonstration and the complete demonstration itself. This is a distinction with strong foundation in traditional logic. "The essential parts of any proof whatever are the material and form or the *Beweisgrund* and *Consequenz*" (*Logik*, K.G.S. IX, 71).

   To translate *Beweisgrund* as "argument" in a context such as this is misleading. It tends to confuse the distinction Kant is making, since in English an argument is thought or intended to establish a position, not to be only the essential foundation for demonstrating that position.

3. Reading with Reich *"von denen anderer abweichen."* Weischedel and the 1763 edition read *"von anderer ihrer abweichen."*

4. Kant employs the verb *erklären* and the noun *Erklärung* throughout the essay. Much later he provides justification for translation of *Erklärung* as "definition." In the "Doctrine of Method" of the first *Critique* he contends that in the strict sense mathematics alone has definitions, for only in that science are there concepts which contain an arbitrary synthesis which can be constructed a priori. "For the object thought is presented in an a priori *Anschauung* which can contain no more and no less than the concept. This way the definition of the concept of the object is originally given, that is without the definition's being derived from anything. The German language has only the one word 'definition' for the expressions 'exposition', 'explication', 'declaration' and 'definition'. We must thus reduce somewhat the strictness of the demand that we deny to philosophical explications *Erklärungen* the honorable title of definitions. We may limit this entire note to the fact

that philosophical definitions [*Definitionen*] are only expositions of given concepts while mathematical definitions are constructions of originally created concepts. The former are accomplished analytically through dissection (the completeness of which is not apodictically certain). The latter are accomplished synthetically and thus actually *create* the concept . . . the former only *explain* [*erklären*] it". (*Critique of Pure Reason* A729-730/B757-758). Contemporary English retains the Latin terms Kant missed in German, but enforces virtually no distinction between them, an improvishment of thought in which contemporary formal logic fully concurs.

5. The imitation of mathematical method in philosophy ". . . has until now been of little value, despite the great advantage which originally was promised for it. Gradually the equivocal honorifics with which philosophical propositions are decorated out of jealousy of geometry have fallen away; for it was modestly understood that it is not good to be defiant in moderate circumstances, and that the difficult *non liquet* [it is unclear] will in no way yield to all this ostentation" (Preface to: *Versuch den Begriff der negativen Grössen in die Weltweissheit einzuführen* [*The Attempt to Introduce Negative Quantities into Philosophy*] 1763, K.G.S. II, 167).

6. Aicht eine einzige Bestimmung ermangle. Cassirer reads "nicht ein einziges ermangle." Weischedel: "nicht eine einziges ermangle."

7. Christian Wolff (1679-1754): *Philosophia prima sive ontologia . . . .* (Frankfurt and Leipzig, 1730), sec. 174; *Vernünftige Gedancken von Gott, der Welt, und der Seele des Menschen* (Halle, 1720) sec. 14.

8. Alexander Gottlieb Baumgarten (1714-1762): *Metaphysica*, 3rd ed. (Halle, 1750), sec. 55.

9. *Critique of Pure Reason* A581-582/B609-610.

10. Christian August Crusius (1715-1775): *Entwurf der notwendigen Vernunft-Wahrheiten, wiefern şie den zufälligen entgegen gesetz werden*, 2nd ed. (Leipzig 1753) sec. 46-48.

11. The wandering Jew. According to legend, because he refused to allow Christ to rest in his home on the procession of Good Friday to Golgatha, he was condemned to wander the earth until the final judgment.

12. Christian August Crusius, *Entwurf der notwendigen Vernunft-Wahrheiten* . . ., sec. 58.

13. See Alexander Gottlieb Baumgarten, *Metaphysica*, sec. 15, K.G.S. XVI.

14. Hitherto Kant has consistently used the expression *das Dasein*. Even in this section he seems to use the terms *das Dasein* and *die Existenz* synonymously.

15. Weischedel reads *anderer moglichen Realität*, "other possible reality."

17. Reading with Reich *einem einigen Principum*.

18. I follow Kemp-Smith in translation of this difficult term. This is a term which Kant used frequently in his early writing and much less often in the *Critiques*.

19. The principle of least action is meant. Pierre Louis Moreau de Maupertuis (1698-1759) announced the discovery of this law in 1746 in a paper, "Les loix des mouvement et du repos déduites d'un principe metaphysique" (*Histoire de l'academie royale des sciences et belles lettres*, 1746, pp. 268-294). This is the principle that: "In the impact of bodies, motion is distributed in such a way that the quantity of motion is the least possible to permit the change." For bodies in equilibrium, "the quantity of action will always be the minimum" (*Essay de cosmologie*, [Leiden, 1751], p. 21). It follows that there must be some minimum natural motion, and Maupertuis calculated such a minimum to be the product of the time of movement within a system by twice the kinetic energy (*vis viva*) of that system. Publication in 1750 of a paper by Samuel König (1712-1757), in which König suggested an

improved formulation of the law and also claimed that Leibniz had anticipated Maupertuis in a letter which Leibniz wrote in 1707, led directly to the bitter dispute involving Maupertuis, the Prussian Academy, Voltaire, and Frederick II.

20. The question set was: "Whether the truth of principles of statics and of mechanics is necessary or contingent." The problem was first set in 1756 to be answered by 1758. The deadline was postponed until 1760, but a prize was never awarded.

21. William Whiston (1667-1752): *A New Theory of the Earth* (London, 1696). German translations appeared in Frankfurt in 1713 and in Wittenberg in 1755.

22. Reading with Menzer *allemeinern* for *allgemeinen*.

23. Johann Peter Süssmilch, in *Die göttliche Ordnung in den Veranderungen des menschlichen Geschlechts* (2nd edition of 1761-1762, pp. 118ff), puts the number of people amongst whom there must be a married couple at from 80 to 115. Kant probably chooses the figure 110 since Süssmilch recommends a ratio of from 1 to 108 to 1 to 115 for agricultural areas "like our Brandenburg villages and those in Finland" (p. 147). Elsewhere in the same book Süssmilch gives the figure for Berlin as 1 : 110 adding that "this almost exactly agrees with the villages of Brandenburg" (p. 121).

24. The Tree of Diana (*Arbor Dianae*) is formed by the reaction of acidic potassium or sodium nitrate, silver and zinc. In a motionless vessel the silver appears in leaf-like configuration (Maupertuis: *Venus physique* edition of 1748, p. 125).

25. In this passage Kant is referring to the controversy between the preformationists, who held that from conception onward each embryo is a miniature of the complete animal, and the epigenists, who contended that the organism develops from simpler to more complex forms during the period of its incubation. Maupertuis's essay, *Vènus physique*, first published anonymously in 1745, had revived interest in the epigenetic theory. The *Critique of Judgment* (sec. 81, K.G.S. V, 374-379) covers much of the same ground as this passage does and repeats the central criticism of preformationism given here. With a greater care for etymological accuracy than was manifested by later writers on biological theory, Kant there terms a system which regards "offspring as mere educts, individualistic preformationism or also evolutionary theory. If the offspring are products, the system is epigenetic."

Insofar as it refers to development or eduction of what already is present, "evolution" is a suitable translation of Kant's expression *Auswicklung*. The term *Fortpflanzung* is neutral with respect to the two competing theories. That is, Kant uses it to refer to perpetuation by evolution and to perpetuation by production. *Erzeugen* on the other hand clearly refers to the production of more complex forms from simpler ones and accordingly is translated as "generation."

26. Georges Louis Leclerc de Buffon (1707-1788), *Histoire naturelle, générale et particulière*, 1749, Vol. II, chap. 2.

27. Maupertuis, *Oeuvres*, 1756, Vol. II, pp. 116-147.

28. Dr. John Hill (1716-1775) an English naturalist and author of *A General Natural History* (London, 1748-1752). Hill's essays were communicated to the *Hamburg Magazine* from 1753 to 1758. Kant is here referring to the thirteenth of these, published in 1757, pp. 233-290.

29. Johann Peter Süssmilch, *Die göttliche Ordnung in den Veränderung des menschlichen Geschlects*, 1st ed., sec. 61. In the second edition Süssmilch proposes an alternative explanation, (sec. 430).

30. Thomas B. Burnet (1635-1715), *Telluris theoria sacra, orbis nostri originem et mutationes generales, quas aut jam subiit aut olim subiturus est, complectens,* 1702, 3rd ed., pp. 37ff.

31. Abraham Gotthelf Kästner (1719-1800). The mining expert probably was Borlach.

32. Voltaire, *Dictionaire Philosophique* article "Causes finales," sec. III *(Oeuvres* [1858] vol. 7, p. 310).

33. No editor has noticed that although Kant speaks of an irregular polygon in this sentence, the context as well as rules of Euclidean geometry require reading *ein jedes reguläre Polygon* for *ein jedes irfeguläre Polygon.*

34. Kant almost certainly is referring to Ray and Burnett.

35. *die Zeugunsfähigkeit, das Auswicklungsvermögen*; see note 28.

36. Kant is probably citing the 1740 translation by B.D. Brockes (p.35), and his citation is not exact.

37. Maupertuis: *Discours sur les différentes Figures des Astres* (Paris, 1732), chap. VI *(Oeuvres,* II). In the *Universal Natural History and Theory of the Heavens* (1755), Kant reports Maupertuis's understanding of the distant galaxies: "In respect to their figure and calculable diameter he holds them to be tremendously large heavenly bodies which, because of their great flattening out caused by rotation about an axis, present an ecliptical shape if they are seen from the side." (K.G.S. I, 254).

38. Buffon, *Histoire naturelle, générale et particuliére* (1749), vol. I, p. 138.

39. Jean Jacques d'Ortous de Mairan (1678-1771): *Dissertation sur l'estimation et la mesure des forces motrices des corps* (Paris, 1741) and *Lettre à Madame du Chastelet sur la question des forces vives* (Paris, 1741).

40. A force attracting to or repelling from a center is a central force and the laws of gravitation according to which heavenly bodies are attracted towards or repelled from a center—the sun in our solar system—are what Kant understands as central laws, *die Zentralgesetze*. See *Critique of Pure Reason*, BXXII, note.

41. *Paradise Lost*, III, 495.

42. *Schwungsbewegung* and *Schwungskraft* are terms Kant employed only infrequently before 1770 and not at all after that.

43. *The Universal Natural History and Theory of the Heavens* gives the time for the revolution of Saturn around its axis as 6 hours, 23 minutes, 53 seconds (K.G.S. I, 294). Both estimates are quite inaccurate. The correct figure is 10 hours, 14 minutes.

44. In this regard see J.G. Daries: *Elementa metaphysics* (Jena, 1754); Alexander Baumgarten, *Metaphysica*, sec. 308-310, sec. 851; F.C. Baumeister, *Institutiones metaphysicae* (Wittenberg, 1738) secs. 780ff.

45. William Derham (1657-1735), *Astro-Theology, or a demonstration of the being and attributes of God from a survey of the heavens* (London, 1715). German translation, J.A. Fabrico (Hamburg, 1732).

46. Bernard Nieuwentyt (1654-1718), *Het regt Gebruik der Wereltbeschouningen*, 1715. The book went through several different French translations and an English one, by J. Chamberlayne, *The Religious Philosopher* (London, 1718).

47. Herman Samuel Reimarus (1694-1768), *Die vornehmesten Wahrheiten der natürlichen Religion in Zehn Abhandlungen auf eine begreifliche Art erklärt und gerettet* (Hamburg, 1754).

An S. Grossman Production